A THEOLOGY OF LIFE

A THEOLOGY OF LIFE

Dietrich Bonhoeffer's
Religionless Christianity

Ralf K. Wüstenberg

Translated by Doug Stott

William B. Eerdmans Publishing Company
Grand Rapids, Michigan / Cambridge, U.K.

To my daughter
Philippa Marie

Printed in the United States of America

03 02 01 00 99 98   7 6 5 4 3 2 1

Translated from the German edition:
Glauben als Leben: Dietrich Bonhoeffer und die nichtreligiöse Interpretation biblischer Begriffe,
© 1996 Peter Lang, Frankfurt

Library of Congress Cataloging-in-Publication Data

Wüstenberg, Ralf K., 1965-
[Glauben als Leben. English]
A theology of life: Dietrich Bonhoeffer's religionless Christianity / Ralf K. Wüstenberg.
p.   cm.
ISBN 0-8028-4266-6 (pbk.)
1. Bonhoeffer, Dietrich, 1906-1945.
2. Christianity — Essence, genius, nature.
3. Religion — Philosophy — History — 20th century.
I. Title.
BX4827.B57W8713 1998
230′.044′092 — dc21   98-17307
                                                              CIP

Contents

II

III

Foreword

It is with great pleasure and satisfaction that I introduce here the translation of Ralf K. Wüstenberg's *A Theology of Life*. Dietrich Bonhoeffer's theology, forged within the crucible of conspiracy, has ignited the enthusiasm of a new generation. On the shoulders of the first generation, and in dialogue with great thinkers of the past century, including both philosophers and theologians, Ralf K. Wüstenberg examines and makes accessible for us today what Bonhoeffer learned from them concerning our own future. Suddenly this material is anything but "dated." Suddenly it is extraordinarily contemporary and unfinished, provoking us to respond to ever-more-urgent questions. How, for example, are we to transmit Christology in view of the Holocaust?

I find his thesis "to live as to believe" to be extraordinarily significant and fruitful. Demonstrating anew and examining critically the continuity of Bonhoeffer's work, he illumines the history of influence of past decades while at the same time revealing new relationships, especially with regard to Wilhelm Dilthey and William James. In this book, Ralf K. Wüstenberg takes each of us to school anew, showing us the way to a new ecumenical adventure.

Eberhard Bethge
President of the International Bonhoeffer Society

Abbreviations

For Bonhoeffer's Works

DBW   *Dietrich Bonhoeffer Werke* in 16 volumes (Munich: Christian Kaiser, 1986ff.). English translation: *Dietrich Bonhoeffer Works.* General Editor Wayne W. Floyd, Jr. (Minneapolis: Fortress Press, 1996ff.). (Citations according to the *Dietrich Bonhoeffer Werke* except for *DBW* 2, *DBW* 3, and *DBW* 5, which are already available as *Dietrich Bonhoeffer Works.* For a comprehensive listing of previous translations of Bonhoeffer's works into English, see Wayne W. Floyd and Clifford J. Green, *Bonhoeffer Bibliography* [Evanston, Ill., 1992].)

DBW 1   *Sanctorum Communion* (Munich: Kaiser, 1986).

DBW 2   *Act and Being* (Minneapolis: Fortress, 1996).

DBW 3   *Creation and Fall* (Minneapolis: Fortress, 1997).

DBW 4   *Nachfolge* (Minneapolis: Fortress, 1989).

DBW 5   *Life Together: Prayerbook of the Bible* (Minneapolis: Fortress, 1996).

DBW 6   *Ethik* (Munich: Kaiser, 1992).

DBW 7   *Fragmente aus Tegel* (Munich: Kaiser, 1994).

DBW 9   *Jugend und Studium 1918-1927* (Munich: Kaiser, 1986).

DBW 10   *Barcelona, Berlin, Amerika 1928-1931* (Munich: Kaiser, 1992).

DBW 11   *Ökumene, Universität, Pfarramt 1931-1932* (Munich: Kaiser, 1994).

DBW 13   *London 1933-1935* (Munich: Kaiser, 1994).

GS   Dietrich Bonhoeffer, *Gesammelte Schriften* in 6 volumes. Edited by Eberhard Bethge (Munich: Kaiser, 1958-74).

HEGEL   *Dietrich Bonhoeffers Hegel-Seminar 1933. Nach Aufzeichungen von Ferenc Lehel.* Edited by Ilse Tödt. Internationales Bonhoeffer Forum 8 (Munich: Kaiser, 1988).

IBF   *Internationales Bonhoeffer Forum* (Munich: Kaiser, 1976ff.).

LOVE LETTERS   *Love Letters* from Cell 92. The correspondence between Dietrich Bonhoeffer and Maria von Wedemeyer, 1943-45. Edited by Ruth-Alice von Bismarck and Ulrich Kabitz (Eng. trans., Nashville: Abingdon Press, 1995).

MW   *Die Mündige Welt* (Munich: Kaiser, 1955ff.).

NL   *Nachlass Dietrich Bonhoeffer. Ein Verzeichnis Archiv-Sammlung-Bibliothek.* Edited by Dietrich Meyer with Eberhard Bethge (Munich: Kaiser, 1987).

WEN   *Widerstand und Ergebung. Neuausgabe* (Munich: Kaiser, 1985³). English translation, *Letters and Papers from Prison* (New York: Macmillan, 1972). Citations according to *Widerstand und Ergebung. Neuausgabe,* translation of Doug Stott. For differences in pagination see Synopsis of *WEN* and *LPP*.

Other Abbreviations

ATR	*Anglican Theological Review*
Bijdr	*Bijdragen. Tijdschrift voor philosophie en theologie*
CJT	*Canadian Journal of Theology*
CQR	*Church Quarterly Review*
ET	*Expository Times*
ETR	*Etudes théologiques et religieuses*
EvT	*Evangelische Theologie*
HTR	*Harvard Theological Review*
RelLife	*Religion in Life*
RelS	*Religious Studies*
RMS	*Renaissance and Modern Studies*
RUO	*Revue de l'université d'Ottawa*
SJT	*Scottish Journal of Theology*
STK	*Svensk teologisk kvartalskrift*
Theol	*Theology*
TLZ	*Theologische Literaturzeitung*
TZ	*Theologie en zielzorg*
USQR	*Union Seminary Quarterly Review*
ZTK	*Zeitschrift für Theologie und Kirche*

Synopsis

Widerstand und Ergebung. Neuausgabe = *WEN* (Munich: Kaiser, 1985[3])
Letters and Papers from Prison = *LPP* (New York: Macmillan, 1972)

IV. After the Failure — July 1944 to February 1945

Introduction

In May 1944, Dietrich Bonhoeffer, the theologian and member of the resistance, wrote to his friend Eberhard Bethge from the military interrogation prison in Berlin-Tegel: "I am currently reflecting on how the concepts of penitence, faith, justification, rebirth, sanctification . . . might be reinterpreted in a 'worldly' fashion. I will write more to you on this."[1] In the ensuing theological correspondence, Bonhoeffer begins using the famous formulations about the "religionless age" toward which we are moving and the "world come of age" that is able to exist without the guardianship of "God." Through such formulations, Bonhoeffer tries to create an interpretive form in which Christ genuinely becomes the Lord of the world again. This form, according to which religion no longer constitutes one of the preconditions for salvation, Bonhoeffer calls a "worldly" or "nonreligious" interpretation. This does not refer to some abstract interpretive form; what Bonhoeffer envisions here is a nonreligious interpretation *of biblical concepts* themselves.

But what does it mean to interpret nonreligiously? Have we, here at the conclusion to the 20th century, really become religionless? What concept of religion is Bonhoeffer really using when he presents this demand for nonreligious interpretation? An almost indeterminable plethora of secondary literature revolves around precisely these questions,[2] though most studies tend to illustrate the multifaceted nature of these problems rather than offer any sustainable solutions. Thus when Bonhoeffer predicts a religionless age, some reproach him as an "atheist" (A. MacIntyre)[3] or "secularist" (A. Loen),[4] while others celebrate him as an "elemental believer" (B. Jaspert)[5] or as a "religious naturalist" (J. Macquarrie);[6] still others view him as the "father of the death-of-God theology" (W. Hamilton *et al.*).[7] Or is he a "gnostic" (C. B. Armstrong, M. D. Hunnex),[8] a "language analyst" (P. van Buren),[9] a "hermeneutician" (most recently K.-M. Kodalle),[10] a "conservative" (E. C. Bianchi),[11] or merely a "recipient" (G. Krause)?[12]

Every possible answer seems to have been proffered. Although we could continue this list even further, we will limit ourselves here to several distinctive views to provide a cross-section of the various forms of misinterpretation that invariably arise whenever Bonhoeffer is interpreted against his own documented intentions — either from the perspective of the regnant religious or secular view of an age or from that of a particular theological school.[13] In the meantime, scholars have for decades repeatedly drawn attention to such misinterpretations.

As early as 1962, D. Jenkins warned against allowing talk of "religionlessness" to degenerate into a "slogan," a warning J. A. Phillips (1967) repeated with reference to Jenkins. J. Mark (1973) then advised against allowing the thesis of religionlessness to become a "springboard" upon which virtually any theology might articulate itself.[14] In 1993, following J. A. Phillips, S. Plant observed that since the 1950s the demand for a "nonreligious interpretation" had become a "slogan for a wide range of theological trends."[15] The British Barth-scholar T. F. Torrance describes the entire scope of this disaster of Bonhoeffer misinterpretations:

> Yet the tragedy of the situation is that in the malaise of recent years instead of really listening to Bonhoeffer, many German thinkers and writers and churchmen have come to "use" Bonhoeffer for their own ends, as a means of objectifying their own image of themselves. And they have been aided and abetted in this by people in Britain and the U.S.A. In this way Bonhoeffer's thought has been severely twisted and misunderstood, especially when certain catch-phrases like "religionless Christianity" and "worldly holiness" are worked up into systems of thought sharply opposed to Bonhoeffer's basic Christian theology — not least his Christology.[16]

Whoever fails to see Bonhoeffer's christological center misinterprets him in the larger sense, even and especially with regard to the notion of nonreligious interpretation. Hence G. Ebeling's admonition that the nonreligious interpretation is for Bonhoeffer nothing other than christological interpretation[17] has maintained its status for nearly four decades as a fundamental insight within Bonhoeffer scholarship. Although virtually every publication in Bonhoeffer studies has cited Ebeling's formulation,[18] it has not yet been examined in any concrete fashion. That is, if interpreting nonreligiously means interpreting christologically, what does this interpretation then mean *concretely?*

The question of the content and intention of nonreligious interpretation provides the underlying guide in the following discussion. Its answer will involve first of all a look at Bonhoeffer's own writings. What does Bonhoeffer himself have to say about *religion?* The approach I will take, which I contend is intrinsic to Bonhoeffer's writings themselves, will then open up the problem of whether he has a concept of religion at all, an issue not previously discussed. The second section explores the influence of both dialectical theology and the philosophy of life on Bonhoeffer's nonreligious interpretation. On this basis, third, I will argue for the centrality of "life" as a theological category in Bonhoeffer's prison theology.

Meanings of "Religion" in Bonhoeffer

A. Religion in the Work of Dietrich Bonhoeffer

1. Reports and Seminar Papers

A survey of Bonhoeffer's references to religion prior to 1927 reveals an interesting picture insofar as hardly a single statement aims at any critique of religion as such. In 1924, he speaks quite unaffectedly about Christianity as a world religion, and discovers that neither Christianity nor Buddhism, in contrast to Israelite piety or to Islam, can be a religion of the law.[1] In a seminar paper on "Luther's Attitude" from 1925,[2] the student Bonhoeffer positively emphasizes Luther's "inwardly religious side": "Despite the most profound world pessimism, his inner religious certainty endures in its most personal manifestation; we must remember this" (300). In a report from the same year,[3] he even places "Christian religion" on the same level as divine revelation. He can then also speak of "religion in the form of church and congregation" (321).

An allusion to a critique of religion can be detected in a note on Luther's lectures on Romans:[4] "The intention of theological logic is to free itself from psychologizing" (324). The catchword "psychologizing" conceals a critique of E. Troeltsch's doctrine of the religious a priori,[5] a concept that will acquire significance in Bonhoeffer's later critique of religion. After this more indirect reference to a critique of religion, we encounter in the following year (1926) the familiar understanding of religion again.

In a study "Joy in Early Christianity,"[6] the Harnack student finds that in the New Testament letters, the notion of "joy" emphasizes even more than it does in the Gospels the commonality of the religious possession (418). But in the Gospel of John, too, he finds that "joy is not essentially an expression of emotion, or joyous agitation, but is essentially identical with the 'certainty of faith,' and is thus an inalienable religious possession" (424). One of Bonhoeffer's sermons from May 1926 on Psalm 127:1 rounds out these early, appreciatory statements concerning religion.[7] The culminating assertion is that "God builds by granting us grace; by speaking the 'yes' to us and to our actions, to our work on ourselves, and to our efforts at elevating economics, health, morality, and religion" (515). This positive coupling of morality and religion reflects the liberal inheritance which Bonhoeffer begins to shed under the influence of dialectical theology.

2. From *Sanctorum Communio* to the *Ethics*

a. As a Doctoral Candidate

Bonhoeffer criticizes religion in his dissertation *Sanctorum Communio* from the year 1927.[8] In addition to formulations such as "religion is the form of the church" from 1925, we now read that the church is not a "religious community" (79), nor an "association of religiously interested persons" (174), but "Christ existing as ecclesial community" (76, 87, 126). Under the heading of the fifth chapter "Sanctorum Communio" (77ff.), the alternative is presented as "not religion, but revelation, not a religious community, but the church. That is what the reality of Jesus Christ means" (97).

Similarly, the understanding of religion as mysticism is reflected in *Sanctorum Communio* (e.g., 82f., 113). The candidate's understanding of religion and morality obviously follows that of his dissertation advisor: "In their real meaning, morality and religion are eliminated from the essence of human beings, and still become visible only in the forms of legal order and of natural religion" (69).[9] Bonhoeffer finally turns against Friedrich Schleiermacher by insisting that the church not be understood as satisfying religious needs[10] (102, n. 18; here he insists that to understand the church as the "satisfaction of needs" is "construe it individualistically"; on the concept of "individualism," cf. esp. 65, 116, 124, 154f.).

b. As an Assistant Pastor

During his time as an assistant pastor in Barcelona, Bonhoeffer occasionally touched on the theme of religion in lectures and sermons, as when in a lecture in December 1928[11] he describes religious partiality metaphorically: "For the psyche of the 19th and 20th centuries, religion plays the role of the so-called quiet room to which one gladly withdraws for a couple of hours before returning to the office."[12]

For the assistant pastor, religion is determined by an anthropological incongruity, namely, the process of beginning with human beings in thinking about God. "The religious path from human beings to God leads to the idol of our hearts which we have formed after our own image. Neither knowledge, nor morality, nor religion leads to God. . . . If human beings and God are to come together, there can be but one path: God's path to human beings" (315). With regard to religion and morality, he concludes retrospectively that "religion and morality can become the most dangerous enemy of God's advent among human beings, i.e., of the good news of the Christian message" (315).

In a lecture to his congregation on prophecy in Israel, Bonhoeffer is also able to speak differently about religion.[13] Following a citation from Amos (3:2), he insists that

> For the person who gives up or defiles religion, religion itself conceals a thorn of death. . . . Defiling religion means to believe one possesses it. It is not we who possess God, but God who possesses us; not the human being who disposes over God, but God who disposes over human beings. To be religious means to recognize that one will never be religious; having God means realizing that human beings can never have God. (296)

Here religion is identified with faith in God. Bonhoeffer seems to be using the concept of religion in various ways, both criticizing *and* positively evaluating religion. This understanding of religion as a path to God is also found in the Barcelona sermons. In a sermon on justification and religion[14] from March 1928, we read that "religion is at once both the most grandiose and the most tender of all human attempts to get at the eternal from within the anxiety and disquietude of the human heart" (457).

In June 1928,[15] he places religion into a pneumatological context and says metaphorically: "We bring forth our most precious, purest trea-

3

sures: our morality and our religion. But behold, the divine fire singes and burns till nothing is left of all our glory" (475). And in September 1928:[16] "Happiness and religion belong together like glitter and gold; religion that does not make a person happy is not religion. But this means we are conceiving religion from the perspective of human beings themselves, and evaluating it only with respect to human beings as the center of the world" (506).

c. As an Assistant

In his *Habilitationsschrift Act and Being*,[17] Bonhoeffer grants Karl Barth the "theological right" with which he attacks Friedrich Schleiermacher's confusion of religion and grace (cf. 154). Put briefly, Bonhoeffer rejects "the equation of religion and revelation in idealism and the transcendental identification of revelation with religion."[18] For Bonhoeffer, faith is "something essentially different from religion" (93).

Bonhoeffer's *Habilitationsschrift* is subtitled "Transcendental Philosophy and Ontology in Systematic Theology." Commensurate with this subtitle, Bonhoeffer believes that both the "transcendental attempt" and the "ontological attempt" have failed to solve the problem of act and being (cf. 33-80). He similarly criticizes the respective understandings of religion associated with the two philosophical premises. Under the heading "1. The Transcendental Attempt" (33ff.), Bonhoeffer writes about Hegel:

> What reason can perceive from itself (as Hegel puts it) is revelation, and so God is completely locked into consciousness. In the living reflection on itself, the I understands itself from itself. It relates itself to itself, and consequently to God, in unmediated reflection. That is why religion = revelation; there is no room for faith and word, if they are seen as entities contrary to reason. (52f.; cf. also 57f.)

Under "2. The Ontological Attempt" (59ff.), Bonhoeffer remarks that

> the object of Scheler's investigation is the essence of the idea of God, rather than the existence of God (Dasein Gottes), and that he does not proceed to the positing of the reality of God. Scheler is not prepared to accept as a proof of God's existence that belief in the reality of God is given as part of the religious phenomenon. (65f.)

For M. Scheler, the "demand for a proof for God [lies] outside the basic religious experience" (66).

In addition to its critique of religion, we also find in *Act and Being* a particular accentuation of a theology of revelation seemingly anticipating the formulations of the Tegel theology. *Act and Being* is thus already concerned with a "concretion of 'what Dasein is called by means of and for God'" (153), and already asserts that "the world . . . 'is for' human beings in Christ the world set free from the I" (153). And it expresses quite pregnantly that "God is free not from human beings, but for them" (90f.).

d. As a Scholar Abroad

Bonhoeffer's inaugural lecture[19] and then his teaching activity at Union Theological Seminary in New York both follow this line, already at work in *Act and Being*, of trying to determine the relation between theology and philosophy. "This at least has to be clear, what we intend to be, Christian theologians or philosophers."[20] In 1931, Bonhoeffer as a scholar abroad places Karl Barth in the tradition of Christian theologians; by contrast, he places religion in the tradition of philosophy. Barth's theology shows how all human attempts to come to God must fail, and condemns "all morality and religion" (438). "It is in the last analysis the great antithesis of the word of God and the word of man, of grace and religion, of a pure Christian category and general religious category, of reality and interpretation" (440). With regard to the natural sciences, Bonhoeffer asserts that "cosmology may come to the assumption of a last ground of the world and may call that 'God'; all we can say in the name of Christian theology is that this God is not the God of revelation and not the creator" (694). The attentive reader can hear the critique of the concept of the deus ex machina resonating here; reference to "God" for the "religious God" — as becomes common in the Tegel theology[21] — is attested for the first time in this passage.

In his report on this stay in America,[22] Bonhoeffer also mentions the scope of his philosophical readings:[23] "I have read almost the entire philosophical work of William James, which captivated me to a remarkable degree" (*DBW* 10.268). William James is reckoned among the empirical thinkers in whom "the key to modern theological language is also to be found" (269). In contrast to the cognitive-theoretical perspective of Transcendental Philosophy, one can say that for pragmatism questions such as the Kantian question of knowledge are "nonsense," and are not a problem in the first place because they do not take life any further. Truth is not "valid," but rather "works"; that is its criterion. Thinking and life are realized here quite visibly in close proximity. (269)[24]

The concept of "life" apparently acquired significance for the student abroad as a result of his having read William James. He also speaks about pragmatism as a "life philosophy" (271), though "life" is allegedly defined individualistically.[25] Bonhoeffer observes critically that this pragmatism in its most extreme form ("growing God") also led to a creative coupling of "religion and faith in progress" (269), with religion becoming social ethics.[26] American ecclesiology allegedly confuses "the church with a religious association," a criticism recalling *Sanctorum Communio*.

Bonhoeffer's criticism is that "instead of the priesthood of believers, we have the right of membership in the association, and instead of the *rite vocatus* we have the pastor as the association chairman" (277). For the theology of the "social gospel," "Christianity is an ethical religion (or indeed is ethics and ethics alone); the Decalogue and its interpretation in the Sermon on the Mount occupy the central position."[27] Bonhoeffer counters this by asserting that "God is not the immanent progressive ethical principle of history, but the Lord who judges human beings and their works; he is the ultimate sovereign."[28]

e. As Private Lecturer

In the winter semester of 1931/32, Bonhoeffer offered a lecture course on "History of Systematic Theology in the 20th Century."[29] He defines the relation between religion and individualism in a contemporary context:

> Individualism has destroyed the Protestantism of the Reformation. In the post-Copernican age, the word *religio* appears in the place of 'faith' (the English Deists), and refers to the ultimate, most delicate human possibilities. The human being is discovered as being related to God.[30]

The process of cultural secularization has come to an end in the 20th century.

Every sphere of life seeks a connection [with this process] within the secular sphere. Laws of action [emerge] from [the] laws inherent in the situation: self-given laws. The appropriate action then means ethically: autonomy. (185f.)

Here "autonomy" acquires significance for the first time as a working concept in historical excursuses (cf. also 190, 191, and 193 [here in connection with W. Dilthey]). The third section of this fourteen-part lecture series deals with the topic "The Concept of Religion as a Concept of Mediation" (147ff.), and addresses critically J. Kaftan, E. Troeltsch, and the neo-Kantians. Criticism of liberal theology is conducted within the framework of dialectical theology. Karl Barth "no longer wishes to confuse religion with God" (195) and "in the name of God turns against religion" (197). "Religion offers not spiritual healing, but only illness with respect to God" (198). Summarizing, Bonhoeffer believes that "theology is absolutely not to be confused with philosophy of religion or with a doctrine of faith" (199).

The lecture series "The Essence of the Church" from the summer semester of 1932[31] seeks the "Locus of the Church" (Part I, 231ff.) "In the World" (Part I.A, 231f.) and "In Christendom" (Part I.B, 233f.), and then concludes with respect to Catholicism and cultural Protestantism that "neither the state church nor the middle class" is the locus of the church (232). The church does not take up residence "at privileged places" (233), nor is it found "on the periphery of life" (233). The implied critique of religion here is ecclesiologically directed and will reappear in the Tegel prison cell in the notions of "religiously privileged persons" and "partiality." In the lectures on "Systematic Theology in the 20th Century," Bonhoeffer concludes that for the relation between religion and individualism "individualization is the basic error of Protestant theology" (238), a criticism referring essentially to Schleiermacher:

His "church" is a voluntary assembly of Christian devotees. This refers the church back to the piety of individuals. The church is not the ultimate presupposition. He puts individual religiosity before the brackets.[32]

Whereas in the lectures on "Systematic Theology in the 20th Century" Bonhoeffer understood this process of religious individualization as having begun with Deism, here he understands it as having begun ecclesiologically after Martin Luther. "The disintegration of the idea of congregation commences immediately after Luther" (238).

In "Your Kingdom Come," a public lecture Bonhoeffer delivered in November 1932,[33] he understands religion on the one hand as flight from the world, and on the other as succumbing to the world. The introductory thesis is accordingly that "we are either provincials or secularists" (270). E. Feil[34] has correctly observed that the critique of religion as secularism and provincialism in this lecture corresponds to the critique of religion as Idealism and Transcendental Philosophy in *Act and Being*.

The lectures on "Creation and Fall,"[35] a theological explication of Genesis 1–3 from the winter semester of 1932/33, do not address the topic of religion, though it is implicit that "Bonhoeffer did not want to speak of life before God the way Hegel did when the latter described people in their practice of religion. . . . Bonhoeffer agreed much more with Nietzsche's criticism of 'afterworldly people' ['provincialists']."[36]

Also in the winter semester of 1932/33, Bonhoeffer held lectures on "Recent Theology" in which he presented and critiqued various contemporary theological outlines.[37] The striking feature of these lectures is a positive presentation of Karl Barth (303-7, 318-21) and almost in contrast to this a critical presentation of K. Heim (307-16). For Bonhoeffer, Barth's theology bears features of religious criticism.

> God's vertical word is judgment over all humankind, over nature, history, even over human inwardness and piety. That he had to come proves that we were not able to come. Hence God's coming is a criticism of all religion. (303f.)

"Inwardness" and "religion" refer to human yearning for God. "The first attack against Karl Barth was launched from the position of religious inwardness" (304). It should be pointed out that the conceptual pair "religion" and "inwardness" thus appears in Bonhoeffer's work as early as 1932. In addition, a sentence occurs in connection with Barth that seems to anticipate statements of 1944: "In his revelation, God is thus completely transcendent and completely immanent" (*Gesammelte Schriften* 5.304). From Tegel, Bonhoeffer writes that "God is beyond or transcendent even at the center of our lives" (*WEN*, 308).

The lecture on "Christology" which Bonhoeffer offered in the summer semester of 1933[38] does not systematically address religion as such.[39] Quite the contrary, closer observation reveals contradictions even in his understanding of religion. He abruptly speaks in a completely positive fashion about religion when he poses the "religious question" in connection with the "who-question":

> The who-question is *the* religious question. It is the question about other human beings and their requirements, about other existence, about other authority. It is the question about love for our fellows. The questions of transcendence and existence become questions of person. That means: Human beings cannot answer the who-question themselves. (170)

Was this capacity for self-answering not associated precisely with religion? Would not precisely the who-question be *the* religious question? Whence this positive understanding of religion? Bonhoeffer seems to be introducing the term "religion" with a certain degree of sovereignty here; in any event, he does make use of it at will in connection with Christology.

Elsewhere in this lecture, he criticizes religion again in his familiar manner. In surveying the various forms of heresy (207ff.), Bonhoeffer also assigns a place to liberal theologians: A. Ritschl as a docetist (211),[40] A. Schlatter as an Ebionite (214), and F. Schleiermacher as a modalist (228). The latter is also suspected of docetic heresy, specifically in the religious sense; for F. Schleiermacher,

> history is the bearer of certain religious ideas and values. History is the appearance of suprahistorical ideas. One of its values is, e.g., the idea of the religious personality of human beings with the "perpetual energy of its consciousness of God" (Schleiermacher, *The Christian Faith*, §94). Jesus is the embodiment or bearer of this idea in history. (210ff.)

Bonhoeffer also held a class in dogmatic issues during the summer semester of 1933, focusing on the religious philosophy of Hegel.[41] The class was based on the edition compiled by G. Lasson, and dealt especially with volumes XII, *The Concept of Religion*, and XIV, *Absolute Religion*. The fragmentary notes from the class attest a thorough discussion of volume XII, something broadly documented in the student notes (13-94). Basically, "Bonhoeffer read Hegel's philosophy as a theologian, more precisely, as an ecclesiologically oriented theologian" (10). Indeed, the student notes reveal that the course was concerned with theologically penetrating and outlining Hegel's philosophy of religion,[42] the result of which is that the specific profile of Bonhoeffer's own understanding of religion recedes.

Only rarely does he depart from Hegel's own works and criticize Hegel himself:

> Hegel allegedly an intellectualist . . . God at the disposal of human beings. Human beings having access to reason. Hegel protects himself from this objection. Comes from rationalism, distances himself from it. Human beings are at God's disposal. Does not come from autonomy. (20f.)

These fragmentary statements from class notes document the critical horizon against which Hegel was read. The evaluation was: "Overcoming the Enlightenment. Philosophical reconciliation between reason and religion. Reconciliation between human beings and reason" (20).

One can at least ask whether this already reflects the theme of religion and modernity. In any case, Bonhoeffer does remark with regard to Hegel's "ideal moments of religion" (vol. XII, 187ff.): "The issue here is the principle of concretion. Direct line from Spinoza to Hegel, which Kant omits" (19). With regard to secularism, Hegel suggests there was "an age in which all science was science of God. Today we know everything, but nothing about God" (12.5).

One participant recalls in this context that

> the word "today" was strongly emphasized; there must have been a reason for this. Was the secularism of modern human beings being addressed, secularism that is our own experience today? (In vol.) XII, pp. 4f. Hegel asserts that "the more our knowledge of finite things has expanded as a result of the sciences themselves having expanded virtually into infinity, all the more has the circle of knowledge of God contracted." In the *Letters and Papers from Prison*, Bonhoeffer raises the question: Where does God still have any room? (18)

f. As Preacher

In addition to Bonhoeffer's lecture activity at Berlin University, we also have a series of Berlin sermons from this period.[43] In a sermon on Thanksgiving 1931, Bonhoeffer juxtaposes God and religion:

> We often hear and say that religion makes a person happy and harmonious and peaceful and satisfied. That may well be correct for religion. But for God, the living God, it is not correct; it is fundamentally false.[44]

10

Anticipating the concept of a deus ex machina, Bonhoeffer writes on the first Advent Sunday in 1931 that

> technology and economics have become independent powers threatening to destroy human beings . . . and religions, too, are unable to help us get even a little beyond this. And in our recognition of this human defeat at the hands of reality, the one great hope arises for a new kind of human being, for a rebirth, for the human being of the future.[45]

According to Bonhoeffer, we must wait for this hope to come to fruition. "If ever a generation had to learn to wait, then it is our own. We wait for better political circumstances. . . . We wait for a new morality, for a new religion."[46] A sermon from 1932 on Colossians 3 expresses the view that this "new religion" will have to do without any religious a priori, and that Christianity cannot simply be conceived in historic continuity up to the modern age:

> . . . we have unfolded before us . . . the entire crisis of our Christian being . . . : If there was a time, if there was a Christianity when one did believe such things, when one did entertain such colossal notions, when one was able to encounter the other . . . at least with that particular certainty that both of them were resurrected in Christ — then our own age, our own Christianity, our own faith constitutes an enormous impoverishment, and we have suffered gargantuan losses.[47]

Bonhoeffer criticizes the development of the modern human being who thinks autonomously: "Our fathers yet said 'in the name of God, amen,' and still lived under the illusion that by saying this they were saying something of import."[48] He does, however, question whether this development of necessity leads to a mourning over past times, for such a view would approximate the German-Christian worldview of the year 1932. "We should once again say 'in the name of God, amen'; religion should be cultivated again and the Christian worldview propagated again."[49]

For the continuation of the present study of Bonhoeffer's understanding of religion, we must remember that as early as 1932 he was already distinguishing between a premodern and a modern-autonomous understanding of Christianity and of religion.

A sermon on Mark 9, also from 1932, recalls the criticism of religion found in *Sanctorum Communio,* where Bonhoeffer distinguishes sharply between faith in God and faith "in our religious community."[50] In a devotional piece at the beginning of the summer semester of 1932, Bonhoeffer critically poses the question of religion's self-understanding:

> We have grown accustomed to finding in religion something that comes from a need within the human soul and then satisfies that need. . . . But we forget here one decisive question, namely, whether religion itself is something true; whether it is the truth; for it may be that although religion is indeed quite beautiful, it is not true, and that although it is all a beautiful illusion, it is nonetheless still just an illusion.[51]

In Berlin, he preached in May 1933 on Exodus 32:

> God has abandoned us, but we need gods! Religions! If you cannot coerce the living God, then make gods for us yourself! . . . Keep religion for the people, give them worship services.[52]

In a lecture on the "Evocation of New Testament Texts" in August 1935,[53] Bonhoeffer again poses the question that was to become so important for his Tegel theology, namely, that concerning human autonomy.[54] He places this question into the context of the various possibilities for evoking the New Testament. Two possibilities emerge: Such evocation can be understood as a justification of New Testament thinking before the world ("this evocation . . . leads directly to paganism" [305]); this, however, lacks honesty. *Or* the course is "not a justification of Christianity before the present, but a justification of the present before the Christian message" (306). In his lecture, Bonhoeffer explicates the second possibility. But where does the notion of autonomy now come into play? He points out that "the New Testament is to justify itself before the present. In this form, the question has become acute for the first time in the age of the emancipation of autonomous reason, that is, in rationalism" (303). He continues:

> To the extent rationalism was nothing more than the appearance of the previously latent human claim to shape one's own life autonomously on the basis of the powers of the given world, this question was admittedly one that had already been raised in the human claim to autonomy itself; that is, autonomous persons who at the same time wish to confess

12

Christianity demand the justification of the Christian message before the forum of their autonomy. If this succeeds, they call themselves Christians; if not, they call themselves pagans. (303f.)

The concepts "autonomous reason," "autonomous shaping of one's life," and "autonomous person" appear here in a peculiarly negative light,[55] reflected as they are in connection with a justification — one Bonhoeffer rejects — of Christianity before the world. In this lecture, autonomy seems almost a hindrance to Christian faith and its understanding of the world. — Not a word on the topic of Christ *and* the world come of age.[56]

In a sermon outline on justification from the same year (1935),[57] Bonhoeffer criticizes the language of salvation as applied to the individual soul. "We must finally get away from the notion that the gospel is concerned with the salvation of the soul of the individual, or with showing the way from the despair of the sinner to the sinner's blessedness" (202). In the same context, he also speaks about religious individualism, which in his opinion Luther at no time advocated. Bonhoeffer continues, asserting that "in this religious individualism and in this methodology, the human being remains at the center" (202).

In a sermon outline at Epiphany 1936,[58] Bonhoeffer places religion into the context of paganism. "All peoples, religions, and human beings like to talk about the victory of light over darkness. This is pagan wisdom and hope" (187).

From the year 1938 we have a homiletic remark on religion in a sermon on Romans 12.[59] On the subject of love for one's enemy, Bonhoeffer remarks that "Jesus Christ, however, was in the midst of his enemies. It was precisely there that he wanted to be. And there we, too, should be. That distinguishes us from all other teachers and religions. The devout want to be among themselves. Christ, however, wants us to be in the midst of our enemies, just as he was" (431). Religion is thus incapable of love for one's enemy.

g. As Leader of the Pastoral Seminar

From the year 1935/36 we have Bonhoeffer's lecture on "The Visible Church in the New Testament,"[60] where he distinguishes between church and religion in the manner of *Sanctorum Communio*: ". . . it is not a new religion that is established; rather, a piece of the world is created anew,

— that is the founding of the church" (330). From this Bonhoeffer concludes that

> the events at Pentecost are thus not primarily a matter of a new religiosity; they are the message of a new creative act of God. And that means that the entirety of life is claimed. This is not even a matter of giving the religious priority over the profane, but of giving God's actions priority over both the religious and the profane. This is the fundamental difference between the church and a "religious community." The "religious community" involves giving the religious priority over the profane, of dividing life into the religious and the profane; it involves a hierarchy of values. The self-purpose of the religious community is the "religious" as the highest — one might even say: God-given — value; the church as that particular piece of world and humanity created anew from within God's Spirit inquires concerning total obedience to the Spirit who creates (both the religious and the profane) anew. (330)

Religion is thus already understood as something "partial," while the church encompasses the "totality" of life. The dialectic of the "prayers and actions of the righteous person" familiar from the Tegel theology (cf. *WEN,* 328) resonates when Bonhoeffer continues the passage just cited as follows:

> Because the church is concerned with God, the Holy Spirit, and his word, it is not concerned specifically with religion, but with *obedience* to the word and with the *actions* of the Father, that is, with the realization of this new creation from within the Spirit. It is not the religious question or any religious concern in the larger sense that constitutes the church — from the human perspective — but obedience to the word of the compassionate new creation. But this also means that it is not any religious formula or dogma that constitutes the church, but the practical doing of what is commanded. (330f.)

If we examine the understanding of religion in the *Cost of Discipleship* of 1937,[61] we find a critical interpretation of religion in connection with Martin Luther. Religion becomes associated with "cheap grace": "And yet the victor in the history of the Reformation is not Luther's recognition of pure, costly grace, but the vigilant human religious instinct for the place at which grace can be had most cheaply" (35). As a student in 1925, Bonhoeffer was still able to speak unaffectedly about Luther's "religious certainty" and his "inwardly religious side."[62] Now, however, religion seems negatively charged in connection with Luther. In fact, "religious knowledge" and discipleship become antitheses:

> An idea of Christ, a doctrinal system, general religious knowledge of grace or of the forgiveness of sins makes discipleship unnecessary, indeed, in truth it excludes it, and is hostile to discipleship. (47).[63]

"Religious immediacy" is also inimical to discipleship. Thus Abraham "accepts the call just as it is issued. . . . Contrary to all natural immediacy, to all ethical immediacy, to all religious immediacy he obeys God's word. He presents his son as a sacrifice" (92f.). In an allusion to National Socialism, Bonhoeffer writes that

> indeed, Jesus also knows those others, the representatives and preachers of the *Volksreligion,* these powerful ones, respected ones, those who are firmly grounded on the earth, inextricably rooted in the spirit of the people, of the age, in popular piety. (102)[64]

In the second part of his book *The Church of Jesus Christ and Discipleship* (213ff.), Bonhoeffer writes about the visible congregation: "Truth, doctrine, religion do not need their own space. They are incorporeal. They are heard, learned, comprehended. That is all" (241). He later interprets this sentence christologically: "God sends his Son — only there can help be found. Neither a new idea nor a better religion is able to achieve this goal" (299).

The reference in these two citations to religion, idea, and God suggests a connection with Hegel's philosophy of religion, which Bonhoeffer rejected in his lectures on Christology in 1933.[65] Similarly, his reference in the sermon on doctrine "in contrast to any sort of religious talk" (242) suggests an allusion to Hegel by way of the concept of "doctrine."[66] The figure of E. Troeltsch allegedly provides the background to Bonhoeffer's reference to a life that "cannot be anchored religiously" (252).[67] Kierkegaard is probably also exercising considerable influence here.[68]

Life Together (1939)[69] reflects themes that the Tegel theology will later treat under the rubric of arcane discipline (such as liturgy and prayer).[70] These themes are *not* understood as *religious.* Bonhoeffer seems to be anticipating here the theme of arcane discipline.[71] He expressly turns against the notion of the "preliminary stage of religion" of the Old Testament, and in connection with an interpretation of psalms of vengeance as prayers, he insists that "nevertheless, these prayers are words of the Holy Scriptures that believing Christians cannot simply dismiss as obsolete and antiquated, as a 'preliminary stage of religion'" (53). This is the only explicit reference to religion in *Life Together*.

h. As a Guest Lecturer

Statements critical of religion can also be found in material from Bonhoeffer's second stay in the United States. On June 18, 1939, a Sunday, Bonhoeffer was disappointed by a worship service he attended and wrote in his diary:

> Simply unbearable. . . . The whole thing was a decent, luxuriant, self-satisfied religious celebration. Such idolization of religion prompts a revivification of the flesh which is accustomed to being held in check by God's word. Such preaching makes one libertinistic, egoistic, indifferent. Do these people really not know that one can get along just fine and even better without "religion" — if only God himself and his word did not exist?[72]

In his report on this stay in the United States[73] in the summer of 1939, Bonhoeffer deals explicitly with Karl Barth in only one instance. The representatives of contemporary American theology, Bonhoeffer suggests, are unanimous in their conscious "rejection of Barth's critique of natural theology" (351). "Failure with regard to Christology characterizes the entirety of contemporary American theology" (352). He then formulates his critique of religion quite in the tradition of dialectical theology:

> American theology and the American church as a whole have never been able to understand what "critique" through God's word means in its entire scope. That God's "critique" is directed also at religion, and even at the Christianity of its churches and at the sanctification of Christians, and that God has established his church beyond religion and ethics — ultimately none of this is understood. One indication of this is the general clinging to natural theology. In American theology, Christianity is still essentially religion and ethics. (354)

16

The diary entry can serve as a commentary here. Concerning the a-religious nature of college students, Bonhoeffer insists that "things have to end up this way if one does not ultimately understand that 'religion' really is superfluous" (300).

The "Prayerbook of the Bible" from 1940[74] contains only one passage critical of religion. As in *Life Together,* the concern is with using the psalms of vengeance as prayer: "All attempts to pray these psalms seem doomed to failure. They really seem to lay before us the so-called preliminary religious stage in relation to the New Testament" (174). And yet these attempts only "seem" to be so doomed, for according to Bonhoeffer, the psalm of vengeance actually does lead "to the cross of Jesus and to the love of God that forgives enemies" (175). "In this way the crucified Jesus teaches us to pray truly the psalms of wrath" (176). Bonhoeffer rejects the notion of the Old Testament as a "preliminary religious stage" to the New Testament, and finds the hermeneutical unity of the Old and New Testaments to be quite clear.[75] The critique of religion on the whole bears a hermeneutical-exegetical accentuation.

In an essay-outline on "Theology and Congregation," also from 1940,[76] Bonhoeffer issues the demand for a congregation that has come of age.[77] He first enumerates the customary misunderstandings of the congregation over against theology, such as

> the Pietist misunderstanding: theology is a matter of the intellect. . . . the Orthodox: all preaching is instruction. . . . the Academic: theology is a strict discipline, a course of study, the university, not something for the laity. (422)

These are followed by "the practical necessities fostering a clear relationship between the congregation and theology," among which Bonhoeffer also includes "independent study and interpretation of Scripture; coming of age in knowledge" (422). He speaks here about coming of age in connection with the "congregation," but not yet with reference to the "world."

i. As Theologian of the Conspiracy

The material associated with Bonhoeffer's *Ethics*[78] was composed between 1940 and 1943, and we thus distinguish between various "periods."[79] With regard to the topic of religion, the years 1940-42 are of particular interest.

Bonhoeffer composed the manuscript "Christ, Reality, and ░░░░," in which he takes up again his thesis about the nonexchange-able character of church and religious community from *Sanctorum Communio.*

> The church can defend its own space not by fighting for him [Jesus Christ], but rather for the salvation of the world. Otherwise the church becomes a "religious community" that fights for its own concerns and ceases to be the church of God in the world. (49f.)

Religion (in the form of a religious community) on the one hand, and the church on the other thus stand diametrically opposed. Bonhoeffer apparently maintained this juxtaposition of religion and church, appropriated from *Sanctorum Communio,* even into the period of his *Ethics.* In addition to marriage, work, and state, the church also has its divine mandate. Following his doctrine of this mandate, Bonhoeffer formulates as follows: "Any subdivision into separate spaces is forbidden here. The entire human being stands before the entire earthly and eternal reality just as God has prepared it in Jesus Christ" (59). The Tegel correspondence will deepen his understanding of how religion fails to maintain this totality of human and divine reality.

The manuscript "Ethics as Formation," also from 1940, contains repeated statements critical of religion. "The church is concerned not with religion, but with the figure of Christ and its formative manifestation among a host of human beings" (84). Here *religion* and *church* are opposed directly, and not, as was the case above, only indirectly the *religious community* and the *church,* a situation probably reflecting the influence of *Sanctorum Communio.*[80] The partial character of religion that will acquire significance in Tegel also resonates when Bonhoeffer writes:

> The church is the incarnate, judged human being in Christ who has been awakened to new life. Thus initially, it has essentially nothing to do with the so-called religious functions of human beings, but with the whole person in that person's existence in the world with all its relationships. (84)

The manuscript "Inheritance and Decay" includes a historical reflection on "western godlessness" (113) which also touches on the topic of religion. Bonhoeffer writes that this godlessness is not the theoretical denial of the existence of a God. Rather, it is itself religion, religion born of enmity toward God. And precisely therein it is western. It cannot let go of its past, it must be essentially religious. Precisely this makes it, in the human estimation, so hopelessly godless. (113)

This passage resonates with terminology from Tegel. The fragment "The Ultimate and Penultimate Things" contains valuable references to Bonhoeffer's continuous thinking in the 1940s. He asks "whether a person can live from the ultimate alone, whether faith so to speak can be temporally extended or whether it always becomes real in life only as the final element of a span of time, of many spans of time" (143). Three years later, from his cell in Tegel, he summarizes these ideas in a pregnant formulation by asking: "We are living in the penultimate and believe the ultimate, is this not so?"[81] He continues in the manuscript to the *Ethics:*

Precisely in extremely serious situations, for example, in the face of someone severely affected by a death, why do I so often opt for "penultimate" behavior, for example by announcing through silence my solidarity in helplessness in the face of such harsh events, instead of expressing myself in what are for me the essentially familiar, accessible words of biblical consolation, even toward Christians? (143)

A letter from the cell in Tegel picks up these ideas and accentuates them with a critique of religion:

As we were again lying on the floor last night, and someone exclaimed "O God, O God" . . . I couldn't bring myself to offer him any Christian encouragement or comfort; all I did was to look at my watch and say, "It won't last more than ten minutes now."[82]

Bonhoeffer did not want to "exploit this moment for the sake of religious extortion." In ethical terms, he thus opted for "penultimate" behavior. From the perspective of religion, this behavior apparently implies acting in a "nonreligious" fashion.

The manuscript "The Love of God and the Decay of the World" from 1942 mentions the word "religion" in only a single passage. Following his portrayal of the Fall, Bonhoeffer finds that "the yearning for a reestablishment of this lost unity is still alive" (306). He continues with the surprising parallel:

> Wherever this yearning violently makes a way for itself, in the sexual union, in which two become one flesh (Gen. 2:24), and in religion, in which a person seeks unity with God — that is, wherever one breaks through this covering, there shame creates for itself the most profound seclusion. (306)

Religion is apparently being treated here as an anthropological phenomenon together with sexual union from the perspective of "shame."[83]

In a letter from June 1942,[84] Bonhoeffer writes to his friend Eberhard Bethge that he "is able to live for days without the Bible" (420). He attributes this to his activity in the "worldly sector" and writes:

> But I sense how a resistance is growing inside me to all things "religious." Often it amounts to an instinctive loathing — which is no doubt not good. I am not religious by nature. But I must think continually of God, of Christ; authenticity, life, freedom and compassion are extremely important to me. It's just that the religious trappings of all this make me very uncomfortable. Do you understand? (420)

Bonhoeffer sensed an antithesis between the "religious nature" on the one hand, and "God" on the other; concepts such as "authenticity" and "freedom" also come into opposition to religion. Bonhoeffer describes the relationship between these antithetical concepts with the catchword "trappings": "God" is, so to speak, religiously "fitted out."

The theologian in the conspiracy continues: "I understand my present activity in the worldly sector in precisely this sense as well" *(ibid.)*. Is Bonhoeffer saying that his entering the German resistance movement is a form of "religiously unadorned" (and thus "nonreligious") interpretation? This question shows clearly how closely related are theology and biography in the person of Dietrich Bonhoeffer.

It should be pointed out that this letter provides a valuable indication of how the critique of religion extends in a continuous fashion even into the Tegel theology.

3. The Tegel Theology

From his prison cell at Tegel, Bonhoeffer confesses on November 21, 1943: "I will definitely not emerge from here as a 'homo religiosus'! Quite the contrary, here my distrust and anxiety with regard to 'religiosity' have become greater than ever" (154). In his letter of December 5, 1943, the prisoner once again picks up and then questions criticism of the "preliminary religious stage" from his book *The Cost of Discipleship:*

> Why in the Old Testament do people so energetically and so often lie . . . kill, deceive, rob . . . despair, blaspheme, and curse for the sake of God's honor, while there is none of this in the New Testament? "Preliminary religious stage"? That is an extremely naive position; it is, after all, one and the same God. But more on this later, and in person. (176)

Unfortunately, we hear nothing more on this topic. Six weeks later, Bonhoeffer writes that during a bombing run he was unable to bring himself "to offer any Christian encouragement or comfort"; he was unwilling, as we saw, to exploit this moment for the sake of "religious extortion" (see the previous discussion in connection with Bonhoeffer's *Ethics*). We observed in addition to the critique of religion ("religious exploitation") a form of "worldly" (religionless?) encouragement: "It won't last more than ten minutes now." "Religionlessness" as a consequence of a "critique of religion" is classified basically under the "penultimate." To the question of April 30, 1944, that introduced the Tegel theology, namely, "what really is Christianity or who really is Christ for us today?" he responds *ex negativo* that except for two movements, "the age of religion" (305) has come to an end among the people of his day. He differentiates between the "sincerely" religious, who "presumably mean something quite different by 'religious,'" and the "intellectually insincere among whom we might land 'religiously'" (305). He asks whether "we should throw ourselves zealously, peeved, or indignantly upon precisely this questionable group of people and try to sell our wares to them" *(ibid.).* He answers his own rhetorical question with a historical reference: For nineteen hundred years, "'Christianity' has been . . . a form (and perhaps even the true form) of 'religion'" *(ibid.).* This derives from Christianity having built upon "the human 'religious a priori'" *(ibid.).* Bonhoeffer now takes issue with this a priori and considers it historically obsolete, concluding that people are becoming "genuinely and radically religionless" *(ibid.)*. In contrast to its portrayal in the *Ethics,* religion here is no longer an anthropological entity.

Because this process of religionlessness has already commenced, the question for the church and for theology is now "how we can speak about God — without religion, that is, without precisely the temporally conditioned presuppositions of metaphysics, inwardness, etc., etc." (306). For Bonhoeffer, Karl Barth clearly set this critique of religion into motion, and he asks how it is possible to live in the world without understanding ourselves as being religiously "privileged" (cf. 306). He then questions terminologically the religious reference to the "human boundaries," a reference ultimately concealing the concept of the "deus ex machina" (cf. 307). Whereas in the letter of April 30, 1944, Bonhoeffer criticized religion in the form of metaphysics and inwardness, in his letter of May 5, 1944, he now explains further that to interpret religiously "means in my opinion to speak metaphysically on the one hand, and individualistically on the other" (312). "Has the individualistic question regarding one's own, personal salvation not almost completely disappeared for all of us?" *(ibid.)*. In the place of one's personal salvation, there now stands the biblical idea of "righteousness" and the "kingdom of God" (312). It is thus now a matter of reinterpreting the concepts of penitence, faith, justification, rebirth, and sanctification in a "worldly" fashion — in the Old Testament sense and in the sense of John 1:14 (313).

The concepts "metaphysics" and "inwardness/individualism" — primary features of Bonhoeffer's late critique of religion — are now interpreted from different perspectives: metaphysics under the aspects of "deus ex machina," "stopgap," and working hypothesis "God"; "inwardness/individualism" under the aspects of "something partial," "religiously privileged," and guardianship of "God."

a. Religion as Metaphysics

Bonhoeffer criticizes religion as metaphysics in the two aforementioned passages (letters of April 30 and May 5, 1944) as well as in the *Outline for a Book.* Here he speaks of "God" "in the conceptual forms of the absolute, the metaphysical, the infinite" (414). In contrast to other oriental religions, he contends, the "faith of the Old Testament" is not a "religion of redemption" (letter of June 27, 1944; *WEN,* 368) insofar as "myths of redemption search outside history for an eternity after death. 'Sheol' and Hades are not constructions of metaphysics" (368). In addition to this explicit reference, Bonhoeffer's critique of religion in the form of meta-physics also appears implicitly under certain other aspects:

> Religious people speak about God when human experience (sometimes as a result of being too lazy to think) is at an end, or when human powers fail — it is actually always the *deus ex machina* that they then march out. (307; my emphasis)

The "notion of the deus ex machina" always involves the "exploitation of human weakness" (307). People speak about God "at the human boundaries," but "this of necessity always lasts only until people, using their own powers, push those boundaries out further, and God as the deus ex machina becomes superfluous" (307). For Bonhoeffer, "having God function as deus ex machina only for the so-called 'ultimate questions'" (374) means that "God becomes the answer to life questions and the solution to life problems and conflicts" *(ibid.)*. In "distinct contrast to all religions," Bonhoeffer points out "the powerlessness and suffering of God" (394): "Human religiosity directs a person in distress to God's power in the world; God is the deus ex machina" *(ibid.)*. The religious interpretation of God as a "stopgap" (341) corresponds substantively to the deus-ex-machina concept. Inspired by C. F. von Weizsäcker's *Worldview of Physics,* Bonhoeffer recognizes "that we should not allow God to function as a *stopgap* for our incomplete knowledge" (341; my emphasis). Regarding the "relationship between God and scientific knowledge," Bonhoeffer believes that "we should find God in that which we know, not in that which we do not know" *(ibid.)*.

God as deus ex machina and as "stopgap" falls under the larger heading of God as a "scientific *working hypothesis*" (393; my emphasis). In addition to the scientific working hypothesis, "'God' exists as a moral, political . . . philosophical, and religious working hypothesis (Feuerbach!)" (393). The guiding theological question of April 30 is accentuated historically on June 8 under the heading "Christ and the World Come of Age" (368; similarly in the letter of June 30).[85] With regard to human development toward autonomy, Bonhoeffer follows a historical excursus in the letter of July 16, 1944 (392f.) by suggesting that "God as a working hypothesis" has been "done away with" and "overcome" (393). He writes similarly on June 8:

> Human beings have learned to come to terms with all important questions without the aid of the "working hypothesis God." In scientific,

artistic, and ethical questions, this has become a matter of course that is hardly challenged anymore; and for the past one hundred years, this has increasingly come to be the case in religious questions as well. (356)

In summary, the first chapter of the *Outline* insists that " 'God' as a working hypothesis, as a stopgap for our embarrassments, has become superfluous" (413).

b. Religion as Inwardness and Individualism

Religion as inwardness and individualism is addressed explicitly in five instances in the Tegel correspondence. The "age of religion" as the "age of inwardness and of conscience . . . is over" (305). Bonhoeffer wants to speak about God "without the temporally conditioned presuppositions . . . of inwardness, etc." (306). "To interpret religiously . . . means on the other hand to speak individualistically. . . . Has the individualistic question regarding one's own, personal salvation not almost completely disappeared for all of us?" (312). In the "preliminary remarks" to the "nonreligious interpretation of biblical concepts," Bonhoeffer writes that "the expulsion of God from the world . . . led to the attempt to retain him at least in the 'personal,' 'inward,' 'private' sphere" (377). In the *Outline*, Bonhoeffer formulates in an abbreviated fashion: "Pietism is the final attempt to maintain protestant Christianity as a religion" (413). Whereas with regard to "metaphysics" Bonhoeffer was concerned with religiously understood transcendence, with regard to "inwardness" he is turning against the incorrectly understood immanence of God.[86]

Bonhoeffer interprets religion as inwardness or as individualism under the aspect of "something partial," those who are "privileged," and the guardianship or tutelage of "God": "Not a word about religious practice; the 'religious act' is always *something partial*, while 'faith' is something whole, an act of life. Jesus calls us not to a new religion, but to life" (396; my emphasis).[87]

What does he mean by "religious practice" that leads only to something partial? In contrast to metaphysics and as a consequence of the drive toward autonomy, people yet try to hold fast to God, for example, in the " 'private' sphere. . . . Chamber-servant secrets . . . became the hunting ground for modern chaplains" (377). The object is "religious extortion," or " 'priestish' . . . snuffling around behind people's sins" (378). The mistake inherent in this practice is that one must first "spy out" people's weaknesses (378) in order to address them then as sinners. Furthermore, the belief is that "human nature consists in a person's innermost, most intimate hidden motives, that which one then calls human inwardness" (379). Bonhoeffer refutes this view biblically and explains historically the origin of inwardness (379f.).

In the letter of April 30, 1944, Bonhoeffer emphasizes the privileged character of religion and asks

> in what way are we ἐκ-κλησία, those who are called forth, without understanding ourselves religiously as being *privileged*, but rather as belonging wholly to the world? (306; my emphasis)

The view here is that religion is to be understood as a privilege, for example, "as a psychic or physical, inborn or acquired gift."[88] Religion as a privilege cannot "be there for others," cannot participate "in God's suffering in the world." Here Bonhoeffer is apparently drawing from the critique of religion he formulated as a private lecturer. In the summer semester of 1932, he similarly criticized the privileged, partial character of religion. If one does criticize religion in its privileged form, the necessary consequence is a deprivileged (= nonreligious?) interpretation: "In my opinion, the Pauline question whether περιτομή is a prerequisite for justification is today the question whether religion is a prerequisite for salvation" (307). From this it follows for Bonhoeffer that "freedom from περιτομή is also freedom from religion" *(ibid.)*.

Just as the conceptual pair "nonreligious interpretation" and "world come of age" belong together, so also "religious interpretation" and "world that is treated as if it were not of age."[89] In this sense, the partial and privileged character of religion falls under the larger heading *"guardianship."* Following a historical excursus understanding human striving for autonomy as having commenced in the 13th century, Bonhoeffer concludes that "one is trying to prove to the world come of age that it cannot live without the guardian 'God'" (357).

Against metaphysics, Bonhoeffer charges that "even if one has already capitulated in all worldly questions, there always remain the so-called 'ultimate questions' — death, sin, — to which only 'God' can provide an answer" (357). In this context, Bonhoeffer also finds the "secularized offshoots of Christian theology, namely, the existential philosophers and the psychotherapists" *(ibid.)*, who "point out to secure, satisfied, happy people that they are in reality unhappy and despairing" *(ibid.)*. The patronage of the world he considers "first meaningless, second undignified, and third unchristian" (358). "Meaningless because it tries to make people dependent on things on which they are in fact no longer dependent" *(ibid.)*. "Undignified because here an attempt is made to exploit human weakness for purposes that are alien to people and not freely chosen. Unchristian because Christ is confused with a certain stage of human religiosity" (358).

B. *Theory of Religion* or Loose Understanding of Religion?

1. Attempt at Systematization

If we survey all of Bonhoeffer's statements about "religion," an initial, formal perusal reveals three groups of "interpretations of religion." Prior to the discovery of dialectical theology we find

a. statements in the foreground that evaluate religion *positively*. These derive from seminar papers and reports from Bonhoeffer's student days.[90] After the discovery and literary involvement with Karl Barth, we find

b. statements *critical* of religion, more broadly represented first in the dissertation *Sanctorum Communio*.[91] The year 1927 marks chronologically a turn from the positive evaluation of religion to criticism of it, criticism that in the following years characterizes his understanding of religion. From this critique of religion, Bonhoeffer derives in 1944 the nonreligious interpretation with which he

c. postulates religion*lessness:* Not only is religion itself criticized (systematically-theologically), but the "age of religion" has (historically) come to an end.[92] He understands Christian faith "no longer merely as anti-religious, but as a-religious."[93]

According to this survey, the three forms in which religion is addressed in Bonhoeffer's overall work are a positive evaluation of religion, a critique of religion, and religionlessness. None of these is systematically developed, nor do the three together reveal any theory of religion. Rather, the three understandings of religion follow loosely upon one another. Bonhoeffer first evaluates religion positively, then criticizes it, and finally demands a nonreligious interpretation of biblical concepts.

Nor should this chronological division be overly pressed. On the one hand, Bonhoeffer does in isolated instances criticize religion even prior to *Sanctorum Communio*.[94] On the other, in 1933 he can describe the christological "who-question" as the "religious question."[95] And still again, as late as 1944 he can speak of Christianity as the "true religion."[96] Hence even during the stage of dialectical theology, we encounter elements of an understanding of religion that chronologically belong to the period prior to 1927, and thus to the influence of liberal theology.[97] Positive statements, critical statements, and statements about religionlessness not only follow developmentally one upon the other, but also occur systematically juxtaposed.

2. Inconclusive Conceptual Definitions

It seems that Bonhoeffer is using the word "religion" in a way that not only makes a definition of its content difficult, but often does not even try to provide any such definition. Rather, "religion" becomes the formal, negative foil against which other important ideas are substantively explicated. As early as 1931, and under the influence of Karl Barth, Bonhoeffer declares that "there no longer can be any general *concept of religion*."[98]

In order to do justice to this situation, we will speak terminologically not of Bonhoeffer's *concept* of religion, and certainly not of his *theory* of religion, but more appropriately of his *understanding* or conception of religion, or of his *thematic treatment* of religion.

Apart from the concept of religion, Bonhoeffer exercises great conceptual care, something a cross-check of other concepts in his theology can easily demonstrate.[99] By not integrating *religion* into his theological thinking, Bonhoeffer distinguishes himself not only from his own age, but also from current systematic-theological outlines.

In his *Church Dogmatics* Karl Barth does not deal with the topic "religion" until after his discussion of the doctrine of the Trinity,[100] while Wolfhart Pannenberg in his *Systematic Theology* does not deal with the topic of religion from the outset under the aspect of the Christian religion.[101] Chapter 3 is subtitled "The Reality of God and the Gods in the Experience of the Religions."[102] Not until chapter 5 does Pannenberg develop the doctrine of the Trinity. We thus find ourselves only on the path toward the "Christian God," and for that reason terminological usage cannot be specifically Christian.[103] Pannenberg concludes rather from a general idea of God a "single concept of religion" which "has its own place in the history of religion and in fact arose only on the soil of monotheistic religion" (149). Pannenberg shares Schleiermacher's view "that the religious disposition belongs inalienably to our humanity" (154). In Pannenberg's own words: "without religion" the human being is "incomplete" (154). Here, there is a "basic difference" between Schleiermacher's concept of religion (154) and that of religion's critics: "Radical criticism of religion stands or falls with the claim that religion is not a constitutive part of human nature . . . [and] will finally wither away" (155). This, however, is Bonhoeffer's own position, and is both the answer and the question regarding why he is not intent on constructing any conceptuality of religion as such. In contrast to him, Pannenberg does not distinguish between modern and premodern thinking.[104] He is able quite self-evidently to draw direct lines from Augustine to Schleiermacher or Hegel without considering the deep cleft which modern striving for autonomy has created in history. As, for example, Wilhelm Dilthey has shown,[105] after the Renaissance and Reformation one can no longer find the kind of immediate relationship with God presupposed in both antiquity and the Midde Ages. In law, the natural sciences, political science, and the humanities, human beings have begun to think maturely, that is, without metaphysics. Pannenberg, too, finds that humanity has extricated itself from its religious roots. Is Pannenberg not calling for the concept "religion" quite against historical developments? Is he not trying to "turn back" history and to draw out the line from Augustine to *religio naturalis* and to E. Troeltsch while simply disregarding the modern striving for autonomy? Augustine's metaphysics are extended into modernity,[106] and "religion" is established anew "as metaphysics."

For Pannenberg, a theory of religion intercepts the distress of God's hiddenness ahead of time, and then prescribes which religious experiences can meaningfully occur in the first place. This basically issues in a denial of the "pathic" constitution of our existence by displacing experiences of suffering and meaninglessness to the end of causal developmental lines, where they are explained religio-theoretically. For Pannenberg, the concept of meaning is from the outset religiously charged, whereas Bonhoeffer's references to meaning remain precisely *non*religious and express "what the Bible calls 'promise.'"[107]

In contrast to Pannenberg, for whose systematic outline a well-defined concept of religion constitutes an integral part, religion begins to evaporate from Bonhoeffer's theological thinking. At the place where religion usually resides in the system of regular dogmatics, the irregular dogmatician asks: "In religionlessness, what do the cult and prayer now mean?"[108] Bonhoeffer answers this question by referring to the arcane discipline of the early church; he himself apparently senses that a void emerges where in religionlessness religious content loses its customary place. That which is associated with the phenomenon "religion," for example, the cult[109] or prayer, is for this reason to be subjected to arcane discipline. Thus, first of all, religionlessness means phenomenologically the homelessness of religion.

Religious content is not to be surrendered, but rather venerated and protected from profanation; in the place of loquacious religiosity, Bonhoeffer demands qualified silence. The glorification of the mystery of Christ's person in prayer and worship corresponds externally to the responsible act, so that arcane discipline finds its "dialectical counterpart"[110] in the nonreligious interpretation. In the words of the *Letters and Papers from Prison,* arcane discipline and religionlessness are related like the *prayer and actions of the righteous.*[111] Or, to use a formulation from the *Ethics,* arcane discipline and nonreligious interpretation are related as the ultimate and the penultimate.[112]

C. Findings

1. Thesis I: Bonhoeffer neither defines religion conceptually, nor develops any closed theory of religion.

2. Methodological Reflections

What does this absence of a theory of religion mean for the rest of the present study? How can we continue to reflect on religion in Bonhoeffer's work if his own statements resist any theoretical formulations? What does this insight into the lack of any unequivocal conceptual definition of religion, an insight gleaned from an examination of his works themselves, mean for our own *methodological* options?

First of all, these interim findings (Thesis I) do make the large number of misinterpretations understandable, all of which presuppose Bonhoeffer to be operating with a fixed concept of religion and then on the basis of this presupposition attempt to explain the nonreligious interpretation.

Previous scholarship[113] presupposes Bonhoeffer to be operating with a fixed *concept* of religion. That is, it presupposes that his concept of religion enables one to draw conclusions regarding the disputed statements about religionlessness and nonreligious interpretation. This particular procedure, which assumes that Bonhoeffer developed a *theory* of religion in his theology, has been unable to produce any persuasive explanatory model for the "nonreligious interpretation" even after forty years of Bonhoeffer-scholarship. Quite the contrary, the continuing paraphrastic renderings of the religious thematic material of the *Letters and Papers from Prison* clearly demonstrate that scholars are still searching for an interpretive key or a sustaining explanatory model for this book. But what if we find that the topic of *religion* as such is not even of fulcral significance for the circle of problems surrounding the non*religious* interpretation, and that the systematic-theological focus does not in fact reside in the critique of religion in the first place, but points rather in a different direction; what if Bonhoeffer was articulating his theme in the guise of a critique of religion merely because he was still under the influence of dialectical theology?

Our first thesis thus advises us to deal with great care with the in-part fragmentary source material. If I am to understand Bonhoeffer's statements concerning religion, I cannot do this directly by way of the primary source material itself, but rather only indirectly by way of the relationships antedating those sources. The question is thus: *What is the origin* of this critique of religion and of the reference to religionlessness? Which writings influenced Bonhoeffer while he was engaged theologically in this critique of religion?

With regard to the *critique* of religion, the next section (Part II.A) will address the significance of Karl Barth in Bonhoeffer's thinking.[114] With regard to the reference to religion*lessness,* the section after that (Part II.B) will then discuss the importance of Bonhoeffer's reading of contemporary philosophy.[115] An evaluation of the various *influences* on Bonhoeffer during this period is advised if one is to do justice to the various source-critical problems attaching to any interpretation of the fragments.

In attempting to clarify substantively the nonreligious interpretation of biblical terms — and thus the question of *what* — we find that the absence of any real theory of religion in Bonhoeffer's thinking prompts us to pursue the question of *origin*.

The Origins of Nonreligious Interpretation

A. From a *Positive Evaluation* of Religion to a *Critique* of Religion: A Systematic-Theological Interpretation

1. From Liberal to Dialectical Theology

a. University

Bonhoeffer essentially grew into liberal theology, and attended lectures by K. Holl and seminars with A. von Harnack to the very last. "With his discovery of dialectical theology, Bonhoeffer acquired a more positive direction that took the place of his previous rather restless roving. He now took a real joy in his work; it was like a liberation."[1] Bonhoeffer's discovery of Karl Barth is dated to the years 1924/1925, and is associated with the collection *The Word of God and Theology*, which appeared in 1924.[2] Bonhoeffer owned a copy of this volume,[3] and probably passed it around to other family members.[4] Eberhard Bethge writes that in 1925 Bonhoeffer made himself the "propagandist for this book."[5] The work contains the essay "Biblical Questions: Insights and Prospects"[6] from the year 1920, in which Barth declares that

> Jesus simply has nothing to do with religion. The meaning of his life is the actuality of that which is actual in no religion, the actuality of the unapproachable, unfathomable, incomprehensible. (94)

The juxtaposition of religion and faith corresponds to this. While religion "is possible for everyone," Barth believes that "the faith commanded in the Bible is not for everyone" (74). Religion is rejected as a "possibility." "Religion forgets that it has a right to exist only if it perpetually suspends itself" (80). The expression "suspension of religion" in 1920 already represents a significant turn in Barth's critique of religion. Right at the beginning of his essay, he asks "what the Bible has to offer us as an aid to interpreting what happens in the world" (70). It is not God's intention "to establish the history of religion, but rather to be the Lord of our lives, the eternal Lord of the world" (85). Elsewhere in the essay, he declares that

> there have already been many expressly nonreligious people who have perceived the whole seriousness and weight of the question of God much more strongly, and have expressed this much more incisively than the most devout and zealous believers. (73)

Several parallels suggest themselves with regard to the late Bonhoeffer. For example, on April 30, 1944 (*WEN,* 306), Bonhoeffer asks, "How can Christ become the Lord also of the religionless?" He continues: "Barth, the only one who began to think in this direction, did not, however, develop this idea thoroughly and think it through" (*WEN,* 306). The Scandinavian Bonhoeffer scholar B.-E. Benktson believes that Bonhoeffer is thinking here of Barth's early essay.[7] On the whole, Benktson was the first to draw attention to this connection between the early Barth and the late Bonhoeffer; we will have occasion to return to this insight in our discussion of the Tegel correspondence.

Eberhard Bethge reports that

> Bonhoeffer's papers include some lecture notes — at that time these were laboriously copied out by hand — under the heading "Karl Barth, dictated notes on 'Instruction on the Christian Religion,' I and II," These constitute the principal points of his lectures dictated to his students by Barth in Göttingen during his dogmatics course in the summer of 1924 and the winter of 1924-25, and they are a brief early version of what was to be expanded into the first volume of his *Prolegomena to Christian Dogmatics* of 1927.[8]

In his notes on Barth's *Christian Dogmatics* (*DBW* 9.473f.), Bonhoeffer makes no mention of Barth's understanding of religion. In *Sanc-*

torum Communio, Barth's *Christian Dogmatics in Outline* is then mentioned extensively, albeit in an ecclesiological connection unconcerned with any critique of religion (cf. *DBW* 1.172ff. and Bonhoeffer's n.120). Bonhoeffer criticized this early dogmatics outline to a fellow student, complaining of its "reactionary gestures." The fellow student defended the Barth of these dogmatics in contrast to the Barth of the *Letter to the Romans,* explaining that Barth first had to "establish a link with the past" in order then to take "two steps forward."[9]

Bonhoeffer was familiar with Barth's *Letter to the Romans* of 1922 (in the 3rd ed. of 1923), as well as with several issues of the periodical *Between the Times.*[10] It is especially Barth's *Letter to the Romans* and the 1924 volume of the periodical that come to expression in Bonhoeffer's work prior to 1927.

We found *positive* remarks regarding religion in Bonhoeffer's report on historical and pneumatic scriptural interpretation from the summer semester of 1925.[11] Nonetheless, Bonhoeffer does discuss the dialectician. He is concerned with the dialectical-theological understanding of Scripture on the one hand, and with K. Holl's presentation of Luther's hermeneutics on the other. Bonhoeffer tries to bring Barth and Holl together — the Reformed and Lutheran traditions — by way of their understanding of Scripture. With regard to Barth, he writes that "revelation is contained in Scripture, i.e., 'attested,' as Scripture itself puts it" (*DBW* 9.311). Following Holl,[12] he writes that

> thus it is not Scripture itself that is revelation, since that would again constitute an objectification through rational means; it is not Scripture itself that is experienced as revelation, but the matter at hand. *(ibid.)*

Bonhoeffer is thus reading Barth with an interest in scriptural interpretation from the perspective of revelation theology (cf. also 313f. with regard to Barth's theology of Israel).

Bonhoeffer's report from 1926 on the church and ecclesiology reveals dependence on Barth's *Letter to the Romans* (*DBW* 9.336ff.). Bonhoeffer makes ecclesiological reference to Barth when he declares that

> the church will never take the fateful step of asserting that "all that exists is sin," but rather must learn to distinguish creation on the one hand from human distortions on the other, and to sharpen its vision.[13]

In his seminar paper on the Holy Spirit in Luther (*DBW* 9.355ff.), the student says that the justified Christian

> is — to use an expression from Karl Barth — "the unintuited . . . *new* subject, the human ego standing and enduring before God . . . for us . . . visible and comprehensible only as non-given." Hence only thus can it be said that the Christian can no longer sin. Thus the Holy Spirit is not in *me;* a second I has split off from me, and lives in heaven, far from here, a "heavenly double" of my earthly I.[14]

The report on John and Paul (*DBW* 9.441ff.) similarly displays a pneumatological dependence on Barth:

> The old person, justified and sanctified by faith and the Spirit, becomes the new person; his sin stands under grace, he stands as a new creature in the world of God's grace, in the beyond of history, in Christ. "In Christ" means "our inclusion in the suspension of this person, revealed in Jesus as the Christ, in which he is established as a new person" (Barth).[15]

Interim findings: On the whole, we can observe that in 1925/1926 Bonhoeffer repeatedly picks up on Barth's writings. We find Bonhoeffer "in a theological interim-position between Barth and the Berlin theologians."[16] For our own study, it is of significance that Bonhoeffer's reception of Barth prior to 1927 derives from a revelatory-theological, ecclesiological, and pneumatological perspective that as yet has nothing to do with a critique of religion.

b. Doctoral Work

Traces of Barth's influence can be found in *Sanctorum Communio* from 1927.[17] In the main chapter with the same title, "Sanctorum Communio" (77-199), the doctoral candidate repeatedly references Barth. He finds first of all that "there are basically two misunderstandings of the church: a historicizing misunderstanding, and a religious misunderstanding" (79).

Bonhoeffer classifies Catholic ecclesiology under the "religious misunderstanding," though one also encounters the "religious misunderstanding" in sociology, specifically in attempts "to analyze the 'church' *qua* 'religious community' . . . as a 'public-legal corporate body' and to establish a sociological morphology for it. Then anything theological would be superfluous" (79f.). Here we encounter the juxtaposition of theology and religion (in the form of a "religious community"). "One cannot deduce externally" that the church claims to be the church of God.

> This path does not basically take us beyond the category of "possibility." From here one of necessity comes across the concept of the "religious community." The concept of church is conceivable only in the sphere of reality posited by God, that is, it cannot be deduced. The reality of the church is a revelatory reality whose nature is to be either believed or denied. (80)

This statement concerning revelation does not take the doctoral student beyond the position of his dissertation advisor.[18]

M. Scheler and H. Scholz try to derive the concept of church from religion or from the religious community. Bonhoeffer shows how Scheler equates religion and metaphysics and thus directs the former against history:

> The error in Scheler's argumentation is that his idea of the holy begins with a metaphysical concept of value that always remains inaccessible to us in its absoluteness, instead of arguing from the perspective of the historically positive revelation . . . in Christ. (82)

Whereas Scheler understands religion as metaphysics, Scholz equates religion and revelation:

> Religion belongs first of all to the ponderables of the human spirit, and is second not a priori, but rather revelation, which are mutually exclusive terms. From this follows the necessity of education in religion. (83)

Scholz begins with the general concept of religion. "The general concept of religion includes no social intentions. . . . This refers us from the general concept of religion back to the concrete form of religion, and for us this means to the concept of church" (84). Bonhoeffer asserts that "only from the concept of revelation [we might add: and thus not from the *concept of religion*, R.W.] can one get to the Christian concept of church" (84). This antithetical juxtaposition of revelation and religion is explicated in the concept of the church:

35

It is not a new religion that is soliciting adherents . . . rather, in Jesus Christ God has posited the reality of the church, of humankind that has been pardoned. Not religion, but revelation; not religious community, but church. This is what the reality of Jesus Christ means. And yet a necessary connection obtains between revelation and religion just as it does between the religious community and the church, something often overlooked today. (97)

With this antithetical juxtaposition of religious community and church, Bonhoeffer is apparently delimiting himself over against E. Troeltsch.[19] To the familiar antithetical juxtaposition of religion and revelation Bonhoeffer now abruptly adds the idea of a connection between the two. This juxtaposition and connection of religion and revelation can be interpreted against the background of Karl Barth on the one hand,[20] and Albrecht Ritschl on the other.

One encounters this antithetical juxtaposition of revelation and religion in Barth's *Letter to the Romans,*[21] especially in the seventh chapter, "Freedom" (211ff.). According to Barth, "the boundary of religion" (211ff.) is posited with Christ. "Christ is the end of the law, the boundary of religion" (220). "The purpose of religion" (222f.) is to confront a person with his crisis, "and the more strongly this crisis asserts itself, the more clear does it become that in this phenomenon we are in fact dealing with conscious or unconscious religion" (225). In religion, "sin becomes a visible entity" (228) standing over against "God's freedom" (236). "The reality of religion is struggle and aggravation, sin and death, devil and hell" (24). In the reality of religion, "the religious human being himself is to come to expression with his unique being and possessions (psychology of religion!)" (240); it is "the discovery of his unredeemed status" (241). The concept of religion of the early Barth takes its orientation from the Pauline theology of the law, and follows a dualistic use of language, whence Barth can say that "religion is incipient dualism" (251). In addition to the equation "law is religion and the gospel is grace," Barth picks up further on the Pauline dialectic: As little as the law is the same as sin, just as little is religion the same as sin; "sin is not identical with the religious possibility" (223). Barth develops a dialectic of sin and religion, not of grace and religion (contra B.-E. Benktson).[22] This relationship remains antithetical: Religion "is a misfortune" (241), the "negative side" of grace (212). The "dialectic" (219) attested in chapter 7 is for Barth a dialectic of religion and sin determined from the perspective of grace alone. From the perspective of grace, "sin becomes a visible entity" (228). The dialectic of sin and law (Paul) and of sin and religion (Barth) is determined exclusively from the perspective of grace, and is not a dialectic of religion and grace. In the *Letter to the Romans* of 1922, Barth picks up basic insights from 1920 again and anticipates the understanding of revelation as the "suspension of religion" in his *Church Dogmatics* I/2 of 1938 when he writes that "Jesus Christ, however, is the new human being beyond the human being possible for us, beyond especially the devout human being. He is the suspension of *this* human being in his totality" (252).

When in *Sanctorum Communio* Bonhoeffer juxtaposes revelation and religion, he is apparently following the terminological usage of Barth's *Letter to the Romans*. He also writes in *Sanctorum Communio,* however, that there is a "necessary connection between revelation and religion": "As a pathfinder, as a model, Jesus Christ is also the founder of a religious community" (*Sanctorum Communio,* 97). "Every shared religion is founded." Thus Albrecht Ritschl's formulation.[23]

Ritschl recognizes "characteristic features in which Christianity manifests itself as a religion" (188), including those of totality and community as characteristic of the Christian religion. "The assertion that the religious worldview takes its orientation from the notion of a whole is indeed demonstrated in Christianity" (190). "The communal cult has a closer relationship with revelation, which constitutes the organizational point of every coherent religious worldview" (192). For the Christian religion, this means that "in Christianity, revelation in the Son of God is the fixed point for all knowledge and all religious action" (192). According to Ritschl, this also applies to the church,[24] which here stands under the catchphrase "communal cult." "In this significance of revelation for the communal cult we also find an unavoidable condition for understanding Christianity. The person of the founder is not only the key to the Christian worldview and the standard for Christians' self-evaluation and moral striving, but also the standard for the disposition of the prayer in which both the individual and the communal worship of God is to consist" (193). Bonhoeffer could very well have acquired from Ritschl an understanding of the relationship between revelation and religion that is not from the outset determined by antithetical juxtaposition.[25] Also of significance in this context is the character of totality which Ritschl ascribes to religion.[26] Following the citation above, we read that at the same time, the advantage of Christianity depends on this acknowledgment of God's revelation in Christ, the advantage, namely, that its worldview is an enclosed whole and that its goal for life is to become, as a Christian, a whole, a spiritual character above the world. (193)

In *Sanctorum Communio,* the liberal and dialectical-theological understanding of religion yet seem to stand disconnected next to one another. Although a critique of religion is prepared, it is not carried through. With regard to the distinction between the Kingdom of God and the Kingdom of Christ, Bonhoeffer then explicitly follows Karl Barth (rather than Seeberg, who nowhere mentions such a distinction): "The church is identical with the Kingdom of Christ; the latter, however, is the Kingdom of God realized in history since Christ" (98).[27]

Following the text of *Sanctorum Communio* further, we notice Bonhoeffer's critique of an individualistic narrowing of the concept of church. According to Bonhoeffer, it is only in the church that one can have community with God.

> Every individualistic concept of the church falters on this one fact. Between the individual and the church, the following intertwined relationship obtains: The Holy Spirit is active only in the church as the communion of saints; thus every person seized by the Spirit must already be in this communion; on the other hand, no one stands in this communion who has not already been seized by the Spirit; from which it then follows that *in the same act in which the Spirit moves the elect in the community posited in Christ, it also leads them into the actualized community.* Entry into the community grounds faith, just as the latter grounds the former. (101)

Bonhoeffer notes that "Schleiermacher, for example, did not recognize this connection" (101, n. 18). With regard to Schleiermacher's *Christian Faith* and *Speeches on Religion,* Bonhoeffer demonstrates further that

> the reason for the religious formation of community is found in the individual's need for communication. The church is the satisfaction of a need, and is individualistically construed. The same thing is implied by the famous assertion in the *Christian Faith* that Protestantism makes the relationship of individuals dependent on their relationship to Christ (*Christian Faith,* §24). (102)

Bonhoeffer understands Schleiermacher's ecclesiology individualistically, and is apparently not directly criticizing his concept of religion. This criticism of Schleiermacher is directed rather against his concept of church and against the lack of any concept of person and humankind in Idealism. Schleiermacher allegedly abbreviates the latter biologically: "Substantively, we reject the biological disposition of the concept of humanity as well as the anthropological disposition of the idea of the pneuma."[28]

The section on the community of the Spirit (106ff.) again shows traces of Barth's influence. The thesis "Christian love is not a human possibility" (108) contains Barthian terminology. According to the *Letter to the Romans,* "love is merely a 'relative' human possibility."[29] This terminological allusion is followed by an explicit debate with Barth on the topic "love of one's neighbor."[30] According to Bonhoeffer, one's fellow is "in and for himself infinitely important," and is not the "One in the other" (110, n. 28).[31] He follows the Lutheran tradition against the *extra Calvinisticum* in whose tradition he believes Barth to be standing.[32]

In his explications on "unity of the Spirit" (128ff.), the doctoral candidate is also able to acknowledge both Luther and Barth together. Following the Luther citation according to which "all are one" in Christ (133), Bonhoeffer adduces the "Word-of-God" theologian in asserting that "this unity is based on Christ being 'the One beyond every other' (Barth)" (134). In *Letter to the Romans,* Barth writes that "it [this unity] is communio . . . it is — the One beyond every other."[33] Bonhoeffer apparently cited Barth from memory.

Interim findings. On the whole, one cannot really call the doctoral candidate a "Barthian."[34] His dissertation advisor remarks regarding the dissertation *Sanctorum Communio* that "although points of contact with Barth can also be found here and there . . . these influences are countered by others" (*DBW* 9.176). In the example of the critique of religion, we observed the considerable extent to which the influence of dialectical theology stands next to that of the liberal inheritance. The young Bonhoeffer "cannot simply be classified with a specific school. K. Holl, R. Seeberg, and K. Barth all influenced him; from all three he appropriated fulcral elements, and over against all three he preserved his independence in theological questioning and searching."[35]

c. Assistant Pastorship

In the congregational lecture "Jesus Christ and On the Essence of Christianity," Bonhoeffer writes that

> ethics and religion and church are all oriented in the direction of human beings toward God; Christ alone, however, completely alone, speaks from the direction of God to human beings, not from the human path to God, but from God's path to human beings.[36]

Bonhoeffer picks up this idea again at the end of the lecture, and in opposition to "religion" as the "new cultural idea" says:

> No, the Christian idea is God's path to human beings, and as its visible objectification: the cross. . . . God comes to human beings, who have nothing other than a space for God, and this empty space, this emptiness in human beings is in Christian language called: faith.[37]

This reference to "empty space" is extremely interesting from the perspective of possible influence insofar as in his own commentary, Barth writes on Romans 2 that "faith, too, insofar as it is in any sense an empty space, is unbelief."[38] Bonhoeffer is apparently following the terminology of the dialectician even while contradicting him substantively. That is, Barth is disputing precisely the possibility of a "space for God in human beings." Here Bonhoeffer yet seems to be basing his argumentation on the doctrine of the "religious a priori."

In the sermons from the time of his curacy, Bonhoeffer picks up on Barth's thinking not only terminologically, but theologically as well. Thus the assistant pastor preaches on Romans 11:6 concerning the significance of the "one thing," namely, "that God is God and grace is grace."[39] The theological dependence on Barth in this sermon is also accentuated with elements of a critique of religion: "Not religion, but revelation, grace, love; not a path to God, but God's path to human beings, that is the sum of Christianity" (458). The expression "not religion, but revelation," borrowed from *Sanctorum Communio,* is repeated once more at the end of the sermon in the manner of a recapitulation: "Not religion, but revelation and grace: that was the redemptive word, and the world closed itself off from this word" (460).

But just as Bonhoeffer's dissertation is not characterized only by this religio-critical juxtaposition of revelation and religion, so also this sermon contains more differentiated statements about religion. "Religion and morality represent the greatest danger for recognizing divine grace, since they bear within themselves the seed prompting us to seek our path to God ourselves" (459). Here the reference is to "difficulty" rather than to "impossibility," to a "seed" rather than a "fundamental mistake."

The sermon on 2 Corinthians 12:9 contains unequivocal allusions to Barth. Parallel to the *Letter to the Romans,* Bonhoeffer's sermon asserts that "religion is the misfortune,"[40] while Barth writes that religion "is a misfortune."[41] Bonhoeffer also writes that "everything that happens in the world is countered by the word of grace,"[42] while in Barth we read that religion is the "negative side" of grace.[43]

A positive evaluation of religion is then found in the sermon on Romans 12:11:

> Nothing existing in time is divine, absolutely nothing, not even the church, nor even our religion. All this is subject to transience, and yet all that is transient of the individual contains a piece of God's will, a piece of eternity.[44]

Hence religion, too, contains a "piece of eternity"!

d. Findings

In summary we can say in retrospect of Bonhoeffer's various developmental stages that the liberal understanding of religion he articulates as a student begins, in 1925, to yield to a critical understanding under the influence of dialectical theology; on the other hand, Bonhoeffer does remain bound to his liberal inheritance, and a cultural-Protestant understanding of religion is still attested in the sermons and lectures we have from his period in Barcelona.

2. Under the Influence of Dialectical Theology

a. Habilitation

"The licentiate of theology, having received his doctorate six months earlier, plans to brook no compromises in his new work; it will be systematic rather than historical, and theological rather than psychological. He had early on contradicted Seeberg's psychological linking of theology to a religious a priori."[45] In the first, introductory part of *Act and Being,* Bonhoeffer distinguishes more sharply than in *Sanctorum Communio* between Kant and German Idealism.[46] He writes about Hegel:

> In the living reflection on itself, the I understands itself from itself. It relates itself to itself, and consequently to God, in unmediated reflection. That is why religion = revelation. (53)

J. H. Burtness[47] suggests in this context that Bonhoeffer and Barth share "a rejection of philosophical Idealism." Closer observation, however, reveals that not only Bonhoeffer and Barth share this rejection, but Bonhoeffer and Seeberg as well. In addition to Barth, Bonhoeffer can also describe his dissertation advisor 'far more as Kantian-transcendental than as idealistic" (55f.). That is, Seeberg's view is that "God is the supramundane reality transcending consciousness, the creator and the Lord" (57). But how is God revealed to human beings? "This is where Seeberg's theory of the religious a priori comes into play; there is in human beings 'a compelling ability' to come to an unmediated awareness of pure spirit. By means of this ability, human beings can receive God into themselves" (57):

> The religious a priori is supposed to be fundamentally open to the divine will; there is, it is said, a mold in human beings into which the divine content of revelation, too, may pour. In other words, revelation must become religion; that is its essence. Revelation is religion. But that is a turning away from pure transcendentalism toward idealism. (57f.)

Bonhoeffer is apparently picking up on an inconsistency in his teacher's philosophical premise that can be demonstrated in the concept of the "religious a priori." For Bonhoeffer, reference to the religious a priori in this passage is linked with the equation of revelation and religion, and therein also with the philosophy of identity of German Idealism.[48] For the rest, Seeberg's pupil follows the Luther interpretation of his Berlin teacher, even though this is not representative for *Act and Being* as a whole:[49]

The natural human being has a *cor curvum in se*. Natural religion, too, remains flesh, and seeks after flesh. If revelation is to come to human beings, they need to be changed entirely. Faith itself must be created in them. In this matter, there is no ability to hear before the hearing. These are thoughts that Seeberg has expressed himself and supported with reference to Luther.[50] Having been wrought by God, faith runs counter to natural religiosity, for which the religious a priori noted by Seeberg certainly holds good. (58)

A revelatory-theological critique of religion of the sort radicalized in the main section under the influence of Barth's doctrine of revelation is thus prepared (with Lutheran elements!) from the perspective of R. Seeberg. Bonhoeffer finds Seeberg to be inconsistent:

> According to Luther, revelation and religion are bound to the concrete, preached word, and the word is the mediator of contact between God and human beings, allowing no other "immediateness." But then the concept of the religious a priori can be understood only to imply that certain mental or spiritual forms are presupposed for the formal understanding of the word, in which case a specifically religious a priori makes no sense. All that pertains to the personal appropriation of the fact of Christ is not a priori, but God's contingent action on human beings. (58)

God and human beings cannot be brought together through the assumption of a formal a priori, but rather only through the word. Bonhoeffer perceives an element of tension in Seeberg's interpretation of Luther, and believes he can relieve this tension in favor of Christology by bracketing out reference to the religious a priori. It is ultimately idealistic and unnecessary from the perspective of Luther. In addition to Seeberg, Bonhoeffer also mentions Karl Barth in connection with the critique of religion. In addition to the *Letter to the Romans* (55, 81), in the main part of *Act and Being* Bonhoeffer is influenced primarily by Barth's *Dogmatics in Outline*[51] (cf. 83-86, 92, 96f., 99f., 130). He portrays Barth as a theologian of the act and offers a broad presentation of his doctrine of revelation (81-87). What Bonhoeffer missed in Seeberg he finds in Barth, namely, consistency in transcendentalism. "God is made known only in acts that God freely initiates" (83). Under the influence of Barth, Bonhoeffer also comes to speak, under the heading "Knowledge of Revelation," of the relationship between a theology of revelation on the one hand, and religion on the other:

> This is where the profound difference between genuine transcendentalism and idealism comes to light. If, as was shown in the latter, revelation was in essence religion as a consequence of the identification of I and being, the two are in sharp contrast in the course of the transcendental project. True, God 'is' only in faith, but it is God as such who is the subject of believing. That is why faith is something essentially different from religion. (93)

The critique of religion is here a critique of the understanding of religion characterizing German Idealism, and results from the use of Kant's phenomenalism, as represented most consistently in theology by Karl Barth. It is against this background, too, that Bonhoeffer's statement is to be understood regarding the "theological right" "with which Karl Barth chides Friedrich Schleiermacher for his 'great confusion' of religion and grace" (154). Bonhoeffer again refers (154 n. 25) to Barth's *Dogmatics in Outline*,[52] in whose §18 ("Grace and Religion," 396ff.), under the heading "2. The Great Confusion (Schleiermacher)" (402), Barth writes:

> Schleiermacher's human being stands from the very outset and always before God. . . . If this is religion, then it is taking place in a different world than does revelation. This has nothing to do with its subjective possibility, with grace, with the outpouring of the Holy Spirit. [p. 404] Schleiermacher's homo religiosus has — and perhaps nothing is more characteristic of it — no counterpart. [405]

Barth does not remain with a critique of religion when under the heading "3. God and Religion" (413f.) he continues:

> By virtue of God's grace, in the concrete reality of revelation, which admittedly is not at our disposal but which on the basis of divine disposal can become a reality for us, too, there is an acceptance of religion, a qualification of human piety as faith and obedience, an acknowledgment of alleged reverence as genuine reverence. (416)

Hence Barth does believe that in the light of revelation, religion can also become "true religion," as he will explicate in *Church Dogmatics* I/2

(325ff.). In this interpretation, too, Bonhoeffer is following the *Dogmatics in Outline* when he writes:

> It must be stated clearly that in the community of Christ faith takes form in religion and that, consequently, religion is called faith — that seen in light of Christ I may and must calmly confess "I believe," only to add, of course, with a view to myself, "help my unbelief." For reflection, all praying, all searching for God in God's Word, all clinging to promise, every entreaty in the name of God's grace, all hoping for reference to the cross is 'religion,' 'credulity.' But in the community of Christ, even though it is always the work of human beings, it is faith given and willed by God, faith in which God may truly be found. (*DBW* 2.154)

We thus observe a parallel movement in Barth and Bonhoeffer regarding a critique and a positive evaluation of religion, a movement deriving from the influence of the word-of-God theologian (cf. *DBW* 2.154, n. 25). In contrast to his position in *Sanctorum Communio,* in *Act and Being* Bonhoeffer is now following Barth's understanding of religion *exclusively;* Barth's doctrine of revelation enables Bonhoeffer to question Seeberg's reference to the religious a priori and thus to rediscover for theology Kant's phenomenalism. The revelatory-theological shift in accentuation to a position asserting that God is allegedly free not *from* human beings, but *for* human beings, emerged in favor of a balance between Barth and Luther, and is to be understood against the background of the ecclesiological concerns of *Act and Being;* it does not contribute to an understanding of the issue of religion. Quite the contrary, here Bonhoeffer can, as we have seen, refer back to both Luther (57f.) *and* Barth (93, 153f.).

The inaugural lecture on "The Question of the Human Being in Contemporary Philosophy and Theology"[53] expands this criticism of German Idealism from *Act and Being* with the addition of phenomenology (360f.: M. Scheler) and existential philosophy (363f.: M. Heidegger). Bonhoeffer summarizes: "Ultimately, philosophy has always formulated the question of the human being such that human beings themselves find the answer, since it is already contained in the question itself" (368). To this, theology responds: "Theology accepts this result of philosophical activity without objection, but interprets it in its own fashion as the conceptual activity of the *cor curvum in se*" (369).

45

Picking up on Luther, Bonhoeffer turns to the Luther interpretation of his teacher K. Holl, for whom the transcendent God manifests himself to human beings at one place:

> The place where God manifests himself must be the same place from which human beings understand themselves, and simultaneously the place from which the unity of the human being is grounded. This place, however, is obviously conscience. . . . Holl defined Luther's religion as a religion of conscience. (370)

Whereas Holl and Seeberg were determinative figures for the student's and doctoral candidate's interpretation of Luther, Bonhoeffer abandons this understanding of Luther after *Act and Being.* And whereas the conceptions of Holl, Seeberg, and Barth all yet stood in an unconnected fashion next to one another in *Sanctorum Communio,* in *Act and Being* Bonhoeffer goes over to dialectical theology and — on the philosophical level — to Neo-Kantianism. Whereas for *Act and Being* it was Barth contra Seeberg in the critique of religion, here is it Barth contra Holl, the latter of whom was subject to

> the most animated criticism from the so-called dialectical theology. The question in which human beings reflect on themselves always remains a question; from within themselves, human beings can find no answer, since there is in them not a single point at which God might gain space in them; . . . their thinking . . . their religiosity remain hopeless attempts to anchor the I in the absolute. (370f.)

For Barth, the dialectical understanding of revelation stands in the place of the "religious conscience":

> God remains the eternally transcendent, eternally distant God even and particularly where in revelation he comes close to human beings. Barth says: "The human being to whom God reveals himself is the human being to whom God cannot be revealed" (*Dogmatik,* I, 287). (371)[54]

The antithetical juxtaposition of philosophy and theology lying behind the inaugural lecture makes an exception in the case of the philosophical outline linked with dialectical theology, namely, Kant's phenomenalism (cf., e.g., 371).

46

b. First Stay in America

Bonhoeffer is probably to be designated as a Barthian during his stay in the United States, and at Union Theological Seminary his advocacy of dialectical theology could probably be called enthusiastic. The influence of Barth's *Letter to the Romans* is evident when Bonhoeffer speaks of the "great antithesis of the word of God and the word of man," "of grace and religion."[55] We also have indications of how Barth incorporated philosophy into his own theological thought. Bonhoeffer first makes it clear that Barth is a Christian theologian rather than a philosopher. In this he is demonstrating the centrality of revelation in the theology of the word of God, a centrality deriving from the exclusive "coming of God":

> It is God's to let men see into these secrets of his revelation. . . . This precisely is the logic of the Bible, God's coming which destroys all human attempts to come, which condemns all morality and religion, by means of which man tries to make superfluous God's revelation. (438)

Religion is criticized from the perspective of God's revelation. According to Bonhoeffer, Barth has introduced the category of the word of God, a category that in particular stands opposed to religious thinking:

> The category which Barth tries to introduce into theology in its strict sense, which is so refractory to all general thinking and especially religious thinking, is the category of the word of God, of the revelation straight from above, from *outside* of man, according to the justification of the sinner by grace. (440)

Here Bonhoeffer is explicitly following Barth's *theological* critique of religion by placing it into the context of the *justificatio impii*. Barth now turns from a Christian theologian into a philosopher as well: "In every theological statement we cannot but use certain general forms of thinking. Theology has those forms in common with philosophy" (440).

With this statement, Bonhoeffer is formulating one of the basic insights attaching to the relationship between theology and philosophy. He finds that in the *Letter to the Romans* and in later writings, Barth has appropriated the philosophical terminology of Kant and of the Neo-Kantians.[56] Over against German Idealism (with allusions to Hegel and Fichte),[57] Kant possesses for Barth the advantage of a self-limitation of philosophical thinking: "There is only one philosophy, which recognizes this fact and states it as the definite and essential limit of man; this is according to Barth . . . the essence of Kantian philosophy" (444).

In his portrayal of Kant, Bonhoeffer is obviously also employing conceptual figures from his *Habilitationsschrift* (cf., e.g., *actus directus-reflexus,* 448). He ascribes to Karl Barth the recasting of Luther's statement from *Act and Being* ("reflecte fortiter, sed fortius fide et gaude in Christo" [*DBW* 2.135]): "So as Luther said pecca fortiter, sed crede fortius Barth could say reflecte fortiter, sed crede fortius" (448). In contrast to *Act and Being* with its formulation limiting the *Extra Calvinisticum,* namely, that God is free not from human beings, but for them, Bonhoeffer now writes in a completely Barthian fashion about the sovereign God: God is "free Lord and Creator; . . he reveals himself in sovereign freedom wherever and whenever he wants" (449). Bonhoeffer shares dialectical theology's critique of religion, and places it into the larger philosophical context of the Barthian reception of Kant.

Interim Findings. In *Act and Being* (1929), in his inaugural lecture (1930), and in New York (1931), Bonhoeffer observes ever more incisively that Barth's concept of revelation cannot be understood without Kant's phenomenalism. Barth concurs when the *thing in itself* becomes for Kant at least unknowable, and for the Neo-Kantians a mere boundary or limiting concept. He argues that in exactly the same way, *God in and for himself* cannot be known unless he first makes himself *known* through revelation. This revelatory-theological influence of Neo-Kantianism culminates in 1931; but this high point simultaneously marks a turning point in Bonhoeffer's adaptation of philosophy. In New York, Bonhoeffer discovers the life philosophy of American pragmatism.

c. Meeting with Barth

"The second great phase of his career" begins biographically with his return from the United States in 1931.[58] This stage includes the first personal meeting with Barth after what has hitherto been a literary debate with the dialectician, and in its own turn, the meeting generates a correspondence between the two (1932f.). Eberhard Bethge remarks concerning the visit with Barth: "The visit to Bonn, arranged through Erwin Sutz, belatedly fulfilled an ambition of his student days" (131). Commensurately, Bonhoeffer wanted to "spend as much time as possible at Bonn before the term there ended" (131). He probably also drew attention to himself in one of the seminars with an utterance critical of religion.[59] He writes in a letter to his university friend E. Sutz (July 1931) about the first conversation with Barth, one that lasted several hours:

> Now, of course, everything is quite or even completely different with regard to *Karl Barth* himself. One breathes a real sigh of relief, and is no longer afraid of suffocating to death in the thin air. I think I have never regretted more having left something undone in my theological past than that I did not go to him earlier.[60]

Bonhoeffer believes that "Barth is even standing beyond his books" (19). "His discussions impress me even more than do his writing and lectures" (19). He also discussed ethical questions with Barth, and was glad finally to hear "a thorough presentation of Barth's own position" (20). "Here really is somebody from whom one can learn something, and here I sit in pitiful Berlin, moping about because no one is here from whom I might learn theology" (20f.). Just how serious Bonhoeffer is about Barth's person and theology is demonstrated by his attempt, by way of family contacts, to have Barth considered for a position at the Berlin University.[61] Eberhard Bethge remarks succinctly: "But the year 1933 intervened, and the appointment went to Wobbermin."[62]

Before Bonhoeffer traveled to England in 1933, he met with Barth again in April and September 1932, first in Berlin, then in Switzerland. "At this time, Barth and Bonhoeffer were on closer terms than ever became possible again" (*Dietrich Bonhoeffer*, p. 134). Yet even the meetings of 1932 already stand in the shadow of the incipient church struggle in Germany, and their conversations shift from theology to church politics, something their correspondence also attests. While in his Christmas letter of 1932 Bonhoeffer yet looks back at the earlier, unencumbered meetings with Barth,[63] the correspondence of 1933 is completely colored by the church struggle. In September, he sent Barth the outline for the Bethel Confession along with a letter[64] soliciting Barth's opinion. In October, Bonhoeffer explains why he has decided to "simply perform pastoral work" in England, namely, because "virtually no one has understood the Bethel Confession, on which I really have worked with great passion."[65] Barth answers from Switzerland that Bonhoeffer absolutely ought to return from London to his "Berlin post." "What can the meaning possibly be of 'move to the periphery' or of the 'quietude of the pastoral office,' and so on, at such a moment when your presence quite simply is required in Germany?"[66]

Bonhoeffer's literary acquaintance with Karl Barth from his student days continues after 1925, with Barth's influence culminating first perhaps in the lectures at Union Theological Seminary in 1930/31; personal contact with the dialectician (1931/32) brings about a further turning point, with Barth eventually functioning as a trusted advisor in biographical decisions against the background of the incipient church struggle (1933).

d. Berlin University

As a private lecturer at Berlin University, Bonhoeffer gives lectures on "Systematic Theology in the 20th Century" during the winter semester.[67] The fourteen-part lecture series culminates in a presentation of dialectical theology and of Karl Barth (cf. §10: The Turning Point, 192ff., and §11: God, 197f.). Bonhoeffer as a private lecturer now seems to have parted company once and for all with the Berlin theology (cf. the presentation of A. von Harnack, §5, 164ff., R. Seeberg and K. Holl, §13, 207f.). This confirms what Bonhoeffer wrote in the earlier letter about "pitiful Berlin." And yet the lecture by no means deals only with Karl Barth, who recedes rather in favor of a historical presentation of systematic theology. Commensurately, the critique of religion occupying the central position throughout the lecture is by no means oriented only toward the Barthian critique of religion. Already at the beginning of the classes, the problem of religion is addressed within the framework of historical considerations. Bonhoeffer is concerned first with presenting, in §2, the "church and theology of the turn of the century within the general intellectual-historical context" (143f.); about religion, he writes: "The religious-moral personality [was] the center of preaching. Christianity is conceived as religion" (145).[68] The regnant view during the Wilhelmian age was that *Christianity equals religion;* that this was not always the case is shown by Bonhoeffer's formulation of Christianity, namely, that it *was* identified with religion. If the equation *religion equals Christianity* is historically bound to the waning years of the 19th century, then how is religion to be defined *prior* to this period? Bonhoeffer observes how in modernity "individualism . . . has destroyed the Protestantism of the Reformation":

> In the post-Copernican world, the word *religio* appears (from the English Deists) instead of the word "faith." This refers to the final, most delicate of all human possibilities. The human being [is] discovered as being

related to God. The Reformation is viewed as the discovery of this human being. (145)

Religion thus enters history as a *substitute* for faith. Whereas during the Reformation we find "faith," after the Reformation we find "religion." Faith and religion apparently emerge as historical antitheses! In any event, theology and history do not seem to be entirely separable in Bonhoeffer's understanding of religion. Ultimately, religion in its entirety is then equated with Christianity. "The concept 'religion' obtained its current meaning, in other words, only in modern times."[69] From the understanding of religion as a "substitute for faith" on the one hand, to the "identification" of religion and Christianity on the other, the problem of religion as such underwent a history during the modern period whose individual stages Bonhoeffer now presents. "Hume already traced religion back to human affections" (148), and Feuerbach allegedly worked this conception out to its completion. "Hence Feuerbach's two questions to religion: (1) that concerning the veracity of its assertions (illusion);[70] (2) concerning its concurrence with real life" (148f.).

If we understand the term "concurrence" in the sense of "honesty, sincerity" we have one of the fulcral catchwords with which Bonhoeffer will be concerned in Tegel, since as a matter of fact he does accuse religion there of failing to concur with *life*. Religion allegedly lacks the character of totality and honesty. As we will see, Bonhoeffer answers this second question himself in Tegel.[71] To the question why the theology of the 19th century (referring to Hegel and Schleiermacher) did not answer the questions raised by Feuerbach, Bonhoeffer responds that "official theology was too strongly . . . tied to the problem of religion" (149).

Following the presentation of Feuerbach, the private lecturer moves on to the understanding of religion entertained by J. Kaftan (149f.), E. Troeltsch (150ff.), the neo-Kantians (153f.), and W. James (157). Over the course of the lecture series, he returns to E. Troeltsch and W. James, who seem to possess a special significance for his own understanding of religion. Bonhoeffer asserts that Troeltsch is indebted to both Kant *and* Schleiermacher (cf. 151).

> Religion must through cognitive-theoretical observation be shown to be a necessary piece of the nexus of reason. A religious a priori is to be uncovered, demonstrating thus the validity of religion. (152)

Bonhoeffer then remarks critically concerning E. Troeltsch:

> Here, too, religion [is] to be understood from the perspective of the world. For Troeltsch, there is no longer any possibility of separating theology and philosophy. Theology [is a] special form of the science of religion, and the latter [a] special form of philosophy. (152f.)

Bonhoeffer seems to be recalling this insight in 1944 when in a letter from his Tegel cell he writes that "the weakness of liberal theology was that it granted the world the right to assign Christ his place in it; in the struggle between church and world, liberal theology accepted the — relatively mild — peace dictated by the world. Its strength was that it did not try to turn back history, and genuinely did pick up the debate (Troeltsch!) even though that debate ended in defeat.[72]

In the brief presentation on W. James, Bonhoeffer is able to draw on his extensive studies in America, mentioning, for example, as one of James's works *The Varieties of Religious Experience,* on which he had given a short report at Union Theological Seminary.[73] In an abbreviated form, he asserts in his lecture that

> pragmatism addresses every problem from the perspective of the living human being. . . . Life [is] the criterion of truth; only what manifests itself [occurs] is true. Religion [is] first of all a psychological phenomenon. (157)[74]

The critique of James which Bonhoeffer expresses on cognitive-theoretical grounds in the report, he articulates here on religio-critical grounds: "Religion [is] assigned a place among the necessities of life; whether transcendentally or pragmatically, it remains anthropology (Feuerbach!)" (158).

But how are Troeltsch and James now related to one another? From James, Troeltsch learned to view the feeling for the presence of the suprasensual as the characteristic feature of all religion. "The characteristic feature of all religion [is] its psychological moment; one must begin with this moment in order to get to the transcendental. Psychology [is the] entry to cognitive theory" (160). Troeltsch and James thus coincide in cognitive theory and religion, their cognitive-theoretical possibility being psychology. At this point, Bonhoeffer could have mentioned yet a third name, one he does indeed mention elsewhere in this lecture, namely, that of Wilhelm Dilthey (146, 177, 192). The Tegel theology is announcing itself when Bonhoeffer writes about "Wilhelm Dilthey's hermeneutic theory" (177) that "the question is whether this philosophy of history can be applied to theology" (177), a question to be answered in the *Letters and Papers from Prison*. Bonhoeffer's reflections in §9 of his lecture, preserved only in fragmentary form, seem to anticipate many of the historical reflections of his Tegel theology:[75]

> Maturation period of the secularization process of culture (medieval cities, Renaissance, Enlightenment, humanity). . . . Every sphere of life seeks a connection [with this process] within the secular sphere [that understands itself as being autonomous].[76] Laws of action [emerge] from [the] laws inherent in the situation: self-posited laws. The appropriate action then means ethically: autonomy. Human beings are basically in a position to allow things to act in their creatureliness without violating anything in them; they need only accommodate themselves to the immanent laws. This is the stage of the pure autonomous culture. (185f.)

What Bonhoeffer here demonstrates using the example of ethics that have become autonomous, in Tegel he develops for theology in its entirety. If I am correct, this lecture marks the first reference to human beings who since the Renaissance and Enlightenment have understood themselves to be *autonomous*. Modern reflections on history are apparently not just issues addressed in the Tegel theology. Franz Overbeck and Friedrich Nietzsche attack Christianity "as the most fateful hindrance to autonomous culture" (186). In this lecture, Bonhoeffer yet abides in historical reflection and does not draw the conclusion he draws in 1944 from this observation of a culture that has become autonomous, namely, to pose the question of who Christ is for us today, that is, for a world come of age.

Instead, he points out in this lecture the futile theological reactions to Overbeck's and Nietzsche's attacks. One is either assimilated or one negates the development; "in any event, one does not want to admit that Christianity is inimical to culture. Of significance . . . here [is] the self-evident nature of the synthesis [of Christianity and culture]" (187). If we understand the expression *religion*, which historically has grown into a universal concept, the way Bonhoeffer himself understands it at the beginning of his lecture with its entry into history (in the 17th century) and extending up to the Wilhelmian age, then one can say that this synthesis has also become a *synthesis of religion and Christianity*.

The universal concept of *religion* undergoes a fundamental critique at the hands of Karl Barth; a "turn" (192ff.) becomes discernible. "The question is: God and human being, and culture ends up exclusively on the side of the human being and of religion. Insofar as Barth no longer wishes to confuse religion and God, this signals the turn" (194f.). "In the name of God, Barth turns against religion" (197), and for Barth,

> religion offers not spiritual healing, but only illness with respect to God. [Religion] perpetually risks believing that it has God, or knows about him, albeit in complete humility and moderation. Religion then becomes merely one sphere among others. (198)

Bonhoeffer's last statement here resonates with the later characterization of religion as "partiality." He is able to articulate Barth's critique of religion historically as well when in the light of dialectical theology he declares any general concept of religion to be obsolete: "There can no longer be any general *concept of religion.*"[77]

Is Bonhoeffer saying here that religion is a historic concept which, having been introduced by the Deists, culminated in cultural Protestantism and ultimately came to an end in dialectical theology? Can we draw a conceptual arc from the beginning of the lecture, where Bonhoeffer introduces religion historically, to the point at which he considers religion to be historically obsolete? In any case, we must note that Bonhoeffer's understanding of an obsolete "general concept of religion" derives from dialectical theology and is connected with Karl Barth's critique of religion; indeed, he radicalizes it and fits it into a historical framework.

Section §11 stands under the title "God" (197ff.), and provides a presentation of Karl Barth's theology. (The title is already of significance!) In the following section (§12; 199ff.), Bonhoeffer explains why theology "is by no means to be confused with a philosophy of religion" (199f.): "Theology no longer has to ground its truth" (199): "In the beginning is an act of acknowledgment. There is only rejection or recognition, and neither [can be] grounded. So also in the beginning of theology is there faith" (200). Nor should theology be confused with a doctrine of faith: "No path can be taken backwards from faith to God. Doctrines of faith always understand God as an object" (200).

Here we quite rightly are hearing the influence of Barth resonating from *Act and Being,* where Bonhoeffer linked the theology of the act (Barth) with the theology of being (Luther). Just as in *Act and Being* Bonhoeffer surrendered a pure theology of the act with its radical concept of God's freedom in favor of the Lutheran predicates of being attributed to God in his word, so also at the end of these lectures does Bonhoeffer offer the following formulation with regard to God's freedom: "Not freedom from, but freedom for" (211). Here, as in *Act and Being,* the reformed Barth is given a Lutheran interpretation and thus rendered fruitful especially for the idea of congregation.

> Each person in the congregation is permitted to forgive the sins of the other. God himself granted this, namely, that I can assure the other person of God; from this the congregation lives in freely bequeathed continuity which is the present Christ himself. (211)

Bonhoeffer's understanding of religion accepts without qualification the radical concept of God's freedom as advocated by Barth. With regard to the critique of religion, Bonhoeffer yet seems to be following Barth unequivocally in 1931/32, apparently considering him to be the appropriate answer to the Feuerbach questions and to the critical objections against cultural Protestantism. This may also explain why he does not independently develop further his historical excursuses, as he does later during the period of the Tegel theology. Instead, these historical reflections flow into dialectical theology, and Bonhoeffer believes that Barth himself has basically fulfilled them. This applies in particular to the understanding of religion and of cultural autonomy.

It does not, however, apply to the relationship between theology and philosophy, where there is still need for "clarification" (212). For Bonhoeffer, Barth's use of neo-Kantianism, particularly of Paul Natorp (cf. 202f.), apparently does not yet constitute the final determination of the relationship between philosophy and theology. Bonhoeffer is able to speak this way possibly because under the influence of his stay in the United States he became acquainted with a different philosophy. As later developments will show, Bonhoeffer does indeed open himself up to a philosophy that is "close to life," a philosophy he already knows at this point in time but which he will not develop fully until 1944. Whether pragmatism provided the impulse for this must remain an open question for now.

In addition to Bonhoeffer's lectures at the Berlin University, we also have sermons from this period. In a sermon on Colossians 3, he underscores the immediacy of a pre-modern consciousness of God according to which human beings continually encounter one another "in the certainty that they are both resurrected in Christ."[78] This immediate certainty of God has become obsolete in modernity.

Bonhoeffer is apparently picking up his distinction between a pre-modern and modern consciousness of God from his lectures on "Systematic Theology in the 20th Century," altering it for homiletical reasons into the distinction between a "past" and "present Christianity." Christianity that "was" was characterized by an immediate "certainty" of Christ; by contrast, "our Christianity" constitutes "an impoverishment" compared with that of the past, that is, the immediacy of faith is no longer a given. Interestingly, too, Bonhoeffer is able to formulate this distinction between modern and pre-modern thinking without recourse to the concept of religion. What comes into view is a critique of *Christianity* rather than of *religion,* in which point the sermon differs from the lectures. Both the sermon and the lectures do, however, share the historical reflections.

In the winter semester 1932/33, the private lecturer Bonhoeffer offers lectures on "Recent Theology"[79] in which he critically presents various theological conceptions of his own time. One noticeable feature of these lectures — recalling the lectures on "Systematic Theology in the 20th Century" — is the positive evaluation of Barthian theology (303-7, 318-21; separated by a critical presentation of Karl Heim: 307-16).

> God's vertical word is judgment over all humankind, over nature, history, even over human inwardness and piety. That he had to come proves that we were not able to come. Hence God's coming is a criticism of all religion. (303f.)

A critique of religion deriving from Barth can yet be found in the Tegel theology. It is of interest that the concept of "inwardness"[80] is marginally attested in connection with a critique of religion even before the *Letters and Papers from Prison.*

The lectures on Christology from the summer semester of 1933 mention the topic of religion only peripherally. We already noticed in our presentation of these lectures in Part I that Bonhoeffer poses the "who-question" in connection with the "religious question": "The who-question is *the* religious question."[81] For Bonhoeffer, the who-question as a religious question is the question of transcendence. According to our findings to this point, particularly with regard to *Act and Being,* we expected to encounter the question of transcendence in connection with a *critique* of religion from the perspective of a theology of revelation. Instead, the question of religion is associated with the question of transcendence. The underlying understanding of religion here does not derive from the influence of dialectical theology, but appears rather to belong to the number of unreflected statements with a positive view of religion that still appear after 1929. One notices that these statements are made outside the context of Barthian theology (cf. also the statements with a positive view of religion dating from the same semester in connection with Bonhoeffer's seminar on Hegel, statements we encountered in Part I).[82]

In the second half of the 1930s, the topic of religion recedes in favor of ecclesiastical-political and practical-theological activities. Interestingly, Bonhoeffer's literary occupation with Barth recedes at the same time. Neither *The Cost of Discipleship* nor *Life Together* explicitly mentions the name Karl Barth even once.[83] Neither is any critique of religion to be found. On the whole, these writings address the topic of "religion" either rarely or not at all.[84] In the sense of an *argumentum e silentio,* we do derive from *The Cost of Discipleship* and *Life Together* an indication that the critique of religion is being conducted exclusively within the framework of dialectical theology.

e. Second Stay in America

In the report Bonhoeffer provided regarding his second stay in America in the summer of 1939,[85] he again criticizes religion with recourse to Karl Barth. He alleges that American theology has not understood that "God's 'critique' also applies to religion" (354), and that this theology is "still[86] essentially religion and ethics" *(ibid.).*

In his diary entries in June 1939, Bonhoeffer underscores the idea of a historically obsolete understanding of religion, alleging that religion "really has become superfluous,"[87] and that people would be "well and even better off without 'religion.'"[88]

Here Bonhoeffer is obviously going beyond Barth's critique of religion insofar as he not only criticizes religion, but intends to get along "without" religion. Indeed, he apparently no longer even wants to address the topic of religion as such nor integrate it into his own theological conception the way Barth does in *Church Dogmatics* I/2, which appeared in 1938, one year before these diary entries. Does this represent an initial reaction to §17 of *Church Dogmatics* I? It is in any event highly likely that Bonhoeffer was already familiar with *Church Dogmatics* I/2 at this time, since he was always "aware of the latest" with regard to Barth's publications.[89] This becomes especially evident in the manuscripts to his *Ethics,* which we will now examine; beforehand he acquired proofs of *Church Dogmatics* II.

f. Fragments to the Ethics

The early manuscripts (1940-41) contain isolated statements critical of religion. Here Bonhoeffer picks up the critique of religion from *Sanctorum Communio,* for example, the antithetical juxtaposition of the religious community and the church (*DBW* 6.49f., 84 = *DBW* 1.97). Here Barth's influence on Bonhoeffer's critique of religion is continued from *Sanctorum Communio* with its alternative of revelation *or* religion.

Other statements obviously prefigure the Tegel theology. Religion allegedly misses the character of totality attaching to divine and human reality (cf. *DBW* 6.59). Religion's character of particularity resonates where the church "deals with the so-called religious functions of human beings," but not "with the whole person" (84). Sentences such as these attest the sovereignty with which Bonhoeffer engages the negatively charged concept "religion" for his own ethical explications (cf. esp. 306!); he does nonetheless still reckon with "religious functions of human beings," obviously returning to the notion of a religious a priori[90] which he had criticized earlier (cf. *Act and Being*) but which he has yet to discard once and for all (cf. the *Letters and Papers from Prison*).

Of all Bonhoeffer's writings, the fragments to his *Ethics* seem least inclined to yield a well-delineated understanding of religion. Religion, religious community, religious society — all these are used interchangeably as the negative foil to "church" (cf. 49, 84).

Although the appropriation of Barthian thought does continue to be significant,[91] it refers now less to Barth's concept of religion than to his ethics: "Bonhoeffer's position is sooner to be found in proximity to Karl Barth's theology and ethics."[92] Although Bonhoeffer continues to deal with Barth's ethics even into the Tegel period,[93] this is not the case with the concept of religion, as we will see with regard to the catchphrase "revelatory positivism."

In the Tegel correspondence, Bonhoeffer is able to explicate ethical ideas from his own manuscripts from the perspective of a critique of religion as well. The ethical explications concerning "the ultimate and penultimate things" (e.g., *DBW* 6.143) become the Tegel question, "We are living in the penultimate and believe the ultimate, is this not so?"

(*WEN,* 176). Bonhoeffer picks up the ethical theme of the "ultimate and penultimate" from the perspective of a critique of religion. "Ultimate" behavior is in "serious situations" "religious behavior"; the penultimate — we may add — is "nonreligious" behavior."[94] A. J. Wesson points out that the ethical theme of "thinking in two spheres" is articulated in Tegel from the perspective of a critique of religion under the concept of "inwardness."[95]

Beginning in 1940, Bonhoeffer debates with Karl Barth in an ethical context. The first encounter with Barth in 1931 was already characterized by discussions of ethics, and now, ten years later, these same discussions are deepened (meeting in August 1941). Whereas with regard to *Church Dogmatics* II/2 a certain proximity between Barth and Bonhoeffer emerges in *ethical questions,* with regard to *Church Dogmatics* I/2 and the Tegel correspondence we will find that the two theologians diverge in their *understanding of religion.*

The fragments to the *Ethics* constitute a turning point in Bonhoeffer's understanding of religion. Whereas from *Sanctorum Communio* to *Act and Being* and on through the *Ethics* he is formulating his critique of religion in the tradition of dialectical theology, *Letters and Papers from Prison* attests the terminological influence of Barth only in isolated instances.

g. Findings

The answer to the question of *influence,* of the *source* of Bonhoeffer's *critique* of religion, is that prior to 1944, every statement Bonhoeffer makes that is critical of religion can be traced back to Barth's *theological critique* of religion. Barth's influence on Bonhoeffer reaches a certain apex around 1930 (inaugural dissertation and lecture, stay in the United States, activity as private lecturer). In *Act and Being,* for example, Bonhoeffer follows the Barthian understanding of religion *exclusively* as presented in the *Letter to the Romans* and in *Christian Dogmatics in Outline.*

While the expression "from a positive evaluation of religion to a critique of religion" is associated with the name of Karl Barth, so also does Bonhoeffer's conclusion from this critique of religion emerge in critical debate with the dialectician, a process we will now examine from the perspective of the key phrase *revelatory positivism.*

3. Out from under the Shadow of Dialectical Theology: The Objection of Revelatory Positivism

a. The Problem

Hardly a concept has become as characteristic of critiques of Barth as has Bonhoeffer's own objection of revelatory positivism. It is astonishing that the content of a term cited as frequently as this one has not yet really been clarified. "Revelatory positivism" has sooner become merely a catchphrase, something evidenced by its considerable history of influence. Whereas Barth himself conceded that, indeed, he has perhaps "occasionally" behaved and expressed himself from the perspective of such revelatory positivism,[96] Barth scholarship has a different accentuation, alleging that Bonhoeffer misunderstood Barth in the first place (F.-W. Marquardt),[97] and thus his provocative expression should be "deleted" from the theological dictionary (S. Fisher).[98]

While some interpreters believe that "revelatory positivism" is aiming at Barth's doctrine of revelation (R. Prenter, E. Feil, R. T. Osborn),[99] others understand it as Bonhoeffer's attack on Calvinism (J. H. Burtness, G. B. Kelly).[100] Still others consider the reference to revelatory positivism to be a methodological problem (H. Ott *et al.*).[101] Or is the issue merely the lack of any political dimension (T. R. Peters)?[102] Is he turning against all "black-and-white thinking" (H.-J. Abromeit)?[103] Does the expression perhaps not even come from Bonhoeffer himself (G. Krause)?[104]

This list of interpretive models can be expanded, and no doubt all these interpreters are observing something of substance. It is merely striking that none of the interpreters just mentioned really seems to examine the source material.

b. The Source Material

Bonhoeffer charges Barth with revelatory positivism in three — and only three(!) — passages. The three letters are dated to April 30, May 5, and June 8, 1944.[105] They develop Bonhoeffer's new ideas about "religionlessness," the theme of the letters being "religion." All three exhibit the same structure: Bonhoeffer first engages in a critique of religion, acknowledges Barth as having begun this critique, and *then* criticizes him with the questionable expression and deduces for himself the nonreligious interpretation. The "logical conclusion"[106] of the *critique* of religion is for

Bonhoeffer a *non*religious interpretation which never appears in Barth, prompting rather the appearance of revelatory positivism. Thus is the criticism of Barth introduced in a completely parallel fashion in all three passages.

Revelatory positivism appears exclusively in connection with Barth's *concept* of religion. Bonhoeffer observes a development in his teacher's understanding of religion, a development whose endpoint he seems to be criticizing.

In addition to more general attempts to illuminate the context of revelatory positivism and the critique of religion (D. Jenkins, J. A. Phillips, C. E. Krieg),[107] scholars also offer concrete suggestions regarding which of Barth's writings Bonhoeffer may have had in mind: Were they Barth's writings from 1919 that were critical of religion (A. Pangritz),[108] those from 1920 (B.-E. Benktson),[109] or those from 1938 (G. Sauter, A. J. Wesson, E. Grin)?[110]

Against what is Bonhoeffer directing his charges? In which writings does he perceive a failure on Barth's part, one to which in all three letters he transitions formally with the word *then?* He is not referring to the *Letter to the Romans* (of 1922),[111] since he emphasizes this work positively in Tegel. Here "the God of Jesus Christ was engaged against religion."[112] Is he referring to an earlier writing? Whereas in the letter of April 30 Bonhoeffer speaks *substantively* about Barth, who was the *only* one who began to think in this direction,[113] in the letters of May 5 and June 8 he asserts *historically* that Barth was the "first"[114] to have begun with such a critique of religion.

B.-E. Benktson[115] relates the remark on April 30, 1944, to Barth's essay critical of religion from 1920, namely, "Biblical Questions, Insights, and Prospects," which Bonhoeffer knew from *The Word of God and Theology.* In this essay, Barth writes that "Jesus Christ is the least appropriate object of religious and mystical experiences."[116] Although B.-E. Benktson quite rightly observes several parallels to statements made from Tegel, he finds such only with regard to the critique of religion. By contrast, Barth's essay attests no evidence of any nonreligious interpretation of the sort following for Bonhoeffer from a critique of religion. Although in Tegel he well may be thinking of this early essay as well insofar as he generally is thinking of Barth when engaging in a critique of religion, still this does not put any emphasis on this particular essay over the *Letter to the Romans* or, for example, the *Church Dogmatics.* By contrast, Benktson's premise is that on April 30 Bonhoeffer is thinking exclusively of this particular essay, an essay delivered, as he himself writes, "a quarter century before the *Letters and Papers from Prison*."[117] In that case, however, one would have expected at least some reference to the nonreligious interpretation in Karl Barth, which, according to Bonhoeffer's statements on April 30, however, was never offered. Benktson does not find any nonreligious interpretation of biblical concepts in Barth's 1920 essay. Neither the early Barth nor the Barth of the regular *Dogmatics* undertook any nonreligious interpretation.

c. The Significance of the Church Dogmatics

Both the *Letter to the Romans* (1922) and Barth's early essay (1920) can be eliminated as sources for interpreting revelatory positivism. One notices furthermore that in Tegel, Bonhoeffer is also able to speak about "true religion." This permits the question whether this attests a *positive* influence of the *Church Dogmatics* I/2 §17 (1938), in which Barth picked up the Reformation distinction between true and false religion.

G. Sauter writes the following about the third section of §17 of the *Church Dogmatics* I/2, "True Religion": "This might have prompted Bonhoeffer to remark that 'Christianity . . . has always been a form (perhaps the true form) of religion.'"[118] Sauter's observation is of significance because it demonstrates the direct influence of *Church Dogmatics* I/2 on Bonhoeffer's understanding of religion during the Tegel period. And yet this seems unlikely with respect to Barth's reference to "true religion." Is it not precisely Barth's *critique* of religion that Bonhoeffer is acknowledging? Is he not expecting precisely from this particular critique of religion a conclusion which Barth's *positive evaluation* of religion in the third section of §17 provides probably the least support? In that case, a more likely choice would be the second and first sections of §17. Perhaps Bonhoeffer's remark — really more an aside — concerning "Christianity as the true religion" does not refer to Barth in the first place. Wilhelm Dilthey, whom Bonhoeffer is reading during this period, also speaks about "true religion."[119] On balance, we have seen that Bonhoeffer always views religion critically when it is standing in the light of dialectical theology. In addition to this, throughout the entire corpus of Bonhoeffer's work one does encounter statements positively inclined or at least neutral toward religion, statements apparently not originating under Barth's influence. For example, in *Sanctorum Communio* we saw how statements critical of religion could be interpreted against the background of dialectical theology, and statements positive toward religion against the background of liberal theology (e.g., A. Ritschl). Beyond this, R. Seeberg's *Dogmatics* also proved to be an important interpretive aid, the first volume of which devotes over two hundred pages to the "nature of religion" and to a "demonstration of Christianity as the absolute religion" (*Dogmatics* 1.15-222); hence R. Seeberg could also have been Bonhoeffer's source for such reference to "Christianity as the true religion."

In Tegel, Bonhoeffer is *not* influenced by the Barthian concept of religion from *Church Dogmatics* I/2 §17. Quite the contrary, he criticizes a change in the dialectician's understanding.[120] Now the fulcral question is whether he is referring perhaps *negatively* to §17. Here we are picking up on the observation that the charge of revelatory positivism is leveled *exclusively* in connection with the Barthian concept of religion.

The view of religion in Barth's *Church Dogmatics* differs from that in the *Letter to the Romans* insofar as Barth develops a theological concept of religion. The critique of religion now becomes "the integrative task of theology."[121] Whereas the young Barth criticizes religion as the "negative side of grace," the Barth of the regular *Dogmatics* acknowledges it as the response to God's action. In §18 of his *Dogmatics in Outline,* Barth already goes beyond a purely critical view of religion and inquires concerning its "acceptance" in the light of revelation. Religion can be "adopted and sanctified."[122] In the third section of §17 of *Church Dogmatics* I/2, Barth speaks in a more fundamental fashion about "true religion." "Revelation can adopt religion and mark it off as true religion."[123] In order to speak about true religion, one must emphasize the element of grace characterizing it. True religion lives "through grace by grace."[124] The gradient grace-religion increases where the question regarding religion is to remain an "uninterruptedly theological question,"[125] where God acts "sovereignly" with regard to human beings.[126]

Revelation and religion cannot be systematically juxtaposed, that is, one cannot "treat them as comparable spheres . . . mark them off from each other . . . [or] fix their mutual relationship" (294). Hence the relationship between religion and revelation cannot be conceived dialectically. Nor does Barth even use the term "dialectical" in this context, referring rather to the "superiority" (295) of revelation over religion. Commensurate with a "theological treatment of religion" (299f.), Barth speaks consistently about religion from the perspective of revelation (e.g., contra Hegel, 298f.). Thus the anthropological question of what religion actually is, is to be answered from the perspective of the theological question concerning revelation. "In revelation God tells human beings that He is God, and that as such He is their Lord" (301). Yet by revealing himself, God encounters human beings not in some "neutral condition" (301), but as "religious human beings," that is, as those who seek to know God on their own (301). Religion thus becomes "resistance" to revelation, "the attempted replacement of the divine work by a human manufacture. The divine reality offered and manifested to us in revelation is replaced by a concept of God arbitrarily and wilfully evolved by human beings" (302). In summary, it is clear that for Barth "it is only by the revelation of God in Jesus Christ that we can characterise religion as idolatry and self-righteousness, and in this way show it to be unbelief" (314). From the perspective of the revelatory event, religion can then be characterized as "non-necessity" (315), "weakness" (316), "mysticism" (319f.), and "atheism" (319f.).

We see that with the *Church Dogmatics,* the critique of religion issues into a *revelatory-positive* view of religion instead of, as Bonhoeffer expected, into a nonreligious interpretation. Instead of the nonreligious interpretation of *biblical concepts,* Barth offers a revelatory-positive interpretation of *religion.*

Bonhoeffer did not derive any guiding impulses for his own critique of religion from Barth's *Church Dogmatics* I/2.[127] When, for example, in *Church Dogmatics* I/2 Barth criticizes the legal elements attaching to religion, Bonhoeffer expects a nonreligious or "de-privileging" interpretation of the biblical περιτομή. He would like to carry Barth's religio-*critical* premise further *critically,* not institutionalize it and develop a theological concept of religion. The logical consequence of a critique of religion is to speak about God without religion. If revelatory positivism is criticizing the *construction* of a theory of religion, then religionlessness for Bonhoeffer means the *absence* of any theory of religion.

For Barth, as for Pannenberg, religion is an anthropological phenomenon. But in contrast to Pannenberg, Barth assigns religion not to history, but to hamartiology. Whereas for Pannenberg religion belongs constitutively to the historic existence of human beings, for Barth it belongs to their sinful being. Just as human beings cannot be without sin, so also religion attaches to them and is justified. Religion becomes a constitutive part of dogmatics and finds a fixed theological place in the doctrine of justification. Within the framework of the Reformational doctrine of *justificatio impii,* religion, too, insofar it is Christian, or true religion, is justified in the light of revelation.[128] By contrast, Bonhoeffer wants to understand human beings *without* rather than *with* religion. Nor does he reflect in a single passage of his work on this connection between an understanding of sin and of religion. Quite the contrary, in the Tegel theology Bonhoeffer is intent on addressing human beings with regard not to their *sinfulness,* but to their *maturity.* He is concerned not with the *religious* person (in Barth's sense), but with the *religionless* person. And does a new understanding of religion help the religionless person? In the letter of April 30, Bonhoeffer suggests that nothing of significance is gained for the "religionless worker" from revelatory positivism, which "essentially has remained restoration" (*WEN,* 306). Rather, arcane discipline allegedly acquires "new importance" in religionlessness *(ibid.).*

Whereas Barth's revelatory positivism is associated with religion, Bonhoeffer's nonreligious interpretation stands in a dialectic with arcane discipline.[129] The "virgin birth" and the "Trinity"[130] are better subjected to arcane discipline, venerated, and protected from profanation than explicated from the perspective of regular dogmatics.

d. Other Voices

Our investigation has determined that the charge of revelatory positivism is directed at Barth's concept of religion rather than at his doctrine of revelation, as other interpreters believe.

R. Prenter[131] views Barth's doctrine of revelation from the perspective of "actualism," "analogism," and "universalism." Actualism implies that "revelation as such has no extension in time; it occurs from time to time" (22). Analogism is "that which in this world points to revelation or reflects it figuratively" (27). Universalism "is an emphasis on the supratemporal nature of revelation" (29). Prenter derives these three perspectives on Barth's doctrine of revelation from the latter's *Letter to the Romans* of 1922, and then treats them in a blanket fashion as determinative for the entirety of Barth's *Church Dogmatics.* And indeed, we did observe a different accentuation from Barth in Bonhoeffer's doctrine of revelation as early as 1929. In *Act and Being,* Bonhoeffer debates Barth's actualism and arrives at the formulation (also cited by Prenter): "God is free not from human beings, but for them" (36). Prenter suggests that in the *Church Dogmatics,* in contrast to the *Letter to the Romans,* Barth turns away from the world — "toward eternity" (38) — and thus falls prey to the speculative proclivities of scholasticism, justifying thus the charge of revelatory positivism from Bonhoeffer's view (41). Prenter defines thus: "By revelatory positivism, Bonhoeffer understands a proclamation of God's revelation that presents its truths only as objects for acceptance without being able to clarify their relation to the lives of human beings in the world come of age" (21). Although this finding may be correct in the broader sense, it still does not explain *what* prompts the objection in the first place. Prenter does not observe the connection between revelatory positivism and the understanding of religion; he tries instead to interpret the accusation of revelatory positivism exclusively from the perspective of Barth's doctrine of revelation, but then finds himself confronted by the problem of having to present the doctrine of revelation in its totality and thus to generalize it.[132] By contrast, we found that, for example, the revelatory-theological shift in accentuation with respect to actualism in *Act and Being* through the *Letters and Papers from Prison* bears a religio-critical accentuation rather than a revelatory-theological one. This corresponds to our formal observation in the letters, namely, that Bonhoeffer criticizes Barth in the context of religion — and only there.

In the Tegel correspondence, the charge of revelatory positivism is directly associated with the Barthian critique of religion, and *cannot* be explained substantively from the perspective of the doctrine of revelation in and for itself, but from that of the revelatory-theological understanding of religion. Hence Prenter's admittedly blanket observation regarding a different understanding of revelation in Barth's *Letter to the Romans* on the one hand, and the *Church Dogmatics* on the other, is essentially correct, and needs only to be applied to the understanding of religion in *Church Dogmatics* I/2 to aid in our understanding of revelatory positivism.

B.-E. Benktson has correctly drawn attention to the close connection between Barth's and Bonhoeffer's *critique* of religion. He also emphasizes the close bracketing of the critique of religion and the nonreligious interpretation in Bonhoeffer's thinking,[133] albeit without applying this observation to the connection between the critique of religion and the positive revelatory-theological estimation of religion in Barth.

This results in part from Benktson not having noticed the formal structure shared by the letters of April 30, May 5, and June 8, 1944, according to which the acknowledgment of Barth's critique of religion and Bonhoeffer's critique of Barth's own positive revelatory-theological estimation of religion are addressed in the Tegel correspondence within the bracket between the critique of religion on the one hand, and the nonreligious interpretation on the other.

Benktson also operates with a substantively different concept of religion in Barth, one not taking into account the revelatory-theological gradient revelation-religion. Benktson understands the Barthian concept of religion "dialectically" without differentiating between the *Letter to the Romans* and the *Church Dogmatics,* and also equates this concept with the concept of religion in both Paul Tillich and Bonhoeffer.[134] By contrast, it has become clear to us that Barth's understanding of religion from the *Letter to the Romans* to the *Dogmatics in Outline* to the *Church Dogmatics* is determined "dualistically" in the sense of a clear gradient revelation-religion. Because Benktson understands Barth's concept of religion dialectically and does not take into account the revelatory-theological gradient of the positive estimation of religion in *Church Dogmatics* I/2, it is not surprising that he finds no solution to the problem of revelatory positivism. That is, if Barth's and Bonhoeffer's concepts of religion were dialectical, Bonhoeffer's own reservations concerning revelatory positivism would be meaningless. It is precisely the dualistic premise and the attendant revelatory-theological gradient (grace-religion) that necessitates the sharp accentuation of revelation. If religion is criticized from the perspective of revelation, any attempt at positively acknowledging religion of necessity prompts an emphasis on revelation.

e. Expansion of the Term?

Revelatory positivism is thus the "result" of Barth's critique of religion,[135] more precisely, the negative and unexpected result. The result Bonhoeffer expected from the critique of religion is the nonreligious interpretation of biblical concepts, and this thus constitutes the "contrasting counterconcept"[136] to revelatory positivism.

Bonhoeffer is trying to think from the incarnation[137] to the world rather than positivistically from grace to the church. In Bonhoeffer, revelatory positivism already undergoes a certain expansion. That is, in the same way he acknowledges Barth's critique of religion even before *Church Dogmatics* I/2, neither is the critique of revelatory positivism restricted to the positive evaluation of religion in *Church Dogmatics* I/2; Bonhoeffer expands it rather to include controversial ecclesiastical-political questions.

In his *Outline for a Book,* Bonhoeffer writes: "Barth and the Confessing Church lead one to a repeated entrenchment behind the 'faith of the church,' and never to a completely honest enquiry and determination of just what one really believes oneself" (*WEN,* 415). Regarding the keyword "Confessing Church," Bonhoeffer draws from the ancient statement of Archimedes: "Theology of revelation; a δὸς μοὶ ποῦ στῶ over against the world; and round about it an 'objective' interest in Christianity" (413). Bonhoeffer seems to be expanding the charge of revelatory positivism against Barth to include the Confessing Church. Although the impact of this concept apparently accommodates such expansion, this keeps it ambiguous. On May 5, 1944, we read first that the "Confessing Church . . . has completely forgotten the Barthian premise" and "has slipped from positivism into conservative restoration" (359). Then we read in the same letter that liberal theology has been "overcome" through a nonreligious interpretation; "at the same time, however, its question really has been taken up and answered (which is not the case in the revelatory positivism of the Confessing Church!)" (360). In one instance, Bonhoeffer reproaches the Confessing Church's "revelatory positivism," and then in another its "restoration" disposition. Bonhoeffer seems to hesitate in expanding the charge originally directed against Barth, something also suggested by the expression "revelatory positivism of the Confessing Church"; that is, the concept has acquired a certain degree of independence.[138]

f. Findings

Bonhoeffer, who had no intention of developing a concept of religion himself, and certainly no theory of religion (cf. Thesis I), uses the expression "revelatory positivism" to criticize Barth's attempt in *Church Dogmatics* I/2 to engage in such conceptual development: Religion is ultimately affirmed as an anthropological phenomenon rather than (as also with the early Barth) viewed as an intellectual-historical phenomenon.[139]

B. From a *Critique* of Religion to Religion*lessness*

1. The Second Change in Bonhoeffer's Understanding of Religion

In section A, we traced Bonhoeffer's path *from a positive evaluation of religion to a critique of religion*. This first change in his understanding of religion was accessible to an interpretation. The objects of the investigation were the statements he made that were *critical* of religion. The question concerned the *source* of the *critique* of religion.

In the Tegel correspondence, we encounter statements that can no longer be interpreted against the background of dialectical theology. As we saw in the case of "revelatory positivism," Bonhoeffer obviously steps

68

out of the shadow of Barthian theology and the Barthian critique of religion. Nonetheless, he acknowledges Barth's critique of religion explicitly even though it no longer appears in its original terminology. Instead of the antithetical dialectical-theological juxtaposition of revelation and religion of the sort yet discernible in the *Ethics,* Bonhoeffer now, in his Tegel theology, sees a religionless time commencing. In this section, we will ask: What is the *source* of Bonhoeffer's reference to religion*lessness?*

a. The New Terminology

The first lengthy theological letter of April 30, 1944, poses the question: "How can we speak about God — without religion, that is, without precisely the temporally conditioned presuppositions of metaphysics, inwardness, etc., etc.?" (*WEN,* 306). Religion is described in terms of the temporally conditioned presuppositions "metaphysics" and "inwardness." The letter of May 5, 1944, also states: ". . . to interpret religiously . . . means in my opinion to speak metaphysically on the one hand, and individualistically on the other" (*WEN,* 312). What religion in the form of metaphysics means, Bonhoeffer explicates under the aspects of "God" as a "working hypothesis" (*WEN,* 393, 413), "stopgap" (341, 413), and "deus ex machina" (307, 394, cf. also 374). The latter two aspects he also subsumes under the collective designation of a "scientific working hypothesis" (cf. 393). Whereas the critique of "metaphysics" is directed against God's religiously understood transcendence, the critique of "inwardness" is directed against misunderstood immanence. "The age of religion . . . was an 'age of inwardness and of conscience'" (305). Bonhoeffer criticizes "religion as inwardness" under the aspects of "something partial" (396, 377f.), "religiously privileged" (306f.), and guardianship "God" (357f.).[140]

A comparison of the religio-critical terminology of the *Letters and Papers from Prison* with that *prior* to 1944 reveals a change. We now pose the question of influence: What is the *source* of the terms "metaphysics" and "inwardness" appearing in connection with Bonhoeffer's thesis of religionlessness?

E. Feil and C. Gremmels discovered simultaneously but independently a connection between these terms and the reading Bonhoeffer was doing during his imprisonment (especially in the early summer of 1944). He dealt intensively with Wilhelm Dilthey's "historical philosophy of life"[141] and, beginning in January 1944, repeatedly requested that he be sent the material explicating this philosophy.[142] Some trace of this reading must be discernible in his letters as well.

In his study,[143] C. Gremmels has juxtaposed Bonhoeffer citations from *Widerstand und Ergebung. Neuausgabe* with statements from Dilthey's *Weltanschauung und Analyse des Menschen seit Renaissance und Reformation*, revealing verbatim agreement in statements concerning

  (I) Giordano Bruno   Bonhoeffer 408   = Dilthey 341   ("friendship")
 (II) Baruch de Spinoza   Bonhoeffer 408   = Dilthey 429   ("affections")
(III) Herbert of Cherbury Bonhoeffer 392f. = Dilthey 248f. ("autonomy")

Beyond this, Gremmels (14f.) also finds that Bonhoeffer appropriated reflections on "coming of age and human autonomy" from fulcral passages of Dilthey's work.[144] "In addition to such formal references, one can also ascertain substantive points of contact elevating Bonhoeffer's reading of Dilthey above the status of mere chance" (15). According to Gremmels, these include the "key interpretive term" equally applicable to Bonhoeffer and Dilthey, namely, "this-worldliness," a focus on the here and now (15).

From Dilthey's observation that "every examination begins with the earth," Gremmels derives a "critique of transcendence in the name of the earth" (15). "The issue is no longer the poorly posed alternative between immanence and transcendence, 'earth' or 'heaven,' but rather a mediation of the intentions attaching to these categories" (16). Bonhoeffer finds this mediation when he formulates: "God is beyond even in the middle of our lives" (cited in Gremmels, 16). We must additionally observe that Bonhoeffer does *not* say that "God is beyond even on *earth*."[145]

Gremmels summarizes the shift in accentuation over against Dilthey in the pregnant assertion that "Bonhoeffer had to replace the cognitive-theoretical critique of 'this-worldliness' with a revelatory-theological critique" (16f., argumentation on 17). Bonhoeffer allegedly goes beyond Dilthey by "bracketing intellectual-historical and christological elements in his reference to 'coming of age'" (22). Gremmels explicates in a double statement:

> The concept of the world come of age interprets the end of a specific world-historical development; it is to be understood historically, or intellectually-historically. . . . The concept of the world come of age interprets the beginning of the salvific-historical development; it is to be understood christologically. (22)

In addition to the concept "coming of age," Gremmels also finds a connection between Bonhoeffer's scientific reading while in prison and the expression "working hypothesis God."[146] This expression becomes one of Bonhoeffer's most important working terms, one he then expands into the "religious," "political," "moral," and "philosophical working hypothesis God" (cf. *WEN*, 393). At the end of his historical reflections in the letter of July 16, 1944, Bonhoeffer then asks: "Where is there still room for God?" (393). In my opinion, this question could just as easily have been motivated by Weizsäcker's book, in which we read in the previously cited passage the following concerning J. Kepler and I. Newton: "For Kepler, the positive findings of science point toward God, while for Newton it is only the gaps in those findings that yet leave room for God."[147]

In Bonhoeffer's letter of July 16, 1944, we can see clearly how he expands the historical reflection concerning the "world come of age," a reflection deriving from Dilthey, in view of modern physics. From Weizsäcker he acquires the concept of the "working hypothesis" which he then applies to Dilthey — for example, with respect to the "moral" and "political working hypothesis" — and at the same time complements by the addition of the "scientific working hypothesis." Bonhoeffer is apparently transferring Weizsäcker's argument into Dilthey's historicism.

Ernst Feil has addressed Bonhoeffer's treatment of religion in various publications.[148] Like Gremmels, so also does Feil observe the clear influence of Dilthey on Bonhoeffer's Tegel correspondence,[149] ascribing great significance to the letters from the first half of 1944, letters individually dated to January 23, March 9, April 30, June 8, and July 16, 1944.

According to Ernst Feil (356), the Lessing citation in the letter of January 23, 1944 (*WEN*, 215), comes from Wilhelm Dilthey, *Das Erlebnis und die Dichtung* (*Poetry and Experience*).[150] The term "worldliness" in the letter of March 9, 1944 (*WEN*, 258), derives from Bonhoeffer's reading of *Von Deutscher Dichtung und Musik* (cf. the letter of February 5, 1944, *WEN*, 235), which he received for his birthday.[151] The terms "metaphysics" and "inwardness," which acquire significance beginning in April 1944 (cf. *WEN*, 305), similarly derive from this reading, and in Bonhoeffer's usage come to designate religion.[152] The concept of "maturity, coming of age," as well as the historical reflections associated with "autonomy" in the letters of June 8 (*WEN*, 356) and July 16, 1944 (*WEN*, 393), derive from *Weltanschauung und Analyse des Menschen seit Renaissance und Reformation.*[153] The following overview is helpful:

Bonhoeffer *WEN*	Concept/Name	Dilthey *Weltanschauung*
June 8 (356)	autonomy	43, 95, 150, 273
July 16 (393)	H. Grotius/ H. of Cherbury	248-57
July 16 (393)	M. de Montaigne	24-39
July 16 (393)	J. Bodin	145-53
July 16 (393)	G. Bruno	297-311 + 326ff.
July 16 (393)	B. de Spinoza	342-58 + 452ff.
July 16 (393)	"as if there were no God" (H. Grotius)[154]	280

In addition, Feil observes parallel with C. Gremmels that the citations from *WEN,* 408, regarding Spinoza and Bruno derive from *Weltanschauung und Analyse des Menschen seit Renaissance und Reformation,* 341.

Our *interim findings* are that both Feil and Gremmels have persuasively demonstrated a connection between Dilthey and Bonhoeffer with respect to individual terms and names from the general sphere of historicism.

Following the lead of these two Bonhoeffer scholars, we now pose the question whether Dilthey's *concept of religion* may also have exerted some influence on Bonhoeffer's Tegel theology. E. Feil has already determined that Dilthey himself represented the kind of religious Christianity (182) which Bonhoeffer criticizes.

Following this to a deeper level, we ask: How in fact does Dilthey understand religion? In his view, Schleiermacher's greatness is that "as the proclaimer of a new religiosity he established an inner relationship between this religiosity and the preceding development of Christianity" (*Weltanschauung,* 339). For Dilthey, religion and inwardness belong together and are affirmed (cf. also *Weltanschauung,* 39, 61, 216). He criticizes metaphysics *historically* (!). Metaphysics can be considered historically obsolete since the 17th century (*Weltanschauung,* 41f., 283, 348). Bonhoeffer agrees with Dilthey's general "opposition to metaphysics."[155] What does this mean? While reading Dilthey, Bonhoeffer observes that the critique of metaphysics actually involves historical criticism emerging from Dilthey's own philosophy of life. Similar to Kant, who is unable to get "behind reason," Dilthey finds that one "cannot get behind life."[156] Knowledge can be acquired only through the realization of life; it cannot be derived from metaphysics.

Bonhoeffer adopts the historical dimension of the critique of metaphysics and applies it to a critique of religion. Whereas for Dilthey metaphysics has become historically obsolete, for Bonhoeffer the "age of religion" has passed; he thus applies historicism to the topic of religion, and in the process adopts Dilthey's conceptuality and especially his argumentation.

b. The Term "Religionless"

Scholarship has been unable to determine the origin of the term "religionless." Even though concepts such as "maturity, coming of age," "worldliness," "metaphysics," and "inwardness" have been shown clearly to derive from Dilthey, no derivation of the term "religionless" has yet been proffered. This is rather remarkable, since the notion of a "religionless time" already occurs first *implicitly,* and then even *explicitly* in Dilthey. In his book *Das Erlebnis und die Dichtung,* we read that "this Christian religion was thus necessary, historically necessary, in order to bring about an age in which it would be superfluous" (86).

By "Christian religion," Dilthey means a particular "circle of dogmas" that developed "in opposition to the religion of Christ" *(ibid.).* These "dogmatic blocks" were allegedly of significance during the "period of the development of reason" (i.e., of the Enlightenment) "to prevent one from falling prey to desolate materialism" *(ibid.).* Dilthey would like to follow Lessing in holding fast to the "religion of the heart," and demands that "we rescue personal Christianity, but leave theology and even the church in the lurch, both of which seem to need to be persuaded on objective grounds!" (74). This recalls Schleiermacher, and, indeed, Dilthey adds Schleiermacher to this family tree as well: "This great, genuine religious idea is at work in all significant moral natures from Spinoza and Pascal on to Schleiermacher" (87).[157] As we have already seen, Bonhoeffer rejects the concept of religion represented by Schleiermacher and Dilthey[158] under the impression of dialectical theology. We must now ask to what extent he adopts at least formally the train of thought involving a "Christian religion" that has had its "time" and has now become "superfluous."[159]

Although Bonhoeffer cannot subscribe to the substantive distinction between institutionalized religion that has had its historical time, and private religion occurring in a timeless-inward sphere, he is indeed able to apply this train of thought to religion in the larger sense. He is presupposing Dilthey when he says that the "age of religion" or the "age of inwardness and conscience" is past. Indeed, his Tegel theology radicalizes this notion further. Rather than viewing some distinction within religion itself, he attacks the modern concept of religion as such (and that of the 19th century in particular). In so doing, he is criticizing Dilthey's (and Schleiermacher's) understanding of religion historically as well — and not just systematically-theologically — as it were in a second line of argumentation.

Remaining for a moment with the concept of "religionlessness," we thus find this concept *implied* in Dilthey's *Das Erlebnis und die Dichtung*. But we also find it attested *explicitly* in his writing, namely, in the *Introduction to the Human Sciences*.[160] Bonhoeffer was familiar with this volume, and mentions it explicitly in his lectures on "Systematic Theology in the 20th Century" from the winter semester of 1931/32.[161] After his explications concerning the "post-Copernican world" in which the word *religio* replaced "faith," he associates this radical "individualization" with the concept of science (*DBW* 11.145f.):

> The object of any science or discipline must reside in evidence; no metaphysics emerges along with the natural sciences. An identity between the categorial system on the one hand, and reality on the other, is presupposed: unscientific science. (Only the theory of relativity and quantum theory first refuted this.) No discipline could escape this: history, philosophy, psychology, and sociology. At the turn of the 19th to the 20th century, one becomes aware of this mistake (Rickert, Dilthey).[162]

Bonhoeffer seems to be well acquainted with Dilthey. The second part of *Introduction to the Human Sciences*, which also deals with theology, presents metaphysics as a historical phenomenon, alleging it to be "a historically limited phenomenon" (*Introduction to the Human Sciences*, 182). By contrast, religion is allegedly a perpetually enduring phenomenon:

> If facts forced us to assume a *religionless condition* at some particular point along the historical continuum extending backwards — which is not, however, the case — this point would simultaneously be a boundary of historical understanding. (*Einleitung*, 138)

Then even more clearly: ". . . thus this excludes the historical understanding of a religionless condition and of the emergence of a religious condition from it" *(ibid.)*. Hence the term *religionless* is attested early, and probably first came to Bonhoeffer's attention through Dilthey's *Gesammelte Schriften* [*Collected Writings*], volume I (= *Introduction to the Human Sciences*). In his *Gesammelte Schriften,* volume II (= *Weltanschauung und Analyse des Menschen seit Renaissance und Reformation*), Dilthey speaks only peripherally of *religionlessness*,[163] so that the answer to the question of influence is probably best answered with reference to volume I. Bonhoeffer critically appropriates the term "religionless"; he does not exclude *religionlessness,* as does Dilthey, but views it rather as a *historical* fact: The *time of religion* has passed.

Bonhoeffer is already reflecting historically on religion while reading *Introduction to the Human Sciences,* and these reflections are evident in his lectures on "Systematic Theology in the 20th Century," where they occur in connection with the previously mentioned Dilthey citation.[164] Religion and faith do not stand here in some yet-to-be-determined (dualistic or dialectical) relationship; rather, religion *replaces* faith (historically). The dualism of faith and religion from Barth's *Letter to the Romans* is heightened here and acquires a historical point: One cannot speak of Reformational faith at all after the 17th century; a modern concept of religion replaced it. Religion as a historical phenomenon had a beginning and must also have an end — at the end of modernity? In any event, Bonhoeffer does reckon with a "religionless Christianity" which at the end of modernity can speak of Christ "without" religion.

Ideas found in Bonhoeffer's Tegel theology are being anticipated as early as 1931/32, and precisely in retrospect coalesce into an overall picture. In both 1931/32 as well as 1944, Bonhoeffer adduces Wilhelm Dilthey in this context.[165]

Just as in the lectures on "Systematic Theology in the 20th Century," so also in a sermon from the same period[166] Bonhoeffer expresses the belief that religion has replaced faith historically.[167] Religion — religion "without God" — has replaced the past notion of Christianity.[168] Religion is placed into the context of history and replaces faith; at the same time, religion is criticized dialectically-theologically: For the sake of a return to faith, religion is subjected to the critique of God's word — thus, "or not at all."[169]

Although the beginnings of a *historical critique* of religion can be ascertained prior to 1944 as well, it is only under the influence of Wilhelm Dilthey, whom Bonhoeffer begins to read in January 1944, that these historical premises are systematized. The philosophical premise of historicism enables Bonhoeffer to organize his understanding of the problem of religion in a fundamental fashion in 1944.

The question arises concerning the relationship in which the historically articulated critique of religion of the Tegel theology stands with the dialectical-theological critique of religion of the preceding period. The problem addressed above concerning *continuity or discontinuity in Bonhoeffer's theology* will now be discussed from the perspective of the topic of religion. First we will examine the meaning of individual concepts within the critique of religion *prior* to 1944 with regard to their meaning within the overall thematic treatment of religion.

c. Individual Concepts[170]

Metaphysics and *inwardness,* two central concepts in the critique of religion of the Tegel theology, occur *prior* to 1944 only once each in connection with religion. In the United States, Bonhoeffer asserts in 1930 that "no *religion,* no ethics, no *metaphysical* knowledge can help human beings get closer to God."[171] In a lecture from 1932/32, Bonhoeffer similarly speaks of inwardness and religion in the context of Barthian theology:

> God's vertical word is judgment over all humankind . . . even over human *inwardness* and piety. That he had to come proves that we were not able to come. Hence God's coming is a criticism of all *religion.*[172]

Although metaphysics and inwardness are attested as concepts in connection with religion, they are not engaged specifically for the purpose of articulating a critique of religion as in the *Letters and Papers from Prison,* but merely occur incidentally.[173]

We have seen that *maturity* or *coming of age* [*Mündigkeit, mündig werden*] as a concept of Bonhoeffer's Tegel theology actually derives from Wilhelm Dilthey. Prior to this, the concept of "maturity," *sui juris,* or "coming of age" occurs in 1933, 1935f., and 1940. In his lecture on "The Leader and the Individual," Bonhoeffer insists that a leader should "guide the individual to real maturity" (*GS* 2.36). Here he applies the concept of maturity untheologically to the current historical situation in which it is precisely immaturity — of the individual over against the leader — that has become the program of the day. The idea of "coming of age" occurs repeatedly in Bonhoeffer's Finkenwalde homiletics. "The Protestant should come of age in dealing with the Bible" (*GS* 4.255). He advises his candidates not to read any other sermons for their own homiletical studies, since this "makes one dependent and makes the path to maturity more difficult" (*ibid.,* 260). Sermons should guide a congregation toward "coming of age in scripture" (*ibid.,* 268). It is not doctrine that the congregation should remember; rather, after the sermon congregation members should themselves "open scripture and read the text" *(ibid.).* Bonhoeffer's demands in his outline "Theology and Congregation" from 1940 tend in the same direction. Here he struggles to come to a clear understanding of the "relationship between the congregation and theology" (*GS* 3.422), and charges the congregation to "come of age in knowledge" *(ibid.).* Hence Bonhoeffer again applies the notion of "coming of age" to the congregation rather than to the world, as is the case in the *Letters and Papers from Prison.*[174] Bonhoeffer demands that the "congregation come of age," but does not yet observe any "world come of age" prompting him to pose the question of Christ *and* the world come of age. Although the *Letters and Papers from Prison* do not retract this demand for a "congregation come of age," it is clear that the concept of maturity acquires new accentuation in Tegel under the influence of historicism.

In contrast to these concepts, that of *individualism* is broadly attested in the context of religion even prior to Bonhoeffer's Tegel theology. As early as his dissertation *Sanctorum Communio* of 1927, Bonhoeffer criticizes any church that serves to "satisfy a need," alleging that such a church is "construed individualistically" (*DBW* 1.102, n. 18). Bonhoeffer also addresses the connection between religion and individualism in his report on his year in the United States in 1931; here the concept of "religious individualism" becomes the key term in understanding the critique of American theology and the American church. The philosophical background of this form of individualism is pragmatism, whose concept of truth is directed at finding "truth in an immanent context and not with respect to its transcendent claims": "It is clear that this basically conceals a purely individualistic understanding of life intent on granting to every individual his or her own happiness, and beyond this is concerned with not very much else" (*DBW* 10.270). The ecclesiological effect of such pragmatically prompted individualism is that American Protestantism bears a "definitively churchless, individualistic character" (*ibid.,* 271). In contrast to Reformational Protestantism with its confessional theology and dogmatics, American Protestantism is grounded solely on religious "individualism of the sort preserved most purely among the Quakers and Congregationalists. . . . Accordingly, the Quakers have no real sermon, no pastor, no 'church'" (*ibid.,* 276).

In the previously discussed lectures on "Systematic Theology in the

20th Century," Bonhoeffer identifies "individualism" and "religion."[175] As in his report on his stay in the United States, he now distinguishes between "individualism" and "religion" on the one hand, and "Reformational Protestantism" on the other. In Europe, Bonhoeffer alleges, "religious individualism" derives not from pragmatism, as in the United States, but from English Deism. He expands this idea in his lectures on "The Nature of the Church" from 1932, where he demonstrates how "individualistic thinking" constitutes one of the most productive sources of errors in Protestantism. "Individualization is the fundamental error of Protestant theology" (*GS* 5.238). As far as knowledge of God is concerned, this means that "the individual becomes the subject of knowledge of God. Troeltsch answers the question of the 'how' in knowledge of God with the religious apriori. Barth answers it with God's revelatory act" *(ibid.)*.

Interestingly, Bonhoeffer also includes Karl Barth (after 1929) among individualistic thinkers. (In *Act and Being*, he also directs the critique of individualism against Barth's theology of revelation; cf. *DBW* 2.122). In a sermon outline on justification from 1935, Bonhoeffer once more formulates fundamental statements concerning individualism and pregnantly articulates the difference between Luther and the post-Reformational period.

> We must finally rid ourselves of the notion that the issue . . . is the personal salvation of the individual soul. . . . In such religious individualism and methodology, human beings themselves remain the central focus. Despite his question concerning the compassionate God, Luther is concerned first with God's salvation, and only thus also with the salvation of our souls. (*GS* 4.202)

Against this backdrop, it is understandable when on May 5, 1944, Bonhoeffer queries: "Has the individualistic question regarding one's own, personal salvation not almost completely disappeared for all of us?" (*WEN*, 312).

Reference to "religious individualism" runs through several of Bonhoeffer's writings and conceals an essential feature of his critique of religion. For Bonhoeffer, "religious individualism" both has a prehistory and, like religion, functions as a concept in his attacks against Schleiermacher *(Sanctorum Communio)*, Barth *(Act and Being)*, James (report on his year in America), Cherbury (lecture), and ultimately Dilthey, who like Schleiermacher represents "private religion." The concept of individualism reveals an unbroken continuity in Bonhoeffer's critique of religion. Nor is this term replaced in the *Letters and Papers from Prison* by Dilthey's concept of "inwardness," but rather is added to the latter in an unconnected fashion. Hence in his letter of April 30, 1944, Bonhoeffer describes religion as "metaphysics and *inwardness*," and in the following letter (May 5) continues: ". . . to interpret religiously . . . means in my opinion to speak metaphysically on the one hand, and *individualistically* on the other" (*WEN*, 312; my emphasis).

The term *autonomy* (or *autonomous*) occurs several times before 1944, first in the inaugural dissertation (*DBW* 2.133), where "autonomous self-understanding" and "autonomous thinking" are opposed to Christology and ecclesiology. Reflections on autonomy in connection with ethics and culture are found in the lectures on "Systematic Theology in the 20th Century" (*DBW* 11.186, 190, 193f.), where Bonhoeffer uses the example of Nietzsche on the one hand to demonstrate the extent to which Christianity represents "the most fateful hindrance to autonomous culture" (*DBW* 11.186), and how on the other hand F. Naumann abandoned "the old attempt at a synthesis" (*DBW* 11.188). "Naumann's thinking concludes with the restless divergence [of Christianity and culture], and yet he does not draw the ultimate conclusion, and again pushes on toward a synthesis."[176]

Bonhoeffer does not yet associate autonomy with religion, though the example of F. Naumann might have suggested such. The name of Wilhelm Dilthey appears later in the context of ethics and culture, within the framework of a reflection on the collapse of "autonomous culture" (*DBW* 11.186). Bonhoeffer discusses Dilthey — again apparently in dealing with the latter's *Introduction to the Human Sciences* — in connection with the "problem of history" (192):

> All three areas (the problems of knowledge, history, and ethics) were concerned with the question of a balance with culture. . . . In the first decade, [there were] more and more whose attempts at accommodation failed. [The] beginning of these was . . . Dilthey. (*DBW* 11.192)

This lecture does not yet associate autonomy as a historical problem with religion, which would have enabled Bonhoeffer to view the concept of autonomy positively. He was not yet familiar with *Weltanschauung und Analyse des Menschen seit Renaissance und Reformation*. The expression "human autonomy" similarly appears in the context of ethical considerations in the lectures on "Recent Theology" (*GS* 5.322), where Bonhoeffer presents Friedrich Gogarten as an individualist ethicist:

The cause of the decline of the world and the collapse of its order is the idea of human autonomy, an idea that since the Renaissance has become increasingly dominant and is linked with an individualistic human self-understanding. The autonomous human being controls the world. *(ibid.)*

The triad "Renaissance-autonomy-individualism" is of significance for our present conceptual study. Whereas in his lectures on "Systematic Theology in the 20th Century" Bonhoeffer had placed individualism *and* religion into a historical relationship, he now relates the conceptual pair individualism *and* autonomy in the same way. It appears that he is gradually collecting the concepts which he will ultimately apply to a critique of religion in the *Letters and Papers from Prison*.

In the lecture on "Evocation of New Testament Texts" from 1935,[177] Bonhoeffer answers negatively the question concerning human autonomy, viewing the question in connection with exegesis and hermeneutics rather than with ethics or ecclesiology. Christianity and autonomy stand in an *alternative*[178] rather than *relational* connection,[179] as is the case later in the *Letters and Papers from Prison*. He views the concepts of "autonomous" reason, life, and human beings all in a negative light, and within the context of a justification of Christianity before the world. The background to this critique of autonomy may have been the positive understanding of "autonomy" within National Socialism.

Prior to 1944, the concept of "autonomy" appears in connection with ecclesiology, ethics, and exegesis, while in the *Letters and Papers from Prison*, it is engaged as a working concept under the impression of Dilthey's systematic writings. The *content* of this concept in Bonhoeffer's understanding is thus discontinuous.

Honesty. In the lecture just mentioned from 1935,[180] Bonhoeffer writes the following about justifying Christianity before the world:

> . . . and it is now merely a question of honesty that one completely loses all interest in this construction and turns away from it. This evocation leads directly to paganism, whence it also follows that the difference between German Christians and so-called neo-pagans is merely one of honesty. (*GS* 3.304f.)

This general reference to honesty becomes concentrated in 1940 in the early ethics-fragment "Inheritance and Decay" into the concept of "intellectual honesty" (*DBW* 1.106). Bonhoeffer formulates under the influence of G. Lessing:

> Intellectual honesty in all things, including in questions of faith: this was the prized possession of liberated *ratio,* and has been counted ever since among the unconditional ethical demands of western human beings. [. . .] We can no longer go back to the time before Lessing and Lichtenberg. *(ibid.)*

Bonhoeffer is thus already viewing "honesty" here as a historical phenomenon that begins with G. Lessing (cf. also Lessing's significance for Wilhelm Dilthey).[181] He similarly alludes to the connection between intellectual honesty and religion in the alternative variant to this sentence: "Intellectual honesty in all things, including in religious matters,[182] was the prized possession of liberated *ratio*" (*DBW* 6.106, n. 52). In the letter influenced by Dilthey (June 8, 1944), Bonhoeffer demands that his observation from the *Ethics* now be implemented: "Intellectual honesty includes letting go of this [religious] working hypothesis" (*WEN,* 393).

A "salto mortale back to the Middle Ages" is thus possible only at the cost of "intellectual honesty" (*WEN,* 393f.). The concept of honesty is incorporated into Dilthey's historicism and addressed in connection with religion.[183] That is, interpreted nonreligiously, the biblical concept of "penitence" means "ultimate honesty" (*WEN,* 394).[184]

"God"/privilege/partiality/preliminary religious stage. Because these individual terms together anticipate the *Letters and Papers from Prison,* we will also treat them together here.[185]

Prior to the *Letters and Papers from Prison,* "God" first appears with this orthography in a lecture given in the United States in 1930/31 (*DBW* 10.448): "Cosmology may come to the assumption of a last ground of the world and may call that 'God.' . . ." Here the orthography emerges that will be used consistently in Tegel to refer to a religious "God" who becomes the answer to the "ultimate human questions" (*WEN,* 357). In the letter of June 8, 1944, Bonhoeffer uses the orthography "God" with particular frequency (cf. *WEN,* 356f.) and, as in 1930/31, also in connection with the natural sciences in reference to the "working hypothesis: God" (introduced here by C. F. von Weizsäcker and incorporated into the historical argumentative framework).

The lecture on "The Nature of the Church" from the summer semester of 1932 addresses the *privileged* character of religion. Bonhoeffer criticizes a church that "settles in preferred locales" (*GS* 5.233), and demands instead that "the church can witness only from the middle of the world, which God alone creates. It must try to make room for God's actions" *(ibid.)*. He continues: "Theology is a function of the church" (*GS* 5.234), while Karl Barth writes: "But theology is a function of the Church."[186] This verbatim concurrence with Barth corresponds to Bonhoeffer's concurrence with Barth's critique of religion during this period. The critique of the privileged character of religion stands in the same context, and extends into the Tegel theology (cf. *WEN,* 306, 327). This critique of religion in the context of the *church* derives from Barth. In the lecture on the *Visible Church in the New Testament* (1935), the church is again juxtaposed antithetically with the religious community. While the "religious community" is concerned with "dividing life up into religious and secular spheres" (*GS* 3.330), the church subscribes to the principle that "the entirety of life is requisitioned" *(ibid.)*. Bonhoeffer thus believes that religion deals with merely a *portion* of life, while by contrast the church is concerned with the whole of life. In the *Ethics,* he picks up this notion again and asserts that the church "thus essentially has nothing at all to do with the so-called religious functions of human beings, but rather with the whole person in that person's existence in the world with all its relationships" (*DBW* 6.84).

From Tegel, Bonhoeffer concludes that "the 'religious act' is always something partial, while 'faith' is something whole, an act of life. Jesus calls us not to a new religion, but to life" (*WEN,* 396). The antithesis "life contra religion" seems to be anticipated in an altered form as "life contra church."[187] "Life" and "religion" are not yet viewed in direct opposition.

Within the framework of an exegesis of the Psalter in *Life Together,* Bonhoeffer enters into the debate with the thesis of the Old Testament as a *preliminary religious stage,* a thesis deriving from the historical-critical school. He is unable to follow this thesis particularly as it relates to the psalms of vengeance (cf. *DBW* 5.39), and then rejects it with respect to the entirety of the Psalter (cf. *DBW* 5.129). From Tegel, he asks in summary: " 'Preliminary religious stage'? That is an extremely naive position; it is, after all, one and the same God" (*WEN,* 176). This anticipates the rejection of a "preliminary religious stage."

Interim findings. We have hitherto limited our analysis to individual concepts that have acquired significance in Bonhoeffer's understanding of religion. Some of these concepts have themselves become characterizing terms for religion (such as "metaphysics" and "inwardness"), and some appeared in the broader context of religion at large (such as "world come of age" or the concept of "honesty"). We will inquire of the relation between *continuity and discontinuity* with respect to the topic of religion first by using the example of these various individual terms. Two groups can be distinguished.

First, we have conceptual groups signaling a *new beginning* in the Tegel correspondence. These include "metaphysics" and "inwardness," which Bonhoeffer did not use *prior* to 1944 in connection with religion. The use of these terms in a definition of religion is something new, and can be understood against the background of Bonhoeffer's reading of Wilhelm Dilthey.

Other terms suggest a certain *continuity* in Bonhoeffer's description of religion. These include especially the concept of "individualism," which from *Sanctorum Communio* on into the *Letters and Papers from Prison* bears features of a critique of religion. In Bonhoeffer's Tegel theology, he uses "individualism" along with "inwardness" to articulate his critique of religion, as we demonstrated in the letters of April 30 and May 5, 1944. The concept of "honesty" is also used in the context of a critique of religion beginning with the *Ethics,* and is expanded in the *Letters and Papers from Prison* into a nonreligious term ("penitence" as "ultimate honesty"). As previously with the concept of the "working hypothesis God," Dilthey's influence prompts Bonhoeffer to incorporate the concept of "honesty" as well into his historical argumentation, something evident in the letter of June 8, 1944. Dilthey's philosophy becomes the historical foil against which Bonhoeffer articulates his own critique of religion systematically and theologically.

One further group of terms is difficult to fit into the schema of continuity and discontinuity. These include concepts such as "maturity, coming of age," and "autonomy." Although our formal conceptual analysis determined that both terms do indeed appear before Tegel, they first acquire significance for a critique of religion only in the Tegel correspondence. Like the concepts "metaphysics" and "inwardness," so also "maturity" and "autonomy" can be traced back to Bonhoeffer's systematic reading of Dilthey in Tegel. It seems as if these terms acquired their real meaning in Bonhoeffer's Tegel theology; after being anticipated earlier, and then gathered together under the impression of historicism.

The evidence of these individual terms suggests that for the time being, we should assume *discontinuity within continuity.* Discontinuity obtains where terms acquire new content in connection with Bonhoeffer's critique of religion (such as, e.g., "autonomy") or are introduced for the first time (cf., e.g., "metaphysics"). Continuity is demonstrated by those terms whose content remains unaltered even into the Tegel critique of religion (e.g., "individualism").

We will now examine whether certain thematic groups already possess significance in Bonhoeffer's work prior to Tegel, or whether they are coined anew in 1944.

d. Thematic Groups

East-West. After his return from America, Bonhoeffer resigned himself to the fact that the Western form of Christianity was coming to an end. He wrote to his friend from his university days, E. Sutz, in October 1931:

> I would still like to see whether one large country might offer the great solution — India; for otherwise, everything seems lost, the great dying-off of Christianity seems to be underway. Is our own age over, with the Gospel being given to a different people, and perhaps preached with *completely* different words and deeds?[188]

In this letter, Bonhoeffer speaks of his activity as student chaplain at the Technical Academy in Berlin, asking what he should preach to the students. "Who still believes this?" (*DBW* 11.33; a similar question arises in 1944, *WEN,* 415: "What do we really believe?"). In a letter from January 1934, still from England, Bonhoeffer picks up again his plan to go to India. "Actually, I was thinking that the next step would finally take me to India and the East" (*DBW* 13.75). And almost as an aside, he continues:

> And because every day I become more convinced that Christianity in the West is coming to an end — at least in its previous form and its previous interpretation — I would really still like to travel to the East before returning to Germany. (*DBW* 13.75)

Bonhoeffer is also already speaking here of an "interpretation," referring apparently to the "religious interpretation" associated with the "Western form of Christianity." Ten years later, he states in the Tegel theology in a virtually parallel formulation that "the Western form of Christianity" is to be viewed "as a preliminary stage to complete religionlessness" (*WEN,* 305f.).

Reference to the "Western form of Christianity" from the *Letters and*

Papers from Prison is thus anticipated earlier in connection with Bon-hoeffer's plans to travel to India.[189] The question now, however, is how this East-West perspective with its *geographical assertion* — namely, that Christianity has come to an end in the West and lives on in the East — is related to the *historical assertion* from the Tegel correspondence that Christianity in the form of religion is on the whole a historic phenomenon that now, at the end of modernity, is coming to an end.

In this regard, Bonhoeffer's train of thought in the letter of April 30, 1944 (*WEN*, 305) is of value. After first posing the question who "Christ is for us today," he presents the *historical* critique of religion deriving from Dilthey: The *age* of "inwardness" and of "metaphysics" has allegedly passed, and Bonhoeffer contests any assumption of a religious a priori. An accumulation of rhetorical questions now follows regarding the possible "addressees" of religious speech. "Are we to fall upon a couple of unhappy souls in their weak moments and, so to speak, rape them religiously?" At this point, the insertion follows:

> If we do not want all this to happen, if ultimately we must judge the western form of Christianity, too, merely as a preliminary stage to complete religionlessness, then what sort of situation arises for us, for the church? (305f.)

Reference to the "Western form" is inserted formally and substantively through the expression "if ultimately we." The sentence remains complete even without this insertion. The impression is that through this insertion, Bonhoeffer is trying, in a kind of second course of argumentation, to introduce the East-West perspective already familiar to him into the historical flow of the letter. He draws the *geographical* argument from 1934 into the *critique of religion* of 1944. An element of *continuity* can thus be assumed for the East-West perspective.

Typology of Names. Remaining for a moment with the letter of June 8, 1944, we notice further the abbreviated classification of philosophers: ". . . Spinoza's pantheism: God is nature. Kant is basically a deist, Fichte and Hegel pantheists" (*WEN*, 393). A parallel to these statements on Spinoza, Kant, and Hegel can already be found in the seminar on *Hegel* from 1933, in which Bonhoeffer is already assuming a "[d]irect line from Spinoza to Hegel that omits Kant" (*Hegel*, 19).[190] In the lecture on Christology Bonhoeffer is quite unaffectedly able to label A. Ritschl as a docetist, A. Schlatter as an Ebionite, and Schleiermacher as a modalist (cf.

GS 3.211, 214, 228). This typification of personal names is a Bonhoeffer peculiarity attested prior to 1944 as well.

Baptism. Although Bonhoeffer's "Thoughts on the Baptism of Dietrich Wilhelm Rüdiger Bethge" from 1944 are already familiar, as early as 1932 he composed a speech for the baptism of the son of his brother Karl-Friedrich. A comparison of the two speeches reveals interesting thematic parallels. The *Thoughts* preserved in the *Letters and Papers from Prison* (*WEN,* 321f.) are familiar especially for their prophetic-sounding concluding thoughts, in which Bonhoeffer sees the advent of a church in which "people are again called to pronounce the word of God such that this changes and renews the world"; he prophesies:

> It will be a new language, perhaps completely unreligious, but liberating and redemptive, like the language of Jesus, . . . the language of a new righteousness, the language that proclaims peace with human beings and the approaching of his reign. (*WEN,* 328)

Before Bonhoeffer gets to these statements dealing with the future form of the church, statements associated with the topic of religion in general, he calls the present church one that "in these years has fought only for its own self-preservation." He predicts at the baptism of the young Dietrich Wilhelm Rüdiger Bethge: "By the time you have grown up, the form of the church will have changed considerably" (*WEN,* 328). This sort of prophecy is not something fundamentally new to Bonhoeffer; in 1932, he was already speaking of what his own nephew would "experience": "Tradition and values — including and especially our so-called Christian traditions and values — are disintegrating; this child will experience this to a much greater degree than we" (*GS* 4.150).

In 1944, Bonhoeffer combines these parallel ideas with the topic of religion in general and prophesies the coming church with an "unreligious language." Yet another idea runs parallel to that in the *Letters and Papers from Prison.* In the baptism speech of 1932, Bonhoeffer offers the following commentary to the baptismal text (Eph. 5:14): "To be awake means to be sober, not to live in dreams and wishes, but in the bright daylight of reality" (*GS* 4.151). In *Stages along the Way to Freedom,* he offers a parallel formulation: ". . . not to hover about in what is possible, but courageously to seize what is real" (*WEN,* 403).[191]

Suffering. This theme occupies considerable space in the Tegel correspondence. The best-known examples are Bonhoeffer's formulations concerning "participating in God's suffering in worldly life" (*WEN*, 395). He demands that one take "God's suffering in the world seriously," and asks: "How can one become arrogant with success or despondent with failure if in this life one suffers God's own suffering?" (*WEN*, 402). Bonhoeffer is sharply distinguishing one's "own suffering" on the one hand, and "Christian" (and thus actually "human") suffering on the other,[192] the latter of which can then also be used synonymously with the suffering of God or of Christ. "Christians stand by God in his suffering," is how a different passage reads (*WEN*, 382). Bonhoeffer also speaks about "selfless participation in the whole and in the suffering of our fellow human beings" (327). The idea of "co-suffering" appears early in the *Letters and Papers from Prison;* even before his imprisonment, Bonhoeffer writes in 1942 under the heading "After Ten Years" (11ff.): In contradistinction to Christ, who experienced "all the suffering of all humanity in his own body as his own suffering," Christians can "only to a very limited extent really experience the suffering of others" (13, 14). This means that

> if we want to be Christians, we must have a portion in the broadness of Christ's own heart through responsible deeds . . . and we should do so in genuine sympathy flowing forth not from fear, but from the liberating and redeeming love of Christ toward all who suffer. (13)

The following lines come from approximately the same time:

> Christ was able to co-suffer because at the same time he was able to redeem from suffering. From the love and power to redeem human beings he acquired the power to suffer along with them. (*GS* 2.597)

One cannot *co-suffer* on one's own initiative, cannot bear the suffering of the whole world, since one cannot also *redeem:* "Wanting to co-suffer on our own power, however, must be stamped out and forced into resignation" *(ibid.).*

Bonhoeffer indicates what the difference is between the genuine co-suffering of Christ and that of Christians (with respect to the redemptive act). To mention but one example to demonstrate how early Bonhoeffer was concerned with the theme of "co-suffering,"[193] I choose the year 1934. In a letter from London in April 1934, Bonhoeffer speaks to his friend E. Sutz about "suffering in faith." Until God commits again to his church, there must be "much believing, much praying, and much suffering" (*DBW* 13.128). In a London sermon from the same year, Bonhoeffer explicates concerning 2 Corinthians 12:9:

> Weakness is holy, therefore we devote ourselves to the weak. Weakness in the eyes of Christ is not the imperfect one against the perfect, rather is strength the imperfect and weakness the perfect. (*DBW* 13.411)

For the rest, he considers suffering to be holy, and asks: "Why is suffering holy? Because God has suffered in the world from man, and wherever he comes, he has to suffer from man again" (*DBW* 13.412). Formulations from the *Letters and Papers from Prison* resonate here.

Structure of the Letters. In his Tegel prison correspondence, Bonhoeffer distinguishes between personal comments and theological explications. This differentiation manifests itself formally through clear and fixed, almost formulaic expressions introducing his theological explications (= "thoughts").[194] With respect to our own inquiry concerning continuity and discontinuity, an examination of this differentiation in Bonhoeffer's letters to Eberhard Bethge *before* 1944 is revealing.

In a letter from February 15, 1941, he brings his friend Eberhard Bethge up to date on the progress of the *Ethics* (*GS* 2.403). This letter first contains personal remarks; for example, Bonhoeffer reports that his mother is listening to the BBC on the radio. He then transitions to ideas he has developed in his *Ethics* and writes: "Otherwise, things have progressed quite well during the last few days. . . . Now I am coming to the topic of the natural right to work, freedom, and thought" *(ibid.)*. So even before Tegel, Bonhoeffer is addressing theological topics in letters (cf. also the letters from 1940 in *GS* 2.374f., with respect to the correspondence with Bethge), though the formulaic expressions of the sort familiar from the Tegel correspondence do not yet appear, not even in pieces that were written contemporaneously with the *Letters and Papers from Prison* but do not address the particular *topic* Bonhoeffer and Bethge were discussing.

As an example, let us compare the letter of June 8, 1944 (*WEN,* 350f.) with lines written on the same day (*GS* 4.595f.). Whereas in the *Letters and Papers from Prison* he transitions after personal remarks to the "thoughts that have concerned me recently" (356) and addresses the problem of "human autonomy" historically (356f.), on the same day he interprets the "Moravian Brethren Textbook" quite "traditionally." He meditates on Psalm 34:20 and 1 Peter 3:9: "The righteous suffers at the hands of the world, the unrighteous does not" (*GS* 4.595). In a loose transition from his doctrine of mandates, he writes about the righteous: ". . . he suffers from the destruction of the divine orders of marriage and family" *(ibid.)*. But what is the response of the righteous person to "the suffering the world inflicts on him"? *(ibid.)*. Bonhoeffer's answer: "To bless, i.e., to lay one's hand on something and to say: despite everything, you belong to God" (596). In this interpretation — also written on June 8, 1944(!) — Bonhoeffer seems to be taking as his premise a different understanding of the world. The question does not address the possibility "Christ *and* the world come of age," but sooner presents the alternative "Christ *or* the world." In any case, the world belongs to the sphere of evil (= "mundus"), just as in the larger sense the conceptuality of this particular exegesis is more theologically traditional than nonreligious (cf. conceptual constructions such as: the righteous, God's blessing, Creator, Redeemer, heaven). We are apparently best advised to remember that from his Tegel cell, too, Bonhoeffer is able to work with completely traditional theological terminology. Of course, the topic concerning him and Bethge at this time is a different one, one that appears and is developed exclusively in the Tegel correspondence. We must remember: These letters are original in both form and content.

e. Findings

The thematic groups demonstrated even more clearly than the previous conceptual exegesis a *continuity* in Bonhoeffer's thinking. Themes that concerned him long before Tegel — for example, the plan to travel to India — are incorporated into the thematic material of the *Letters and Papers from Prison,* where they acquire new import. As was the case with the "concepts," so also does Bonhoeffer radicalize the various "thematic groups" under the influence of his Tegel theology. Just as, for example, in a continuous train of thought he imported the concept of "individualism" and then, under the influence of historicism, coupled it with Dilthey's term "inwardness" as a designation for religion, so also does he incorporate other themes into his historical argumentation. What at first (1934) was a plan without any connection with the theme "religion," in 1944 becomes the East-West perspective: India as the model for *nonreligious* Christianity!

The theme of suffering permeates Bonhoeffer's entire theology, and in Tegel acquires a place in his critique of religion: Religion is incapable of co-suffering. With respect to the theme of baptism, one must remember that even before 1932 Bonhoeffer was envisioning an end of Christianity as the end of genuine values. The "prophet Bonhoeffer"[195] is announcing himself. One final Bonhoeffer peculiarity, also attested as early as 1933, is the typification of names and abbreviated classification into philosophical or theological currents (cf. "Kant as deist" or "Ritschl as docetist").

2. Continuity or Discontinuity in Bonhoeffer's Understanding of Religion?

The *individual terms and concepts* as well as the *thematic groups* associated with Bonhoeffer's understanding of religion both demonstrated an element of *discontinuity within continuity.* The more fundamental question is now

a. Must We Choose between the Alternatives of a Historical or Systematic-Theological Understanding of Religion in Bonhoeffer?

This question will describe the problem of a possible antithesis, as has been presupposed within Bonhoeffer's understanding of religion. Ernst Feil has drawn attention to the discontinuity in Bonhoeffer's understanding of religion. The *Letters and Papers from Prison,* he alleges, "do not speak of a dialectical, and consequently somehow static, juxtaposition of faith and religion, as had been the case in dialectical theology. Instead, the work develops a historical concept of religion which permits Bonhoeffer to move beyond that juxtaposition."[196] Feil believes that Bonhoeffer understands the expression "religionless" not as "a systematic static category but also one of *Geistesgeschichte* in the sense of a world come of age."[197] This antithesis is thus observed in close connection with Bonhoeffer's reading of Dilthey on the one hand, and with his debate with Barth on the other.

As far as Dilthey's influence on Bonhoeffer is concerned, we will follow Feil's argumentation. Three questions arise: (1) Does Dilthey acquire significance for Bonhoeffer only in 1944 rather than as early as 1931/32? (2) What acquires significance for him in 1944 in his reading of Dilthey: historicism or (also) the concept of life? (3) What is the origin of the critique of religion in the *Letters and Papers from Prison?*

We have already seen that, for example, the term "religionless" already appears in Dilthey, specifically in a volume Bonhoeffer cited in 1931/32. In addition to examining terminological dependency, in Part III we will also inquire whether in 1944 he is also basically ascribing theological significance to Dilthey's philosophical conception; that is, did Bonhoeffer merely apply historicism to a formulation of his own *critique* of religion, or did he also appropriate Dilthey's *concept of life?* In any event, the philosophy of life in the form of American pragmatism already acquired significance for him as early as 1930/31 in the United States. We will return later to William James (under "b").

Let us first examine the problem of continuity in Bonhoeffer's understanding of religion. Ernst Feil distinguishes between a "systematic-theological" and a "historical" concept of religion. While the early Bonhoeffer's systematic-theological concept of religion allegedly derives from Karl Barth, the historical concept is to be traced back to Wilhelm Dilthey. Feil views this distinction as an antithesis: *first* "static and systematic," *then* "dynamic and historical"; it is an either-or situation, or genuine discontinuity.

Indeed, the statements *critical* of religion can be shown to be influenced by the early Karl Barth (cf. section A), while the reflections on religion*lessness* stem from Dilthey's historicism (cf. section B). But does this mean that the influence of Barth is thus antithetical to that of Dilthey? We have already demonstrated that Dilthey's historicism acquires importance at the latest in the lectures on "Systematic Theology in the 20th Century" from the winter semester of 1931/32; even *before* 1944, one finds a historical argumentative structure in Bonhoeffer's thinking in connection with religion. If, then, we are to make some distinction in his understanding of religion, we must first ask *when* this distinction came about: 1944, 1931/32, or sometime between? If one assumes an antithesis at all between a systematic-theological and a historical understanding of religion, one must at least inquire what the nature of such an antithesis might be. The assertion that it consists in the antithesis between "static" and "dynamic" is according to our observations insufficient, as is the antithesis between historical and systematic — as if in 1944 Bonhoeffer ceased to think systematically and theologically? Feil differentiates between a dialectical and a dualistic concept of religion in Karl Barth. Our own presentation of Barth's critique of religion revealed as a matter of fact *no* such distinction between a dualistic and a dialectical concept of religion.

From his early essays to his *Church Dogmatics,* Barth's own concept of religion is determined dualistically in the sense of a revelatory-theological gradient faith-religion. A dialectical convergence of faith and religion can certainly not be presupposed for *Church Dogmatics* I/2, which from the outset precludes precisely every systematic equalization of these concepts. Religion is a problem *in* theology. It is precisely the revelatory-theological gradient that is of central significance for the development of a *concept* of religion and that makes reference to "true religion" possible for Barth in the first place.

From the *Letter to the Romans* to the *Church Dogmatics,* Barth's critique of religion is oriented toward a dualism between grace and religion. If we now ask against what Barth is actually directing his critique of religion, we cannot but observe that it, too, is characterized by historical accentuation. For Barth, it is clear that the "word religio" has been acquiring its present meaning "for the past two hundred years." He confesses:

> I can no longer utter the word "religion" . . . without the repugnant reminder that in more recent intellectual history, it is actually the banner indicating the refuge to which Protestant . . . theology began to withdraw more or less in flight.[198]

Barth also reflects on the concept of religion in an *intellectual-historical* context, and has in mind specifically the modern concept of religion as developed fundamentally by Schleiermacher. Barth criticizes the 19th century's understanding of religion from the perspective of the 20th century, and believes — as does Bonhoeffer — that the concept of religion developed by liberal theology replaced the concept of faith of Reformational theology; theology, he believes, became anthropology.[199]

In his own lecture from 1931/32 mentioned above, Bonhoeffer probably also understood Barth in this historical sense, radicalizing historically the antithetical juxtaposition of faith and religion from Barth's *Letter to the Romans,* an antithesis he shared from *Sanctorum Communio* to the *Letters and Papers from Prison.* After the 17th century, Bonhoeffer maintains, one can no longer speak about Reformational faith, though he is able to say this only from the perspective of dialectical theology, since it is from this perspective alone — that is, from that of the 20th century itself — that one can *again* speak about Reformational faith. Thus also does his lecture culminate in a presentation of Barth and of dialectical theology. Systematics and history are not alternatives in Bonhoeffer's understanding of religion. As early as the 1930s, Bonhoeffer uses historical argumentative structures in connection with religion alongside systematic-theological considerations: in the lectures on "Systematic Theology in the 20th Century" with its thesis that religion replaces Reformational faith in the 17th century;[200] in the sermon from 1932, when after distinguishing between a modern and premodern understanding of God he suggests that through dialectical theology faith now again replaces religion in the 20th century;[201] in his 1939 assertion that "religion" has become superfluous in the larger sense, and that "one can get along just fine and even better without 'religion' ";[202] in his *Ethics* in 1941, when he identifies religion with "Western godlessness,"[203] or when in a letter from 1942 he confesses that the concepts "God," "Christ," and so on must be religiously "uncloaked";[204] and finally, when from his Tegel cell he proclaims the "religionless time" toward which we are moving.[205]

Historical and systematic-theological considerations stand next to one another everywhere in Bonhoeffer's treatment of religion, occasionally complementing one another as in the lecture from 1931/32 and in the sermon from 1932 with the assertion that religion as a historic phenomenon had its time from the 17th to the 19th century. The dialectical theology of the 20th century rejects the modern understanding of religion that has emerged since the 17th century. Bonhoeffer's understanding of religion in Tegel radicalizes this critique with systematic recourse to Wilhelm Dilthey and anticipates the historic end of religion in the larger sense.

b. Historically Articulated Critique of Religion in 1931/32: The Significance of William James

We have seen that Bonhoeffer entertained a historical understanding of religion as early as the 1930s. *When* did this happen? *Where* is it first attested? To answer these questions, we will turn our attention to a largely neglected area of Bonhoeffer research. In addition to Dilthey (from 1931/32 onward), the pragmatic philosophy of life[206] also becomes increasingly significant for Bonhoeffer after 1930. In America, he associates this philosophy primarily with the name William James. In 1931 he wrote: "I read almost the entire philosophical work of William James, and it really captivated me."[207]

Bonhoeffer was obviously especially familiar with James's concept of religion. He delivered a paper[208] on the "Conclusions to the Varieties of Religious Experience" which James drew from his *Lectures on Pragmatic Psychology of Religion* from 1901/1902.[209] James opens his "Conclusions" by picking up, from a cognitive-theoretical perspective, on the historical philosophy of life and associating it with the concept of religion, asking: "Ought it to be assumed that in all men the mixture of religion with other elements should be identical? Ought it, indeed, to be assumed that the lives of all men should show identical religious elements?" (760). For an understanding of religion, these questions are answered with "no," since the life situations of human beings allegedly vary too widely. What does the "science of religions" have to say? For it, religion has become historically obsolete, and "there is a notion in the air about us that religion is probably an anachronism, a case of 'survival,' an atavistic relapse into a mode of thought which humanity in its more enlightened examples has outgrown"; ". . . the days are over when it could be said that for Science herself the heavens declare the glory of God and the firmament showeth his handiwork."[210] At best, science acknowledges only a "God of universal laws." In a word, religion is "pure anachronism" (767). To that extent, James portrays the "scientific view of religion" of his own age as a "survival theory" *(ibid.)*.

Direct parallels with Bonhoeffer's understanding of religion in Tegel suggest themselves. Bonhoeffer applied in a consistent fashion Dilthey's historicism (and probably also James's pragmatism) to the modern concept of religion and proclaimed the end of religion. He did this contra Dilthey's own understanding of religion and, as we will see, also contra that of James.

In the continuation of his "Conclusions," James criticizes the scientific "survival theory" of religion, rejecting it "without hesitation," since he wants to preserve the "religion of the individual" and of our "private realities." "Well, it is still in these richer animistic and dramatic aspects that religion delights to dwell," James writes; "it is the terror and beauty of phenomena, the 'promise' of the dawn and the rainbow, the 'voice' of the thunder, the 'gentleness' of the summer rain, the 'sublimity' of the stars, and not the physical laws which these things follow, by which the religious mind still continues to be most impressed."[211] We must "rehabilitate the element of feeling in religion," individuality being grounded, James alleges, in feeling.

These statements suffice to locate James's concept of religion within the series of thinkers from Schleiermacher to German Idealism on up to Dilthey. James also remains consistent in his pragmatism in this positive estimation of religion, since religion does something, and has a specific effect. God "proves to be useful." Thus is religion also "true" in the sense of the pragmatic theory of cognition. "The love of life is the religious impulse." For James, the philosophy of life and the theory of religion are inseparable.

As we saw above, Bonhoeffer rejected "religion" in the form of "individualism" from *Sanctorum Communio* on to the *Letters and Papers from Prison* in connection with Schleiermacher, James, and Dilthey. What is his response to James's "Conclusions"? In his report on James, Bonhoeffer clearly observes the transition from James's presentation of the scientific critique of religion to the positive pragmatic estimation of religion in the "Conclusions." His concise rendering is: "Science is impersonal, religion personal" (*DBW* 10.408). Bonhoeffer also observes the historical mooring of the question of religion in pragmatism. The question for James is "whether religion be only a survival of primitive thought and whether now science takes its place" (*DBW* 10.408). In his James lecture, Bonhoeffer criticizes this swing over to a positive estimation of religion signifying an attempt at balancing religion and natural science. We must assume that he is subscribing to the scientific critique of religion. He rejects the pragmatic concept of religion and initially contests methodologically any pragmatic theology; God's "efficacy" cannot, Bonhoeffer maintains, be given priority over his "reality" (*DBW* 10.409). In other words, what is "true" is not just what "works," and certainly not in the question of God. In his Tegel theology, Bonhoeffer uses the orthography "God" to identify a God who proves real only through his actions.[212]

Bonhoeffer also associates the rejection of a pragmatic doctrine of God with his second critical objection to William James, for whom religious knowledge of God is a matter of the "subconscious" as the mediator between the religious individual and God. For James, however, this is an anthropological phenomenon and does not reside "outside the individual person" (cf. *DBW* 10.410).

For Bonhoeffer, who in 1930 is following the position of dialectical theology with respect to knowledge of God, any "religious experience" not really residing "outside" the individual person can be viewed only as an "illusion." Put philosophically, Bonhoeffer counters James's pragmatism with Kant's phenomenalism. Still, he does take pains to familiarize himself with the pragmatic philosophy of life, and is both influenced by it and prompted to criticize it.

In James, Bonhoeffer became familiar with a critique of religion from the perspective of the natural sciences that became possible as such only in a modern context.[213] This particular form of a critique of religion differentiates sharply between the natural sciences on the one hand, and religion on the other, a view Bonhoeffer explicitly shares: "So it seems to me not to be possible to find a mediating term between religion and science" (*DBW* 10.410). From Tegel, he summarizes the same idea in the sentence: "an edifying natural scientist . . . is a hermaphrodite" (*WEN*, 393).

Bonhoeffer shares the critique of religion developed by James in connection with the philosophy of life, but rejects the entire pragmatic concept of religion.

c. Findings

We thus do *not* have to choose between a systematic and a historical understanding of religion in Bonhoeffer. Quite the contrary, our analysis has shown that this question is not even possible in this form. The articulation of a critique of religion stands in its various contexts together with his appropriation of philosophical conceptions; the three most important names are Kant, James, and Dilthey, for all three of whose philosophical conceptions "religion" is an integral part. To that extent, Bonhoeffer's appropriation of philosophical ideas is eclectic; he does not share their concepts of religion.

It is especially Karl Barth who mediates to Bonhoeffer the phenomenalism of Kant. The revelatory-theological key to articulating the critique of religion is found in the phenomenalism that in neo-Kantianism became a limiting or boundary concept. Beginning in the 1930s, Bonhoeffer complements and radicalizes his understanding of religion historically. The dualism between faith and religion is radicalized and bracketed historically. William James becomes the pioneer for the "historical philosophy of life" of the Tegel theology and for Bonhoeffer's reference to "religionlessness." I personally consider Bonhoeffer's encounter with pragmatism to be his most important after that with neo-Kantianism, and more important even than that with historicism.[214] Although Bonhoeffer does not share the cognitive-theoretical premise of pragmatism, he does share both James's and Dilthey's opposition to metaphysics. He remains a Kantian in the sense of Barth, and this changes only under the systematic influence of Dilthey, through whom he discovers a new side to Kant. The (re)discovery of Dilthey prompts a modification of his philosophical premise (1944): Where Kant refers to reason, Dilthey refers to the cognitive-theoretical significance of life. This, however, also prompts a critique of Barth. Kant and Dilthey combine for Bonhoeffer a common position against the philosophy of identity of German Idealism.[215]

Bonhoeffer rejects Dilthey's *concept of religion* while yet following him terminologically and with respect to the cognitive-theoretical issue. He applies *historicism* against Dilthey's own concept of religion and shows it to be modern. He sees a clear line in the positive estimation of religion running from G. Lessing to F. Schleiermacher and W. Dilthey up to W. James. From Barth he acquires the critique of Schleiermacher's concept of religion, a critique already attested in *Sanctorum Communio:* religion as individualism.

Bonhoeffer historically expands this dialectical-theological position backward to include the 17th and 18th centuries, and forward with respect to the waning 19th and the 20th centuries. This understanding of "religion as individualism" appears throughout from *Sanctorum Communio* (1927) on up to the *Letters and Papers from Prison* (1944), directing itself against the modern concept of religion in general and against that of German Idealism in particular. Here the names of Herbert of Cherbury, G. Lessing, F. Schleiermacher, W. Dilthey, and W. James all play a part.

The independence and originality of Bonhoeffer's understanding of religion become evident in the early 1930s, issuing in 1944 in the thesis of "religionlessness." No antithesis in the articulation of his critique of religion is discernible, while a modification in his terminological and conceptual development can be traced back to the varied influence of theology (Barth) and philosophy (Kant, James, Dilthey).

Bonhoeffer's understanding of religion is characterized by *discontinuity in continuity.* This applies in an expanded sense also to his appropriation of various philosophical conceptions. The neo-Kantian premise (beginning in 1929) is modified (beginning in 1931) into historicism under the influence of pragmatism (1944).

C. Findings

1. Reflections on Content

The path taken by Bonhoeffer's treatment of religion leads from a *positive estimation* of religion to a *critique* of religion to religion*lessness.* In following his path, we observed two transformations in his understanding of religion, both of which are associated with the name of Karl Barth.

The reference to "transformations" is intentional, since these represent flowing transitions rather than abrupt caesurae. That which applies to Bonhoeffer's theology on the whole has been confirmed here with regard to the topic of religion specifically. Along with Eberhard Bethge and other Bonhoeffer scholars, we presuppose an element of *continuity* in the theological and ecclesiological queries of Bonhoeffer as a Christian theologian.[216] In the specific terminology of the Tegel theology, we do admittedly encounter terms which with respect to other, earlier statements regarding a critique of religion leave the impression of *discontinuity*. This impression recedes, however, when we examine the topic of religion against the background of the whole of Bonhoeffer's theology.

The three modes of articulation of religion encountered in Bonhoeffer's overall work could not be interpreted in any isolated fashion; because Bonhoeffer does not develop any *concept* of religion in his own writings, we had to look at the question of *influence:* What is the *source* of Bonhoeffer's *positive* or *critical* view of religion? What is the source of his thesis of religion*lessness?* We can now answer these questions.

I. Statements reflecting Bonhoeffer's positive estimation of religion are to be interpreted against the background of liberal theology (A. von Harnack, A. Ritschl).

II. Statements critical of religion arose under the influence of dialectical theology (K. Barth).

III. His thesis of religionlessness presupposes philosophical historicism (W. Dilthey, W. James prior to that).

The following questions now arise: How are these modes of articulation of religion in Bonhoeffer's theology related? How are the critique of religion and religionlessness related? What is the relation between Bonhoeffer's appropriation of Barth and his appropriation of Dilthey? What is the connection between the analyses in sections A and B?

To answer these questions, we introduce the key concept from Bonhoeffer's Tegel theology, namely, the *nonreligious interpretation of biblical concepts*. This theological program presupposes *both* the thesis of religionlessness *and* the theological critique of religion. Nor can the nonreligious interpretation of biblical concepts be explained solely on the basis of Bonhoeffer's familiarity with Dilthey. We saw that Dilthey did *not* engage the concept "religionless" critically. Quite the contrary, he understands religion consistently from the perspective of history; "religionlessness" is excluded.

Bonhoeffer applies the critique of religion to this particular term from Dilthey, and gives it a new, critical meaning by reversing the term's poles, as it were; the constructive impulse of dialectical theology is maintained into the Tegel theology. We can answer as follows the questions posed above:

In his demand for a nonreligious interpretation, Bonhoeffer combines dialectical theology with philosophical historicism. Bonhoeffer scholarship has previously given insufficient attention to this combination of an impulse critical of religion on the one hand, *and* a historical examination of religion on the other, a combination making the nonreligious interpretation possible in the first place. The result of Part II is the following thesis.

2. Thesis II

> From the perspective of *influence,* the nonreligious interpretation represents a combination of Karl Barth's theological critique of religion and Wilhelm Dilthey's philosophical historicism.

Thesis II answers the question of *influence* raised by Thesis I, namely, the question regarding the *source* of the nonreligious interpretation of biblical concepts. In Part III, we will inquire of the content of this interpretation, namely: *What* does it mean to interpret nonreligiously?

The Philosophy of Life
and Nonreligious Interpretation

Bonhoeffer learned to criticize religion from the perspective of faith. The alternative was *religion* or *faith*. From his Tegel cell, he writes: "The religious act is something partial, faith is . . . an act of life."[1] Faith is explicated as an act of life. He continues: "Jesus calls us not to a new religion, but to life."[2] The alternative is now *religion* or *life* instead of *religion* or *faith*. Bonhoeffer interprets the concept of faith as the concept of life, the abbreviated thesis being: *to live as to believe.* In what follows, we will establish this thesis and inquire whether any connection obtains with the so-called philosophy of life of the waning 19th and the early 20th centuries. In addition to Friedrich Nietzsche and the Spanish philosopher of culture José Ortega y Gasset, the outstanding representative of this direction in philosophical thought is Wilhelm Dilthey.

A. The Significance of Bonhoeffer's Prison Reading
for His Tegel Theology

Even before Bonhoeffer began to read Dilthey systematically in the spring of 1944, he had beginning in 1943 acquired some writings by Ortega y Gasset; in addition, he mentions and reads philosophers and poets associated with the philosophy of life, including C. F. Meyer (*WEN*, 102),[3] F. Nietzsche and S. Kierkegaard (e.g., 257),[4] L. Feuerbach (393),[5]

M. Heidegger (92),[6] J. W. Goethe (e.g., 258),[7] L. Klages (257),[8] F. Hölderlin (363),[9] and J. Pestalozzi (437f.).[10] He also reads and cites a great deal from Adalbert Stifter's *Witiko*.

1. José Ortega y Gasset

In a letter from his cell on October 4, 1943, Bonhoeffer asks his parents to send him two essays by Ortega y Gasset: *System of History* and *On the Roman Empire* (*WEN,* 136). On April 26, 1944, that is, six months later, he writes again to his parents: "Could you please try to get me the new book by Ortega y Gasset, *The Nature of Historic Crises* . . . and if at all possible also the previous *History as System* . . . ?" (303).

By *History as System* and *System of History,* Bonhoeffer is probably referring to the same work[11] by the philosopher of culture, namely, *History as System* from 1941.[12] Bonhoeffer's repeated requests suggest that this particular essay was important to him. That Bonhoeffer did not again request *On the Roman Empire* from 1940[13] suggests that he had received this and had indeed read it.[14] He has thus been reading the philosopher of life[15] since the fall of 1943; his interest in Gasset's work continues, and he makes additional requests in the spring of 1944.

a. Description

In *On the Roman Empire,* Bonhoeffer could at the end of 1943 already be reading about the historic significance of the concept *religio* in Cicero. "This attitude, leading us not to live frivolously, but to comport ourselves with thoughtful reflection, reflection before the transcendent reality — this is the exact sense the word *religio* had for the Romans, and it is truly the essential sense of every religion."[16] Religion allegedly does not mean a binding to God, but quite simply "conscientious" in the sense of "religiosus," "that is, any person who behaves with thoughtful reflection instead of frivolously."[17] Religion as a religion of conscience thus acquires significance for political life. "The concepts of faith and the state permeate one another. In politics there are epochs of religion and epochs of carelessness, of thoughtful reflection and of negligence, of conscientiousness and of frivolity" *(ibid.).*

Apparently, Ortega y Gasset reckons with a time in history without religion, that is, in his terminology, with a time of "negligence, carelessness, frivolity." Religion is thus a historic phenomenon appearing at one time and not at another, since for Ortega y Gasset *religio* does not mean simply the "binding of a person to God" and thus does not represent an anthropological phenomenon *(ibid.)*. As long as a person behaves "conscientiously" and "with thoughtful reflection," that person is religious. "The opposite of *religio* is *negligentia* . . ." *(ibid.)*.

Bonhoeffer quite possibly acquired impulses for his own view of religion as a historical phenomenon as early as the autumn of 1943, if not earlier. Ortega y Gasset played a significant role in the adaptation of historicism and of the philosophy of life both prior to and parallel with Wilhelm Dilthey. To support and deepen this thesis, let us turn our attention to the two writings by Ortega y Gasset which Bonhoeffer read parallel with Wilhelm Dilthey.

F. W. Kantzenbach has persuasively disclosed the connection between Ortega y Gasset's *The Nature of Historic Crises* and Bonhoeffer's Tegel correspondence. In Ortega y Gasset, Bonhoeffer could "read that it is one thing to acknowledge changes in the world, and quite another to judge them: 'The world has changed!' But in contradistinction to the medieval notion that the natural world conceals our true reality as it were like a mask, and that true reality is actually 'our dealings with the absolute or God,' Bonhoeffer contradicted — quite consistent with his own variously presented understanding — the paradox that finds the solution to this situation in the most extreme reversal of perspective. That leads to capitulation before life, to a turning away from the natural world."[18] Kantzenbach also sees the connection with Dilthey, whose analysis Bonhoeffer shares, "though he rejected Dilthey's flight into inwardness and private religious affections" *(ibid.)*. Kantzenbach ultimately arrives at the surprising conclusion: "Where Dilthey was no longer able to guide Bonhoeffer forward positively, Ortega y Gasset already drew attention more specifically to the existential embarrassment . . ." *(ibid.)*. I believe this conclusion can take us further, since among the generation of Dilthey students, Ortega y Gasset apparently did overcome the concept of religion that was determinative for the 19th century. While Dilthey views religion as an anthropological phenomenon, Ortega y Gasset, as we saw, views it as a matter of behavioral expression manifesting itself in different ways in different historical epochs, and which can even be completely absent. For Dilthey, religionlessness is historically incomprehensible; by contrast, for Ortega y Gasset it is quite possible.

The (genetic) connection between Ortega y Gasset and Dilthey has hitherto been presupposed. Kantzenbach also presupposed it. Let us now establish this on the basis of the third writing, *History as System.*

In this study, Ortega y Gasset follows a clear line from the perspective of the philosophy of life, namely that of a rejection of rationalism, beginning with the thesis that "life is a task" (366). It is not something "finished," but something that must be shaped. To this end, a person must "decide what is to be done. This decision, however, is possible only if a person possesses certain convictions with respect to things around him, to other human beings, and to himself. Only with respect to this conviction can a person choose as preferable one course of action over another; that is, only thus can a person — live" (366).

Rationalism is taken to mean "faith in reason" (372). But according to Ortega y Gasset, this "certainty of faith" does not suffice for an examination of life. "Descartes himself already wrote a tractate on the human being. Today, however, we know that all the in principle inexhaustible miracles of the natural sciences must always come to a standstill before the unique reality that is human life" (380). "Physical reason," he alleges, has grown accustomed to "neglecting human life" (380f.). "Physical-mathematical reason" (389) views human beings as things. "A person is not a thing, but a drama — that person's life, a pure, all-encompassing event that happens to every person and in which every person, too, is merely an event" (389f.). Ortega y Gasset also finds that "life is a gerund, not a participle, a *faciendum*, not a *factum*" (390). He again picks up his starting thesis: "Life is a task" (390).

O. F. Bollnow describes what happens in the ensuing pages as follows: "Recently, it was especially Ortega y Gasset, specifically in his *History as System,* who has picked up Dilthey's ideas and formulated them in a persuasively clear fashion."[19]

When Ortega y Gasset speaks about "life experience," he is picking up, for example, Dilthey's notion of a life that is always "in flux" between past and future: "Thus it is that a person's being is irreversible, since it is ontologically forced to move perpetually forward" (396). Although one could find many other parallels, we will leave it at this; the thrust of the entire study, the rejection of rationalism, corresponds to a typical, basic feature of Dilthey's historical philosophy of life.[20]

"Over against pure physical-mathematical reason, there is thus also narrative reason. In order to understand anything human — personally or collectively — one must tell a story. . . . Only through historical reason does life become even marginally transparent" (399). These simple words actually describe basic hermeneutical ideas of Wilhelm Dilthey, and Dilthey is also mentioned explicitly in this context. Ortega y Gasset writes that Dilthey is the person "to whom we owe the most regarding the idea of life, and who in my opinion is the most significant thinker in the second half of the 19th century" (400).

Following Dilthey in yet another feature, Ortega y Gasset is intent upon not falling prey to the subjective inclination of some abstract philosophy of life, and to this end acquires from history his objective standard for examining life. In an allusion to the thesis underlying the subtitle of his study, the philosopher of culture writes: "History is a system, the system of human experiences constituting one, single, unrelenting chain. . . . Every historical expression, if it is to be exact, must be established functionally on the whole of history . . ." (404). The concept of totality that becomes so important theologically for Bonhoeffer could also be prefigured here in Ortega y Gasset's philosophy of life.

b. Findings

The writings of Ortega y Gasset make it possible for Bonhoeffer to become acquainted with the "whole" Dilthey *in nuce*. Ortega y Gasset's presentation of Dilthey reveals with particular clarity the interdependence between life and history.

We are also led to suspect that Bonhoeffer read Dilthey's *Weltanschauung und Analyse des Menschen seit Renaissance und Reformation* under the influence of Ortega y Gasset with particular attention given to the concept of life.

2. Wilhelm Dilthey

Bonhoeffer's reading of the Dilthey volume laid out before him the great historical development that in modern times has brought human beings both autonomy and maturity. Regardless of the sphere in which Dilthey may be observing this striving to come of age and to become autonomous, his point of departure is always human life as it is actually lived in a particular epoch. Dilthey develops his philosophy of life in conceptual constructions such as "life feeling," "life comportment," and "life attitude."[21] Hence Petrarch, for example, was "the most original philosopher of life" because he "was prepared to surrender all scholastic ruminations for a single moment full of life."[22] For Dilthey, the antithesis to life is metaphysics, and throughout this volume he never tires of demonstrating this basic insight with new examples from history.[23] He bases this critique of metaphysics on the cognitive-theoretical foundation of his philosophy of life, namely, the assertion that one cannot get behind life.

a. Description

Again and again, Dilthey begins his analysis of human beings in the Renaissance and Reformation with the riddle of life. Insofar as he views life in a historical context, life acquires an objective feature in contrast to the subjective philosophy of life of Friedrich Nietzsche.[24] Dilthey observes that in the Renaissance, Machiavelli brings about "a complete secularization of morality and politics without reserve and without any backdoors" (29). Prior to Machiavelli, in Petrarch, for example, the idea of autonomy is not yet fully developed; here, "when the struggle of life becomes too severe for the ratio, one engages divine powers . . . as auxiliary troops. For him [Petrarch], life is a battle" (22). Dilthey judges this as a "problem of the philosophy of life," as a "half measure" *(ibid.)*. We can see that Dilthey is obviously reflecting on the concept of autonomy within the context of the philosophy of life.

The concept of "inwardness" characteristic of Dilthey occurs first in his description of Humanism. According to Dilthey, "religious-moral inwardness" replaces metaphysics, and "in its course makes human moral and religious autonomy the foundation of our intellectual life" (39). Dilthey concludes that "[t]he theological metaphysics of the Middle Ages dissolved itself" (40).

Dilthey thus uses the concepts of "inwardness," "autonomy," and "life" together, and evaluates them positively in contrast to "metaphysics."

The "need" associated with "inwardness" is also decisive for Luther. Dilthey's own conclusion regarding the reformer is that "life is the primary element for him." "For Luther, all knowledge about our relationship with the invisible derives from and remains bound to life and from the moral-religious experiences accompanying it" (58). With regard to faith, Dilthey writes that ". . . the inner process of faith finds its expression and its sphere of manifestation in the shaping of the entire external order of society" *(ibid.)*. Dilthey finally cites Luther's own words: "Life never rests" (60). Regarding Philipp Melanchthon and the "new life ideal of German Protestantism," which endures through "the progressive moralization of the world" (164), Dilthey again emphasizes "God's presence in life" *(ibid.)*. For Melanchthon, "faith" allegedly fills "all of life" (164), with "faith" here meaning something like the "believing inwardness" with which Melanchthon reestablishes "a balance between Humanism and Reformation" (162). "The essence of Reformational religiosity" allegedly describes a "higher stage" (211) over against Catholicism. Here the "new religious estimation of life" (215) played an important role; there arose "everywhere" a "deep reflection on life and on human things" (214). Dilthey elsewhere describes the progress of the Reformation over against Catholicism as a turn from "asceticism" to a "shaping of life" (243). In his treatment of Ulrich Zwingli's writing *De vera et falsa religione* (255), one can see the enormous extent to which Dilthey associates religion and life. With regard to human beings and their relationship with religion and life, he alleges, "God brings about in them that religiosity that is their true life" (226). Calvin, he suggests, emphasizes several of Zwingli's religious motifs, such as the "Calvinistic estimation of life" (231). For Calvin, "the religious filling of all of life emerges from the principle of . . . the election of grace" (232).

We can see how reference to the "entirety of life" permeates Dilthey's portrayal. He relates conceptually life and religiosity in their various manifestations in the era of the Reformation. Dilthey remarks in an expressive formulation:

> The idea of a truth containing the core of all religions emerged with irresistible power. Thus arose the concept of natural religion. When the Protestant system of faith, grounded on the principle of Scripture, with humanistic clarity then employed all the historically critical aids for determining purely the inner context of biblical statements, there arose within Socinianism the annihilating inner critique of all theological half-truths and compromises between biblical statements and old-Catholic symbols. (247)

In the following section (246-96), Dilthey describes the "autonomy of thought . . . in the 17th century" (246). In the 17th century, Herbert of Cherbury steps into the inheritance of Hugo Grotius from the 16th century, establishing the "autonomy of religious consciousness" (248). "Reason possesses within itself the capacity for all truths, including religious-moral truths" *(ibid.)*. Herbert of Cherbury introduces the "basic proof of the sufficiency of reason" (249). "The autonomy of human reason with respect to the moral comportment of the life of the individual person was first validated" by Francis Bacon in England and by Pierre Charron in France (260). Dilthey also finds that the tendency toward "autonomous morality" was continued in Italy by, among others, Giordano Bruno and in France by Michel de Montaigne and Jean Bodin (260f.).

Dilthey elsewhere uses a pregnant formulation to render the "political formula" of Jean Bodin emerging from the latter's program of "autonomous morality": "The universal foundations of all social human life are the divine and natural laws" (274).

In the first three decades of the 17th century, Charron, Bacon, and Cherbury articulate the theme that H. de Groot ultimately expounds more fully: the "natural system of the moral world" (276).

Dilthey views Grotius's *task* as being "to establish the new order of society on the basis of reason independently of religions and to ameliorate and if possible end the struggle between the various confessions" (277). Grotius defines the juridical *method* as "that of deduction of the various national legal principles from generally valid concepts" (278). "These concepts, however, are concepts of life, not categories of thought." The *concepts* themselves "inhere in the entirety of life and draw from life their persuasive power. Insofar as either de Groot or Grotius takes these concepts of life as his premise," so Dilthey's concludes: "he is merely renewing the true intention of Roman jurisprudence" (279).

According to Dilthey, "power, life, teleology, and *ratio* are all identical": Within the "teleological nexus," "*ratio* is life and life *ratio*" (279). The "legal concepts" Dilthey analyzes in Grotius are all "life concepts" (cf. 280), whose "validity does not depend on faith in their grounding within a teleological order resting in God. 'Even if there were no God,' the principles of natural law would maintain their independent and universal validity" (280).

Dilthey classifies within the larger context what he has analyzed thus far, observing "progress" from the "natural system" to the "autonomous rational system" (283). In the first stage this historical progress consists of a compromise, supported by "regnant metaphysics," between "dogmatic faith on the one hand, and the science of reason on the other," while the latter stage subscribes wholly to the ideal of establishing "life on the autonomy of reason" *(ibid.)*. The "rationalism" underlying the "autonomous rational system" "consisted in two forms": deism and pan(en)theism. With reference to Bruno, Spinoza, and Shaftesbury, Dilthey explains that "the affirmation of life, nature, and world, which the Renaissance expresses, becomes a metaphysical world formula in the pantheistic or panentheistic monism of these three thinkers" (284).

Dilthey adds a section on "Bruno's Life" (297-311) in which he graphically illustrates the life of Giordano Bruno against the background of Bruno's own age. Here Dilthey proceeds according to the method he elsewhere describes programmatically: "What a person is, is found only in that person's history."[25] "Giordano Bruno was the philosopher of the Italian Renaissance. He elevated its artistic life feeling and its life ideals to the status of a world view and a moral formula" *(ibid.)*.

Dilthey observes from the beginning of "the 14th century to the beginning of the 17th century" a "total shift of interest" *(ibid.)* ". . . from the otherworldly to the this-worldly . . . of life in the midst of the orders of what is real. This gradually progressing alteration of culture is what first made modern pantheism possible" (322).

It is in passages such as these that the great cognitive-theoretical orientation of Dilthey's philosophy of life emerges: "this-worldliness" as a "methodological principle."[26]

In the section "The Function of Anthropology in the Culture of the 16th and 17th Centuries" (416ff.), Dilthey picks up much of what he explicated at the beginning of *Weltanschauung und Analyse,* thus creating an arc from the beginning to the end of the book. He begins with a basic characterization of the 15th century. In "contrast to the world negation of the Middle Ages," Dilthey describes the Renaissance with the basic assertion: "The affirmation of life was the basic feature of the new age" (416). Here he is picking up again on familiar material. Thus does the word "philosophy of life" (417) acquire conceptual meaning in connection with the mention of Petrarch; here the arc is extended from Petrarch to Hugo Grotius (cf. 417), and thus the material from the beginning of *Weltanschauung und Analyse* acquires fundamental significance in connection with anthropology.

The question of the relationship between anthropology and the philosophy of life in Dilthey's work receives a clear answer here. He defines the "new anthropology": "In contrast to modern psychology, it examines the content of human nature itself, the life nexus in which the contents and values of life come to expression, the developmental stages in which this occurs, the relationship with the surroundings, and finally the individual forms of existence into which human beings are differentiated, and thus there emerges from this anthropology quite commensurately a doctrine of life comportment, an evaluation of life values, in short: a philosophy of life" (417).

The definition of anthropology thus issues into an examination of life, confirming the judgment of one Dilthey scholar according to whom "Dilthey's anthropology . . . is simultaneously a philosophy of life."[27] Human beings are interpreted from the perspective of the "entirety" of life; in Dilthey's words: "the vision of this age is naive, intensively oriented toward the senses, encompasses the entire corporeal-spiritual human being, and is full of brilliant details" (418). This new anthropology is "not an individual discipline, but the study of the soul as the key to understanding and dealing with life" (423). Dilthey mentions G. Cardano as a representative of the new anthropology, about whose autobiography Dilthey says: "The foundation of the understanding of life presented here, however, is found in his anthropology" (430). Dilthey presents the details of his observations regarding Cardano's anthropology and philosophy of life in an excursus (430f.), and also mentions B. Telesia (433f.), Michel de Montaigne (436), and finally Giordano Bruno, who "concludes this entire series of thinkers" (435).

Under the heading "Anthropology and the Natural System of the Humanities in the 17th Century" (439f.), Dilthey shows what the "age needed: the establishment of new orders independent of previous authorities; autonomy of the spirit in the regulation of its practical dealings in everyday life; unassailable principles for the regulation of society according to its new needs" (441).

We note again that Dilthey speaks not about autonomy as such, but about the "autonomy of the spirit"; again, the context is *life*. That these demands are put forward in the 17th century derives from the renaissance of the Roman Stoics. Dilthey shows in various writings that "*one* form of anthropology" is regnant, asserting "*one* function of anthropology" (449). "Its background is the new vivacity permeating all of worldly life" *(ibid.).* The concepts of autonomy and life are finally joined by the concept of "inwardness" (450), so that once again we encounter in Dilthey the triad "autonomy-inwardness-life." He again traces his observations back to the Roman Stoics:

> The schema of the course of an *inward life* firmly grounded in its own *autonomy* was found particularly in the doctrines of the Stoics regarding a teleological nexus of nature, of self-preservation, . . . regarding the human fall into the turmoil of the affections and into servitude to these

affections, and finally regarding the liberation of human beings from such servitude through a recognition of life's values. (450; my emphasis)

The "culmination of this movement, a movement independent of the natural sciences, is Hugo Grotius" (450, cf. the excursus on 450f.). According to Dilthey, the "application of anthropology to the humanities" was carried out by Thomas Hobbes, Spinoza, and Gottfried Wilhelm Leibniz (452). By contrast René Descartes grounds his own anthropology on the "new mathematical natural sciences" (452; concerning Descartes, cf. 453-58). Dilthey places Descartes (483ff.) into the context of metaphysics and rationalism, and compares him with other "dualists" — "they deny the life energy."

Put briefly and in an extremely simplified form, Dilthey observes how Descartes reduces the totality of life to the mere activity of thinking. The antirationalistic element in Dilthey's philosophy of life emerges clearly here and is articulated as a critique of Descartes's anthropology.

The final section taken up into the volume of *Weltanschauung und Analyse* stands under the heading "The Basic Motifs of Metaphysical Consciousness" (494f.). Dilthey writes about religion and life: "Religion is rooted not in egoism, but in this need to assert higher consciousness in life" (497). The formulation "*in* life" should be kept in mind; Dilthey is demanding a religion that can be *lived,* a religion of this-worldliness.

In the critique of metaphysics characterizing the first part of this section, Dilthey asserts that metaphysics has finally been overcome. In his own words: "The dreams of the modern metaphysicist exist only in the scholar's study, and there, too, does their paper existence end" (498).

In the second part, he interprets "Christianity in the Ancient World" from the perspective of the concept of experience and life (499f.), applying the concept of experience[28] to religion. "The religious experience is defined through dealings with the invisible" (500).[29] "The transformation from the sensuous to the divine through God's grace in Christ as a fundamental experience becomes an issue in modern consciousness in a process encompassing all of life" (503). Concerning the character of Christ as a model, Dilthey explains: "Every doctrine of *imitatio Christi* through model and religious *imitatio*[30] (not doctrine!) is Christian only insofar as it maintains the relationship according to which it is only through Christ that one can receive grace" (504).

Dilthey evaluates positively the religiosity of the "Reformation" (512f.): ". . . it itself resides in the assumption of the whole richness of human life, of the most profound striving for life, happiness, efficacious activity within religiosity" (515). This picks up what Dilthey had already explicated at the beginning of *Weltanschauung und Analyse* (58ff.). Religion and life are thus placed in a particular relationship in Reformational theology. Finally, he writes about the Protestant "concept of faith" (516): regarding the faith and religiosity of Martin Luther, one can say that it "brings about blessedness *in life* itself" (516; my emphasis).

b. Findings

As an interim summary, let us draw attention to several observations from Dilthey's outline. The concept of "autonomy," of such significance in *Weltanschauung und Analyse,* also became important for Bonhoeffer. Both Ernst Feil and Christian Gremmels have shown Bonhoeffer's formal dependence on Dilthey with respect to the historical dimension ascribed to the concept of "autonomy," first in Dilthey and then in Bonhoeffer.[31]

    Our presentation of *Weltanschauung und Analyse* has shown that the concept of autonomy does not occur only in historical contexts. The guiding cognitive motif for Dilthey is the question concerning "life," and it is only after this question has been addressed that he adds observations about history, anthropology, and so on. Whether in the case of Petrarch (22), Bacon (261), or Grotius (248f., 280f.), Dilthey reflects on the concept of autonomy in connection with the philosophy of life. In reading and considering Dilthey, one also notices that he obviously is not concerned with the transmission of historical knowledge as such, but rather with the interpretive rendering of history. Again and again, we notice the "interpretive foil" against which any given material is being viewed.

    H.-U. Lessing offers this definition:

> In the form represented by Dilthey, the philosophy of life thus means a consistent renunciation of "abstract thinking," it means the concretization of the subject of cognition, the historicizing of cognitive structures, and the task of an "Archimedean" point of cognition.[32]

Dilthey's work gives one a sense of the significance of the historical philosophy of life, something we have tried to illuminate in our portrayal of the course of Dilthey's volume.

The question forces itself upon us whether Bonhoeffer could have, as it were, read past the key interpretive concept of life, whether he could have appropriated the terms and concepts of historicism without acknowledging their attendant status in the philosophy of life, that is, whether one can have the one from Dilthey without the other as well. Did his reading of Dilthey also prompt the interdependence of life and cognition to acquire significance for him?

B. Life as a Fulcral Concept in Bonhoeffer's Tegel Theology

We have seen how through Dilthey "a new attitude toward the world and life"[33] emerges, how the "new view of the world" is emphasized by the "significance the philosophy of life has for one's world view."[34] We will now examine the concept of life in Bonhoeffer's work against this background; in so doing, we will complement the correspondence between Bonhoeffer and his friend Eberhard Bethge as documented in the *Letters and Papers from Prison* and in his letters to his fiancée Maria von Wedemeyer *(Love Letters from Cell 92),* to which we can also add archival material.[35] In this way, the *whole* Dietrich Bonhoeffer of the Tegel correspondence will come to expression.

1. Life as a Theme in the *Letters and Papers from Prison*

At the end of 1942, Bonhoeffer writes: "Ten years are a long time in any person's life" (*WEN,* 11). He wants to protect himself against "abstractions from what is actual, from life itself that is actually lived" *(ibid.).* In Tegel, the prisoner remarks concerning the "fullness of life":

> We still love life, but I believe that death can no longer surprise us much. After the experiences of the war, we hardly dare to admit our wish that it might overtake us not fortuitously, or suddenly, away from those things that are essential, but in the fullness of life and in the wholeness of engagement. (26)

Just as "what is actual" and "life that is actually lived" were earlier identified, so now "those things that are essential" and "the fullness of life." The theme of life is apparently being associated with ethics.[36]

On April 25, 1943, the prisoner in Tegel requests that the work of Adalbert Stifter[37] be sent to him (*WEN*, 37), and on June 4 we find the first evidence of this reading. "I read a bit of Stifter almost every day," he writes, remarking that "this atmosphere, the secure, sheltered life of his figures . . . is very comforting, drawing one's attention to the essential contents of life" (63). In a letter at the end of July 1943, Bonhoeffer writes that "in my present reading, I am living entirely in the 19th century. Gotthelf, Stifter, Immermann, Fontane, Keller — in these last months I have read all these writers with new admiration" (95). Bonhoeffer also mentions Stifter in a letter to Maria von Wedemeyer (November 1943), reflecting on the "pain of deprivation."[38]

He begins reading Stifter's *Witiko* in November 1943 (cf. *WEN*, 143), remarking in December to Eberhard Bethge that "for me, Stifter's greatness is that he forgoes intruding into a person's interior, that he respects the outer covering" (177). Bonhoeffer incorporates Adalbert Stifter into his own theological reflections. "God himself made clothes for human beings, i.e., 'in statu corruptionis,' many things in human beings should remain covered." After the "fall," "there must also be cloaking and mystery" (*ibid.*). Bonhoeffer thus finds the theological idea of a concealment of sin in Adalbert Stifter, and gives it a twist with respect to the theme of life: There is "an impermissible intrusion into the mystery of life. This is the direction of Stifter" (*ibid.*).

At the end of January 1944, Bonhoeffer mentions Stifter's *Witiko* explicitly: "We read once that the young Witiko went out into the world 'in order to do the whole'" (*WEN*, 225). Bonhoeffer interprets this clause (which occurs in Stifter's book on page 28)[39] biblically as an exegesis of Matthew 5:48:

> At issue is thus the ἄνθρωπος τέλειος (τέλειος, after all, originally meant "whole" = complete). . . . Witiko "does the whole" by trying to find his way in the real world, and to that end always listens to the advice of those with experience, that is, by himself being a member of the "whole." A person does not become a "whole" alone, but only together with others.[40]

Bonhoeffer interprets the biblical term τέλειος from Matthew 5:48 ["perfect," according to the NRSV] as it were "life-theologically" with respect to "real life"; what he reads he interprets christologically for life itself, ascribing a theological quality to the concept of life. Whereas earlier we found "what is actual" and "essential" being identified with "life," so here what is "real." During this period when Bonhoeffer was reading *Witiko* (autumn 1943 to winter 1943/44), he also wrote a series of letters in which he reflected further on life. He is disturbed to see the "gradual dissolution of all genuine ties and orders of life" (*WEN,* 141), and criticizes the "godless openness" that makes such a "chaotic impression" (164). Chaos becomes the counterconcept to life here; Bonhoeffer the "ethicist of order" emerges.[41]

Several remarks in the "Drama Fragment" (1943)[42] similarly appear cast in the light of the outlines to the *Ethics,* as do some conversations in "Attempt at a Novel" (1943/44).[43] In the dramatic fragment, Bonhoeffer has "Christopher" say that "we[44] have learned to distinguish . . . between the authentic and the unauthentic, the true and the false, the noble and the base, between what is decent and what is low."[45] In dialogue with the dramatic figure of Heinrich, the "stranger" says: "Dying is interesting, but not being dead, and dying lasts a long time and is just as varied as life itself."[46]

This reference to the multiplicity of life is no accident; some find a connection with Nietzsche's philosophy of life behind this reflection on life.[47] In his attempt at a novel, Bonhoeffer has the Major succinctly circumscribe "the final teaching of history and of life" as "love for real life."[48] Right at the beginning of his novel, he reflects critically on "the dissolution of all the structures of life":[49] "On Sunday, today's human being both seeks and needs not quietude, but distraction, not composure, but dissipation, not poise, but relaxation."[50]

——— The concepts of authenticity, reality, and life also concern Bonhoeffer apart from his theological correspondence during this period. The concept of life, however, is not christologically expanded, and on the whole, these fragments, especially the dialogues, seem like an instruction in the philosophy of life[51] *in nuce.*

In December 1943, Bonhoeffer admits how concerned he is at this time with ethics and with the fragments to his *Ethics:* "Sometimes I think my life is now actually more or less behind me, and all that remains is for me to finish my *Ethics*" (*WEN,* 182). At the same time, however, he is already raising questions that seem to transcend his *Ethics* and are inclined in the direction of the nonreligious interpretation. He often merely interjects such questions and does not reflect further on them.[52] The letter just cited contains such a statement, one that seems rather impulsively interposed: "By the way, I miss worship services so peculiarly little" (183). The abrupt order to his friend from the same month points in a similar direction: "Eberhard, try to find out what the people around you really believe" (200).

Bonhoeffer is apparently prefiguring what he will later explicate more fully in chapter 2 of the *Outline for a Book* from the perspective of the question "What do we really believe?" (415).[53] Nor does Eberhard Bethge seem uninvolved in his friend's work, something we will observe in other passages as well. The unabridged publication of Bethge's letters in volume 8 of *Dietrich Bonhoeffer Werke* will provide the details that fully illuminate his own contribution to Bonhoeffer's theological work.[54]

Bonhoeffer is ascribing fulcral theological significance to the concept of life when on December 18, 1943, he admits to his friend: "I believe we should love God in our lives and in the good he gives to us" (*WEN*, 189). As early as this passage, Bonhoeffer is already indirectly juxtaposing *life* with religion. That is, "the religious fantasy gone wild" is countered by the notion that "one should find God in that which he gives us just now" *(ibid.)*. To Maria von Wedemeyer (*Love Letters*, 203),[55] Bonhoeffer writes that "God subsists . . . in everyday life," in real life. The falsely understood transcendence of God is countered by an understanding that seeks God "in the facts themselves" (*WEN*, 214), in life. Bonhoeffer uses a parallel formulation in his letter of January 23, 1944:

> I believe that we honor God better when we become familiar with the life he has given us in all its value, when we become familiar with it, exhaust it, and love it, and for that reason also perceive strongly and sincerely the pain brought about by those particular life values that have been damaged or lost. (*WEN*, 215)[56]

To be "fully a person" means to be "a Christian in the full scope of this term" (*WEN*, 217). Bonhoeffer's christological interpretation takes as its orientation the concept of life as a totality. He understands God completely from the perspective of life itself (cf. also the exegesis of the passage from Job, *WEN*, 215).

On his birthday (February 4, 1944), Bonhoeffer reflects on the genuine experience of joy, remarking in an aside that it is not easy "to live out joy correctly, to order it and tie it in to daily life" (*WEN*, 233).[57]

The following letters contain repeated reflections on the *whole* of life and on *fragmentary* life whose background is the character of life as a totality, as the 19th-century ideal (and thus as the ideal of Stifter and Dilthey). On February 20, 1944, Bonhoeffer writes to his parents:

This is probably the greatest element of renunciation imposed upon and required from those of us who are younger, who still have our lives in view. This is probably why we sense with particular intensity the incomplete and fragmentary character of our own lives. (*WEN*, 242)[58]

What must remain visible, however, is "how the whole was planned and conceived," even though "external events" are able to shatter "life into pieces" *(ibid.)*. He uses a parallel formulation three days later in a letter to his friend Eberhard Bethge: "The important thing is probably just whether one can yet see from the fragment of our life how the whole was actually designed and conceived" (*WEN*, 246).

On February 21, 1944, Bonhoeffer reflects first on the concept of fate, which will concern us again in connection with the *Outline for a Book;* he then comes to the question of resistance to fate, and relates this to the example of Don Quixote, who is also mentioned in Dilthey.[59] He concludes his considerations with the statement: "The boundaries between resistance and submission [German: *Widerstand und Ergebung*] can in principle not be determined" (244); he concludes concerning the relationship between faith, life, and action: "Faith demands this mobile, living action" *(ibid.)*.

In his thoughts on the "life's work" (246), Bonhoeffer explicates more fully that to which in the letter of February 20, 1944, to his parents he merely alluded: "The longer we are torn away from our real vocational and personal life spheres, the more do we sense that our life — in contrast to that of our parents — has fragmentary character" (245). In addition to the concept of totality so important for the philosophy of life, he now also introduces the concept of "counterpoint," one borrowed from music theory, into his examination of life. He compares the "fragmentary life" with a fugue in which different "themes sound in harmony" and in which "the great counterpoint is maintained from the beginning to the end" (246). Bonhoeffer could have read a great deal about counterpoint in Wilhelm Dilthey.[60]

At the end of March 1944, Eberhard Bethge writes to his friend from Italy: "I am very curious to hear what you are reading about music in Dilthey" (*WEN*, 272). This remark probably refers to Bonhoeffer's reading of *Von deutscher Dichtung und Musik* [*On German Poetry and Music*], a collection of Dilthey's essays Bonhoeffer received in February 1944. Although Bonhoeffer does not address Bethge's remarks explicitly in subsequent letters, the fact that Bethge was correct in assuming that his friend was indeed reading Dilthey intensively is attested by the enduring significance the book had for Bonhoeffer. It was there that he could read about J. S. Bach and G. F. Handel what several months later he would offer as his own evaluation: "I believe Handel is much more focused on the listener and on the effects he elicits than is Bach, and that is why he seems a bit like a facade. Handel is trying to accomplish something with his music, Bach is not" (*WEN*, 391). Handel is given preference over Bach, being able "to comfort us so broadly and so directly" *(ibid.)*. Dilthey judges Handel as unreligious in comparison to Bach, asserting that "the mystical side of religion is alien to his active nature" (*Von deutscher Dichtung und Musik*, 249). He continues: "How different is Handel from Bach! He could never have composed a mass" (250). By contrast, Dilthey appraises Bach as the "expression of Protestant inwardness"; ". . . here was the possibility of elevating Protestant religiosity as it were into eternity" (206). In Bach, "the inwardness of religious life is brought to consciousness" *(ibid.)*.

Once again these citations clearly reveal Dilthey's understanding of "religion as inwardness" — here in connection with music. Bonhoeffer rejects this decisively. Although at the time he is reading *Von deutscher Dichtung und Musik* the thematic material of religion does not stand in the foreground of his reflections, it does in July 1944, and this may also explain why it was only later that he came back to this book. He seems to share the appraisal of Bach and thus to give Handel preference over Bach; the latter represents inwardness and religion in music, while Handel is the unreligious, "direct" one, as Bonhoeffer writes. The positive estimation of Handel could be a result of Bonhoeffer's earlier reading of Dilthey; furthermore, references to "polyphony" and "counterpoint" had become important for Bonhoeffer as a result of his reading *Von deutscher Dichtung und Musik*. Following Dilthey, he speaks about the "polyphony of life."[61]

On March 2, 1944, he asks his parents from his cell: "Could you please get me Dilthey's *Weltanschauung und Analyse des Menschen seit Renaissance und Reformation?*" (*WEN*, 255), a book he will now be reading in addition to *Das Erlebnis und die Dichtung* and *Von deutscher Dichtung und Musik*.

In the letter of March 9, 1944, he praises the " 'Christian,' though also anticlerical worldliness" of the Middle Ages (*WEN*, 258). This could allegedly still be found in Lessing and Goethe, and later also in Stifter and Mörike *(ibid.)*. Whereas Bonhoeffer could have read a great deal about Lessing and Goethe in Dilthey's *Das Erlebnis und die Dichtung*,[62] his mention of Stifter is probably to be traced back to *Witiko,* a novel in which he could read much about Christian worldliness during the Middle Ages. The character Witiko himself can be understood as a representative of this worldliness.[63]

The question arises whether some connection exists between Bonhoeffer's reading of Stifter and Dilthey, and if so, what it might be. An overriding common denominator might be found — put quite generally — in a certain view of human beings and in a particular quality of one's life form, both of which live in the ideals of the 19th century that made such an enduring impression on Bonhoeffer. Another question is whether the "basic humanistic concepts" he mentions over the course of the letter do not ultimately represent concepts finally acquiring significance in the tradition of the philosophy of life, concepts including "humanity, tolerance, gentleness, moderation" (*WEN,* 258). The concept of *moderation* continues to be of significance even into the *Outline for a Book,* where this concept, in addition to others, becomes an exemplary concept for the human "model"-function (cf. *WEN,* 416, where "moderation" is mentioned first[!]).

He writes to Eberhard Bethge in the middle of March 1944: "News of the severe battles near you makes me think of you continually and relate every word I read in the Bible and every hymn verse to you" (*WEN,* 262). He tries to comfort Bethge, referring to the "character of wholeness" attaching to his life. In contradistinction to someone who is "growing up," or is "unfinished," who "is never completely there where he is," a grown "man[64] is always a whole person, and takes nothing away from the present" (262). In the sense of this totality of life, Bonhoeffer is able to write to his friend Bethge that "there can be a fulfilled life despite many unfulfilled wishes" (263). Reference to the "wholeness" of life runs through the Tegel correspondence like a red thread.

On March 25, 1944, the prisoner in Tegel is shaken by the previous night's bombing raids: "The view of the city from the roof was shocking" (*WEN,* 267). Bonhoeffer reflects on how in this night his fellow prisoners and he himself "repeatedly and quite involuntarily were seduced into wishing upon other cities . . . that which was scaring us; 'maybe they'll stay in Magdeburg, in Stettin, etc.' — how often one utters this in despair" (268). He then immediately reflects *theologically* on what he has just *lived* through: "At such times, one becomes extremely aware of the *natura corrupta* and the *peccatum originale;* to that extent, they are perhaps quite beneficial" *(ibid.).*

If in this passage Bonhoeffer is reflecting on the dogmatic *locus* of *peccatum originale* from the perspective of a theology of life, then this represents a parallel to the previously adduced passage in which he interpreted dogmatic reference to the *status corruptionis* with respect to experience (cf. *WEN,* 143).[65]

In two letters from April 1944, the prisoner picks up the dialogue on the course of his own life again, writing on April 11: "I . . . am completely under the impression that my life — as peculiar as this sounds — has gone in a completely straight and unbroken line" (*WEN,* 297). This statement is significant because it has been adduced repeatedly in answer to the question about continuity and discontinuity in Bonhoeffer's thinking. The passage is important for us because we can see how the question of continuity is associated with the theme of life; here he arrives at the unequivocal conclusion: "My life has gone in a completely straight and unbroken line." From the perspective of life's character as a whole, Bonhoeffer understands himself in continuity. "Everything appears to me to be inevitable, necessary, straight, guided by a higher providence" (301). Thus does he write on April 21, wanting to include his friend in this as well: "Is this not also the case with you?" *(ibid.).*

Bonhoeffer has already anticipated the answer when half a page before this question he includes Eberhard Bethge: "Neither of us has really experienced any caesura in his life" (*WEN,* 300). For Bonhoeffer, it is important that "one not lose sight of the whole" (301), something applying especially to "daily life" (297), about which he would like to hear more from Bethge. As a whole, and with respect "to the whole," Bonhoeffer understands his own life in perfect continuity. Despite this, certain aspects of his theological thinking may well be subject to development and transformation, that is, to discontinuity.[66]

In a theological passage to Maria von Wedemeyer on April 23, 1944, Bonhoeffer writes similarly about life, immediately trying to understand it christologically: " 'Pray' and 'follow' go hand in hand — there can't be one without the other. Praying confidently and following readily: there's a full life for you" (*Love Letters,* 223).

Whereas the content of life as a guiding concept is described here in the pair "prayer" and "discipleship," in his "Thoughts on the Baptism" a month later it is expanded into the triad[67] "prayer," "action," and "waiting" (cf. *WEN,* 321ff.).

The letter of April 30, 1944 poses the initial question of the Tegel theology: "What really is Christianity or who really is Christ for us today?"[68]

(*WEN,* 305). Bonhoeffer concretizes the christological "who-question"[69] with respect to the cognitive-theoretical locus of revelation, trying "to speak of God not at the boundaries . . . but in life and in human good" (307). We must at least ask to what extent his reference to God "in human good" is recalling formulations from the *Ethics.*[70] In any event, we do notice that the double determination of knowledge of God "in life and in the good" is a parallel formulation to the letter of December 18, 1943, where we inquired of the connection with Bonhoeffer's *Ethics.*[71]

The ethical-christological "distinction . . . between the penultimate and the ultimate" from the same manuscript in the *Ethics*[72] also acquires "new importance" (*WEN,* 396) in view of the relationship between arcane discipline and religionlessness. Here he classifies the theme of religionlessness under the sphere of the "penultimate" from the *Ethics,* while arcane discipline belongs to the sphere of the "ultimate."

On April 30, Bonhoeffer continues discussing the cognitive-theoretical locus of God: "The 'beyond' of God is not the 'beyond' of our own cognitive capacity! Cognitive-theoretical transcendence has nothing to do with God's transcendence" (308). This observation is followed by a sentence that will retain its significance for other theological formulations in the *Letters and Papers from Prison* as well: "God is beyond even in the middle of our *lives*" (*WEN,* 308; my emphasis).[73] With regard to its cognitive-theoretical locus, the christological who-question becomes the question of life, and the understanding of knowledge of God as the transcendence of life retains this form on into the *Outline for a Book* (413f.; hereafter referred to as *Outline*). There is continuity between this initial, significant theological letter of April 30 and the *Outline* of August 3, 1944.[74]

Eberhard Bethge reacts for the first time on May 8 to the "nonreligious interpretation" presented in this letter, and does so with remarkable involvement: "Some of the things are expressed a bit more naively and primitively in my previously described questions" (*WEN,* 310). This reaction confirms the repeated observation that Bethge was obviously involved in his friend's new ideas, ideas emerging from the theologically qualified dialogue between the two friends.

On May 5, 1944, Eberhard Bethge writes to his friend that he is now trying "to understand and comprehend things, people, and relationships, and to do so 'from a human perspective.' "[75] He previously asked whether Bonhoeffer might be able to say something about the fact that "actually all feeling and thinking now is concentrated on personal experience"[76] (309). The two friends seem to be reflecting theologically as well on what they experience personally; Bethge introduces the reference to "humanity" into the theological dialogue, something that will later bear fruit for Bonhoeffer. The impression arises that the theological level of dialogue between the two friends again and again revolves around the Christian interpretation of their experiences as well,[77] though they by no means stay on this personal level, but move on to more fundamental issues. Thus Bonhoeffer asks, also on May 5, whether "the biblical message . . . affects people today" (312), concluding the necessity of a "nonreligious interpretation of biblical concepts." In his view, that which applies according to Romans 3:24ff. would also apply to such an interpretation: "At issue is not the beyond, but this world, how it is created, maintained, ordered into laws, reconciled and renewed. That which is beyond this world the Gospel insists *is there for* the world" (312; my emphasis).

The letter of April 30 showed that the counterconcept to "the beyond" is "life"; here, in the letter of May 5, Bonhoeffer specifies the significance of life more precisely in the formula *being for*. The formulation concerning the *gospel* that is *there for the world*, in the *Outline* becomes an essentially christological program: *Jesus* is *there for others* (cf. *WEN*, 414). The reference to *being for* is anticipated within the *Letters and Papers from Prison*,[78] where it appears in a context critical of metaphysics, namely, in the letter of May 5 with its criticism of incorrectly understood individualistic faith in the beyond, and in the *Outline* in the criticism directed essentially against any form of incorrectly understood transcendence of God.[79]

Some of the concepts that according to the letter of May 5 are to be interpreted in a "worldly fashion" are then also found in the list of concepts in the *Outline* that are to be interpreted nonreligiously, including especially those of "penitence" and "faith" (*WEN*, 313 = 414).

The *Thoughts on the Baptism of Dietrich Wilhelm Rüdiger Bethge* (*WEN*, 321f.; hereafter referred to as *Thoughts*) include concepts and themes taken up in parallel form in the *Outline*. For example, as an introduction Bonhoeffer adduces the concept of "modesty," whose basis is allegedly "inner contentment" (321). "Earthly values" such as these, he suggests, provide "a firm foundation in all life situations for living together with others, for genuine accomplishment, and for inner peace" *(ibid.)*. The *Outline* counts the concepts of "modesty" and "authenticity" among those virtues that make the church into *the* church that "is there for others" (415f.). Just as the concept of "moderation" at the beginning of the catalogue of virtues (cf. 416) is anticipated in the letters, so also are the (life) concepts "modesty" and "authenticity." Bonhoeffer admits in the *Thoughts* that "there are basic human truths to which life sooner or later always returns" (322).[80]

Picking up on reflections on "fragmentary life," Bonhoeffer writes — with the inclusion of his friend — that "our life, in contrast to that of our parents, has become formless or at least fragmentary" (324). He speaks of the "life goal" *(ibid.)*[81] that his own generation was unable to plan in the way his parents' generation did, and expands his vision to the generation of the child being baptized:

> Differentiated perception, intensive *experience* both of one's own pain and of that of the stranger, are both the strength and the weakness of our life form. Through having to do without and having to endure pain and severe tests of patience, your generation will early on become harder and *closer to life.* (326; my emphasis)

There then follows an Old Testament reference from Lamentations, as well as reflections on the "age of colossal organizations" toward which Bonhoeffer believes we are moving (326; cf. the *Outline, WEN,* 413!). He concludes that "in broad-minded and selfless participation in the whole and in the suffering of our fellows, we will prove our life strength" (327).

If we examine the structure of the *Thoughts* thus far, we find that the adduced section follows a three-step progression according to which Bonhoeffer first refers to experiences, then tries to render these in pregnant formulations ("closeness to life," "life strength"), and finally reflects biblically on the life experience thus articulated (here from the perspective of the Old Testament!). This procedure makes the biblical statements accessible to the "experience" of the reader, as it were; that is, biblical sequences are made transparent for life.

Bonhoeffer concludes the *Thoughts* christologically: ". . . what *life* in Christ and discipleship mean is so difficult and so distant from us that we hardly even dare to *speak* about it anymore" (327f.; my emphasis). What then follow are the famous — as it were, "prophetic" (Eberhard Bethge)[82] — statements about the day that is coming when "people are again called to *pronounce* the word of God such that this changes and renews the world. There will be a new language, perhaps completely *unreligious*" (328; my emphasis).

The question arises regarding just what Bonhoeffer thought was lacking in previous religious language, and what he thought unreligious language might accomplish. Our own analysis of the *Thoughts* — and of the *Letters and Papers from Prison* on the whole — offers a clear answer to this question: In Bonhoeffer's view, the previous *religious language* of the church was incapable of expressing what life in Christ and discipleship in Christ mean. Accordingly, *nonreligious language* should be able to tell us what "life with Christ is, what it means 'to be for others'" (*Outline, WEN,* 416). Here it becomes clear how the *Thoughts* issue directly into the *Outline,* and how they reach their final goal there: Bonhoeffer finds that religious language is unable to express the relevance of the gospel of Jesus Christ for life here and now. *Life with Christ* is the final goal of nonreligious interpretation. (Here the expression *life with Christ* becomes the guiding concept of the double formula *life in Christ and discipleship in Christ.*)[83]

The letter of May 20, 1944, picks up again the notion of the "polyphony of life" (331); Bonhoeffer explains:

> I believe this: God and his eternity want to be loved with all our hearts, not such that this diminishes or weakens earthly love in any way, but as it were like a *cantus firmus* to which the other voices of life resound as counterpart. *(Ibid.)*

This observation acquires concrete form through the question: "Is musical polyphony perhaps so close and important to us because it is the musical reflection of this christological fact[84] and thus also of our own *vita christiana?*" *(ibid.).* Bonhoeffer concludes this idea pointedly: "Life becomes whole only when a person is standing in this polyphony" (323).

Here the idea of the wholeness of life is again linked with the concept of polyphony; we observed something similar in the letter of February 20, 1944. Bonhoeffer draws on imagery from music theory to illustrate Jesus Christ's significance for life.

On May 21 he confesses that "the image of polyphony is still pursuing me" (333), and writes further, picking up on present experiences: "When today I felt a bit of pain at not being with you, I had to think about how pain and joy belong to the polyphony of the whole of life" (333f.). The concepts of wholeness and polyphony again serve to describe life filled with the this-worldliness of Christian faith — "it really is the polyphony of life" (334). It seems as if the concept of polyphony might become a life concept, or, better, a christological life concept, since it is being interpreted for Christian life.[85]

On May 29, 1944, the imprisoned theologian reflects on the "daily hazards" (340) of life in war, and writes to his friend Bethge: "One gradually learns to gain a little inward distance from the hazards of life" (340). He immediately corrects himself: "'Gaining distance' actually sounds too negative, too formal, too artificial, too stoic; it is probably more correct to say that one accepts these daily hazards into the whole of life" (340). Bonhoeffer is again arguing from the perspective of the wholeness of life; in the course of the letter, he then underscores the concept of life theologically (more exactly: christologically). After rereading C. F. von Weizsäcker's *Weltbild der Physik* [*Worldview of Physics*] he writes about knowledge of God:

> Here, too, God is not some stopgap; we must recognize God not at the boundaries of our possibilities, but in the *middle of life;* God wants to be recognized in living, not just in dying. The reason is found in God's revelation in Jesus Christ. He is the *center of life,* and by no means "was added to it" simply to answer unresolved questions for us. From the center of life, certain questions disappear entirely. (341f.; my emphasis)

We already encountered references to Christ as *center* in the earlier lectures on Christology.[86] When Bonhoeffer now speaks about the center of *life* (or *in the middle of life*), he is considerably expanding his insight from the lectures on Christology, namely, by the addition of the concept of life, which he incorporates into the horizon of revelation under the influence of his reading in the natural sciences. He answers the question *where* God can be revealed with reference to the concept of life: "in" life, "in the middle of life," "from the center of life," and so on. Influenced by Weizsäcker's book, Bonhoeffer identifies the counterconcept to life as the concept of the "boundary" or "gap"; in religion, God allegedly becomes the "stopgap." The reference to God as a stopgap (elsewhere: the "working hypothesis God"), a reference critical of religion, is thus countered by the theologoumenon "Christ in the middle of life," and thus "religion" is countered by "life."

The considerable extent to which Bonhoeffer is able to include his dialogue partners in this new discussion can be seen, for example, in the letter of June 2, 1944, to H.-W. Schleicher (*WEN,* 343f.), from whom Bonhoeffer would like to learn what interests the "young people" of his "generation" — "to what are these people *attached? . . .* What do they *believe* and according to what views do they order their *lives?*" (344; my emphasis). Bonhoeffer hopes to acquire new ideas for his own work from the sociological sphere of his nephew. In the second chapter of his *Outline,* we read: "What do we really *believe?*, i.e., such that we are *attached* to it with our very *lives?*" (415; my emphasis). Even individual words (cf. the emphases) seem to anticipate the later explications of the *Outline,* whereby June 2, 1944, by no means represents the *terminus a quo.* We have already cited above the letter of the second day of Christmas 1943 containing the request that Eberhard Bethge find out "what the people . . . really believe" (200). The requests to Bethge and H.-W. Schleicher show that Bonhoeffer is developing his own ideas on religionlessness dialogically in his correspondence.

Something similar is also suggested by Eberhard Bethge's letter of June 3, 1944, in which he observes "the need of people today . . . for a space separated off from the present world for rest, contemplation, and shelter in the calming activities of the cult."[87] Bethge concludes these reflections with the following remark to his dialogue partner: "But you are already thinking about all this" (*WEN,* 348). And, indeed, Bonhoeffer is thinking along the same lines when, for example, in his following letters he picks up the reference to the "space separated off from the world" (an explicit reference to Bethge's letter is found on June 8, p. 360, bottom).[88] The letter just cited makes clear the considerable extent to which Bonhoeffer's best friend is involved in Bonhoeffer's reflections on life; Bethge remarks concerning the "multidimensionality of life":[89]

> What do you really mean when you say that in truth, faith alone makes life possible in multidimensionality? You need to explicate again a bit more precisely why the ground for "God in health, strength, in action" is found in the "revelation in Jesus Christ"; what does "center of life" mean here? (348)

Although Bethge's letter breaks off here, his questions make sufficiently clear the extent to which he, too, is interpreting the theme interrogatively from the perspective of life. Bethge would like Bonhoeffer to ground precisely this christological accentuation given to the concept of life, an accentuation Bonhoeffer actually introduced in a more thetic fashion in the letter of May 29, 1944.

The poem "The Past" (*WEN,* 351f.) contains several lines of impressions on the riddle of life showing clearly how Bonhoeffer is reflecting on the theme of life even in his most personal thoughts: "This only do I know: you went — and all is gone / Do you feel how I now reach out for you . . . / you full, corporeal, earthly life? . . . Life, what have you done to me? / Why did you come? Why did you slip away? / Past, though you flee from me, / do you not remain my past, my own?" (*WEN,* 351 = *Love Letters,* 248f.). Bonhoeffer composes this poem after a visit by his fiancée Maria. In the accompanying letter of May 29, 1944, to his fiancée (*Love Letters,* 244ff.), he writes a great deal about his own "life"; the poem, he alleges, is "part of the story of my life" (*Love Letters,* 247).

Bonhoeffer begins his letter of response to Eberhard Bethge of June 8, 1944 with the words: "You have raised so many important questions about the things I have been thinking about recently that I would be glad if I could answer them myself" (*WEN,* 356). He thus incorporates Bethge's questions from June 3 into his own reflections and now intends to explicate what on the back of the Bethge letter he noted in telegraph style: "Without God — Cathol. Protest. unified in rejection! God not therein. Distress! Exist. philos. Psychother . . ." (348). "I want to try once," the prisoner writes from Tegel, "to determine my own position historically" (356). The ensuing historical reflections on "autonomy" (356f.) in the various scientific disciplines derive from his reading of Dilthey's *Weltanschauung und Analyse.*[90]

It is interesting to observe what twist Bonhoeffer now gives to his first historical excursus. He writes: "Just as in the scientific sphere, so also now in the general human sphere, 'God' is pushed further and further out of life, he is losing ground" (357). The historical determination of position is given an accentuation from the perspective of life. "God as working hypothesis," the "religious God" stands counter to life; he is the God that has been pushed out. Bonhoeffer refers to him formally as *"God"* to distinguish him from the God of Jesus, who is to be found precisely *in life* itself. In the following, he criticizes the reaction of "Christian apologetics": "One tries to prove to the world come of age that it cannot live without the guardianship of 'God'" *(ibid.).* Neither "Christian apologetics" nor the "existential philosophers" nor the "psychotherapists" (357) are able to focus on "daily life" (358).[91] Bonhoeffer finally summarizes his basic christological query: "Christ and the world come of age" (358).

Following this formulation of his theme, he enumerates the many attempts undertaken against this historical development toward a world come of age or which succumb to it. He concludes: "The maturity of the world is no longer the occasion for polemic or apologetics; it really is better understood than it understands itself, namely, from the perspective of the gospel, of Christ" (*WEN,* 360). This is why, according to Bonhoeffer, an interpretive form must be created that explains biblical "concepts" "without presupposing religion as the precondition of faith (cf. the περι-τομή in Paul!)" (360). This comparison of religion with circumcision or with the law occurs in various guises in Bonhoeffer's writing (cf. also 358), appearing first on April 30, 1944 (308).

This comparison is likewise historically motivated. Just as after the Apostolic Council (in the year A.D. 49) the question of circumcision for Gentile Christians began to lose theological-historical significance, so also, after the world has come of age, the question of religion has become "obsolete," and can no longer be made into the condition for faith in Christ. Religion is a historic phenomenon within modern Christianity, and for Bonhoeffer has become historically obsolete. For him, the relationship between religion and περιτομή derives from the historic dimension of the two concepts. This also makes it understandable why Bonhoeffer considers the "attack of Christian apologetics on the process of the world coming of age" to be "un-Christian" (*WEN,* 358). "Un-Christian — because it confuses Christ with a certain stage of human religiosity, that is, with a human law" *(ibid.).*

He writes to Eberhard Bethge on June 27, 1944: "I am currently writing my interpretation of the first three commandments" (*WEN,* 368). In this exegesis, we can observe immediately the focus on life characterizing Bonhoeffer's interpretation. He introduces the Ten Commandments: "What it means for our *life* that God is Lord and is our God, this is related to us in ten short sentences" (*GS* 4.603; my emphasis). In this letter, Bonhoeffer reflects further on the significance of the Old and New Testaments in contradistinction to "myths of redemption": Human beings are directed "toward their lives on earth" (*WEN,* 369).

> Unlike believers in the myths of redemption, Christians do not always have in the eternal a final refuge from earthly trials, but must completely partake of earthly life as did Christ ("My God, why have you forsaken me?"). *(Ibid.)*

Earthly life and discipleship in Christ belong together; in the interpretation of the *Outline,* we will see how precisely this quotation from Mark 15:34 becomes central to Bonhoeffer's interpretation of *Jesus' life* as *being for others.* "The here and now[92] may not be prematurely suspended; here the Old and New Testaments remain in agreement.[93] Myths of redemption originate from within the human experience of boundaries.[94] Christ, however, addresses human beings at the *center of their lives*" (369;

my emphasis). Here, too, Bonhoeffer's christological reflections tend toward an accentuation of the "center" of life. This christological understanding of the "middle" or "center," one already discernible in the *Ethics* fragments from 1940,[95] acquires in the Tegel theology an incisive accentuation from the perspective of life.

On June 30, 1944, Bonhoeffer criticizes the "in*authenticity* of a merely intellectual existence" (*WEN*, 372; my emphasis), and observes biblically: "Jesus never questioned a person's health, *strength, happiness* . . . why else would he have made the sick healthy and restored strength to the weak?" (374f.; my emphasis). We see again how Bonhoeffer interprets the Bible from the perspective of life; in this particular instance, we even encounter concepts clearly deriving from the philosophy of life: happiness, authenticity, strength.[96] Bonhoeffer summarizes the significance of Christology for the philosophy of life in the pregnant assertion: "Jesus *lays claim* for himself and for the Kingdom of God to the entirety of human life in all its manifestations" (375; my emphasis). He then reformulates the theme of June 8 as the "*appropriation* of the world come of age by Jesus Christ" (*ibid.;* my emphasis). Both statements refer to "claims" or "appropriation"; if we ask about what is actually being claimed or appropriated, it is first of all Jesus' claim "to the entirety of human life," and then also "to the world come of age." The more abstract reference to the "world come of age" thus refers concretely to nothing other than "the entirety of human life." The hinge concept of "claim" or "appropriation" both allows and requires this parallel or concrete specification, since Bonhoeffer is concerned with Jesus' significance for the entirety of human life (i.e., life come of age).

Bonhoeffer formulated his theme on June 8, 1944: "Christ and the world come of age" (*WEN*, 358). Here, on June 30, he gives this theme a dynamic gradient: "The appropriation of the world come of age through Jesus Christ" (375). Bonhoeffer makes the theme more concrete through reference to life.[97] Both formulations conceal the theme *Christian faith and life come of age* — expressed dynamically: "the appropriation of life come of age through Jesus Christ."

In July 1944, inspired by Dilthey's explications in *Weltanschauung und Analyse*, Bonhoeffer remarks concerning the problem of a confession of faith: "A confession of faith does not express what someone else 'must' believe, but what one believes oneself."[98] The question of a "must" of faith then becomes the object of theological reflection in the *Outline* (*WEN*, 416f.).

On July 8, 1944, Bonhoeffer reflects critically on the concept of "inwardness" (379; cf. also 377f.). One-sided talk about "that which is inward, personal, and private" (377) does not correspond to biblical thinking. "The Bible knows nothing of our distinction between the external and the internal. . . . It is always concerned with the ἄνθρωπος τέλειος, the whole person" (379). Following Dilthey's understanding of inwardness, Bonhoeffer writes: "The discovery of so-called inwardness is not made until the Renaissance (probably in Petrarch[99])" (379). By contrast, "the 'heart' in the biblical sense refers not to that which is internal, but to the entire person before God" *(ibid.).* Inwardness and religion run counter to the wholeness of human life. Bonhoeffer suggests "that one simply acknowledge that both the world and human beings have come of age, and that one not 'put down' human beings in their worldliness, but confront them in their strongest position with God" (379).[100] There follows the familiar double delimitation over against psychotherapy and existential philosophy.[101] He concludes with the words: "Well, now it is time to speak concretely about the worldly interpretation of biblical concepts. But it's too hot!" (380). What he has already written is to be understood as "preliminary remarks" to the "nonreligious interpretation of biblical concepts" (377).[102]

The poem "Christians and Pagans" addresses "God's distress": "People come to God in His distress" (*WEN,* 382). For Christians, it is accordingly not their own "human distress" that stands in the foreground, the distress with which they themselves have to deal, but God's "weakness and death." It is for Christians to "stand by God in His suffering" *(ibid.).* This poem could also be understood from the perspective of the letters of May 8 and July 8 with their critique of existential philosophy and psychotherapy, which in Bonhoeffer's opinion focus on human distress. Christians take as their point of departure not their own distress, but that of God, that is, they participate in God's suffering in the world. The existential-philosophical interpretation and the nonreligious interpretation seem in this view to be mutually exclusive. If we were to describe this poem thematically, the title "The Christian in a World Come of Age"[103] would be appropriate.

In the long letter of July 16, 1944, Bonhoeffer writes about the theme he and Bethge share (= "our" theme): "I am only gradually making progress toward the nonreligious interpretation of biblical concepts" (*WEN,* 392). In so doing, he again — as on June 8 — begins "historically" in order to demonstrate the "great development leading to the autonomy of the world" *(ibid.)*. Bonhoeffer shows how the human striving for autonomy has developed in the spheres of reason, morality, politics, and so on, with his observation of, for example, autonomous morality clearly betraying his Dilthey reading: "In morality: Montaigne, Bodin, who set up life rules instead of commandments" (393; cf. *Weltanschauung und Analyse,* 261).

It does not escape Bonhoeffer's attention that in Dilthey, the historical argumentation figures are anchored in the concept of life. It is not that the notion of morality in and of itself has become autonomous; rather, it is that life's morality is no longer bound to commandments. For the rest, Dilthey ultimately links the concept of morality with the concept of life. Bonhoeffer takes this into account in speaking about the autonomy of *human beings* (*WEN,* 356) or of *the world* (392f.).

In Part I, we discerned in addition to Dilthey also the influence of C. F. von Weizsäcker, under whose concept of the "working hypothesis" ultimately all forms of a religiously understood notion of God are subsumed. "God as a moral, political, scientific working hypothesis has been done away with, overcome" (*WEN,* 393). Thus Bonhoeffer at the end of his historical excursus; this excursus (along with that in the letter of May 8) will in the *Outline* become the basis of the first chapter, "Stocktaking." "Stocktaking" describes the situation obtaining "before" the nonreligious interpretation. (In order to interpret nonreligiously, one must first show what it means to "interpret religiously"; this is the purpose served by the excursuses and by Dilthey's historicism.) These issue into the question concerning life, and demand nonreligiously that biblical concepts be interpreted from the perspective of life here and now. Bonhoeffer recognizes that we cannot return to the religious world of the Middle Ages in which "God" was yet discernible, or we can at best only at the price of "intellectual honesty" (394). Instead, the human being come of age must acknowledge that we live in the world "etsi deus non daretur." By acknowledging this, a person performs what the Bible calls "penitence." Bonhoeffer thus interprets this concept nonreligiously as "ultimate honesty" *(ibid.)*.

The considerable extent to which the nonreligious interpretation aims at the concept of life becomes clear in the ensuing sentences: "God lets us know that we must live as those who come to terms with life without God" *(ibid.)*. Bonhoeffer ultimately considers this to be that which is really Christian, or — better — that which is commensurate with Christ: "Before and with God, we live without God" *(ibid.)*.

The addendum to the letter of July 18, 1944, underscores these observations; the idea of co-suffering from the poem "Christians and

Pagans" is taken into the theme of life. On July 18, Bonhoeffer repeats that "Christians stand by God in His[104] suffering" (395), and remarks: ". . . and this distinguishes Christians from pagans. 'Could you not keep awake one hour?' Jesus asks in Gethsemane. This is the reversal of everything a *religious* person expects from God. Human beings are called to suffer God's own suffering at the hands of the godless world" (395; my emphasis). In the next sentence, the theme of suffering enters into the more fundamental theme of life:

> That is, [human beings] must genuinely *live* in the godless world, and are not permitted to conceal or transfigure its godlessness in some religious fashion. . . . They are permitted to live in a "worldly" fashion, that is, are liberated from all false religious ties and hindrances. (395; my emphasis)

Bonhoeffer apparently picks up yet another idea in his formation ethics. In the fragment "Ethics as Formation," he writes: "Jesus is not *a* human being, but rather *the* human being."[105] In the Tegel letter, he picks up this formulation again in a critique of religion: "Being a Christian does not mean being religious in a certain way . . . *rather, it means being a human being; Christ creates in us not *a* type of human being, but *the*[106] human being" (395; my emphasis). Just as Christ was *the* human being, so also he creates *the* human being in us. Bonhoeffer uses one of the significant insights of his formation Christology in illustrating his critique of religion in Tegel. Genuine, whole, Christian life stands over against the religious act; put fundamentally, *religion* stands over against *life:* "It is not some religious act that makes a person a Christian, but participation in God's own suffering amid worldly life" (395). In this sentence, the triad religion-suffering-life is overcome once and for all: The religious person does not suffer and does not live in the Christian sense; the nonreligious person suffers and lives by being drawn "into God's messianic suffering in Jesus Christ" (395).

Bonhoeffer asks what persons such as Jairus or Cornelius in the New Testament have in common: "The only thing these people have in common is participation in God's suffering in Christ. That is their 'faith'" (*WEN*, 396). This prefigures even the wording of the formulations in the second chapter of the *Outline,* where Bonhoeffer will write: "faith" as participation in Jesus' being (cf. *WEN*, 414).[107] He explicitly juxtaposes religion and life — and with clarity unsurpassed in the *Letters and Papers from Prison* — when following the material just cited he writes: "Not a word of religious practice; the 'religious act' is always something partial, while 'faith' is something whole, an act of life. Jesus calls us not to a new religion, but to life" (396). After defining the content of "faith" as participation in Christ's being, Bonhoeffer delimits the preliminary definition of the "concept of faith" over against religious partiality, and adds: faith as participation in Jesus' being *and* as a total act of life. This means that Bonhoeffer is developing a "nonreligious" triad of faith, participation (in suffering), and life (as a totality), formulating this contra the "religious triad" of unbelief, nonparticipation (in suffering), and non-living (religious partiality).

He then asks in the sense of a "nonreligious interpretation" how this "life" will look, "this life of participation in God's powerlessness in the world?" (*WEN*, 396). Unfortunately, he does not provide an answer in this letter, though he does raise the question of "life" showing the way. Passages such as these remind us what was once said about Bonhoeffer's prison theology, namely, that he "makes us face the right questions."[108]

On July 21, 1944, Bonhoeffer reflects intensively on the theological profile of a "profound this-worldliness" (*WEN*, 401).

> Not the flat and banal this-worldliness of the enlightened and the busy . . . I mean the profound this-worldliness full of discipline, in which a knowledge of death and of the resurrection is always present. I believe that Luther lived in such this-worldliness. (*WEN*, 401)

We have already seen the considerable extent to which the concept of this-worldliness, too, derives from Bonhoeffer's reading of Dilthey.[109] Now we will see that the concept of this-worldliness is decisively linked with that of life. Bonhoeffer confesses on the same page that "only in the full this-worldliness *of life* does one first learn to believe" (*ibid.;* my emphasis).

For Bonhoeffer, this-worldliness means the this-worldliness of life. Just as earlier the concept of coming of age was specified more closely through a substantive genitive attribute (cf. the coming of age *of the world* and *of life*), so also here: the "this-worldliness *of life.*" In what follows, Bonhoeffer comes back to the understanding of faith as μετάνοια as explicated on July 18: Learning to believe in the full this-worldliness of life means doing without "making something of oneself" (*WEN*, 402), which would be conceived religiously, that is, conceiving the human being as "homo religiosus" (401). Believing means to take seriously "God's suffering in the world," to keep watch "with Christ in Gethsemane"; "and thus does a person become a human being, a Christian" (402). Bonhoeffer finally asks rhetorically: "How can one become arrogant with success or despondent with failure if in this life here and now one suffers God's own suffering?" (402).

In his subsequent reflections on "Stages on the Path to Freedom" (*WEN*, 403), Bonhoeffer indicates the significance of the expression "suffering along with God's suffering in life." After his explications regarding "discipline" *(ibid.)*, about which he had already spoken in the letter of July 21 (401, cited above), he writes about "suffering" (403): "Miraculous transformation. Your strong, busy hands / are tied. Powerless, lonely you see the end / of your deed . . " (403). Given what Bonhoeffer has said in the letter of July 21, these ideas are to be related to life and understood christologically.

Bonhoeffer is no doubt also reflecting on his own biographical position here. In that case, this third section on "suffering" would also introduce the final stage of his own life.[110] But he wanted more; Bonhoeffer seems to be taking this reference to life as it were into his own basically christological reflections on faith as genuine participation in God's suffering in the world. Here the strong hands are "tied," here one is "powerless" while watching, here one sees the end of the "deed" (cf. Christ's powerlessness on the cross, Mark 15:34). The "miraculous transformation" is the transformation into Christ's suffering in the world.

In two further letters, Bonhoeffer provides concrete explications of his basic christological question of April 30, 1944, namely, concerning *who Christ is for us today.* On June 8, he wrote: "The question is: Christ and the world come of age" (*WEN*, 358). On June 30, he demands programmatically "the appropriation of the world come of age through Jesus Christ" (375).

We have seen that he came to associate his reflections on life with these formulations. This observation is confirmed when on July 28, 1944, Bonhoeffer writes about the Old Testament concept of "blessing": "This blessing is the *appropriation of earthly life* for God" (*WEN*, 496; my emphasis). As early as June 30, he was already speaking about the appropriation *of the world* and *of life.* Here, on July 28, reference to the appropriation *of the world* recedes in favor of the concept of life; Bonhoeffer is concerned with the "appropriation of earthly life for God" (406). Much suggests that it was only here — at the time of the composition of the

Outline — that Bonhoeffer defined the "life-theological" dimension of the "theme" with which he and Bethge were concerned.

We also see that it is apparently only here that the repeated references to the earthly significance of Jesus Christ[111] and of life focused on the here and now are finally clarified. "This blessing is the appropriation of earthly life for God, and it contains all promises" (*WEN*, 406). In this letter, Bonhoeffer is arguing completely from the perspective of the Old Testament, and quite consciously does not want to oppose the cross with the blessing of the Old Testament. The "difference between the Old Testament and the New Testament is . . . that in the Old Testament, blessing also includes the cross, while in the New Testament, the cross also includes the blessing" (407). The concept of life encompasses both Testaments, something demonstrated most clearly by the formulation of an "earthly Christology" (cf. the christological exegesis of Canticles as an earthly love song! *WEN*, 345).[112]

In his reflections on the Old Testament, Bonhoeffer is apparently also adopting ideas of his friend. "You say that the Bible does not say much about health, happiness, strength, etc." (406). He contradicts Bethge's view here.[113] "In any case, this is certainly not the case in the Old Testament. The theological conceptual link in the Old Testament between God and human happiness, etc., as far as I can see, is the concept of blessing" *(ibid.)*. The next sentence is that cited earlier concerning "blessing" as the "appropriation of earthly life for God."

Bonhoeffer points out the significance of the Old Testament for life, and is obviously interpreting the theological-biblical concept of *blessing* with the aid of the anthropological concept of *happiness* derived from the philosophy of life. In so doing, he is taking the Old Testament as his orientation for explicating the reflections in the letter of June 30, 1944, in which in his interpretation of the New Testament he drew on precisely these concepts of human "health," "strength," and "happiness" (*WEN*, 375). In that letter, the section ended with the remark: "Jesus lays claim for himself . . . to the entirety of human life . . ." (375). What Bonhoeffer said about the significance of the concept of life in the New Testament on June 30 he complements on July 28 with respect to the Old Testament, using the same concepts which in our interpretation of the letter of June 30 proved to derive from the philosophy of life. "Life" becomes the central interpretive concept for the entire scriptures of the Old and New Testaments.

One notices that during the period in which the concept of life acquires such significance, Bonhoeffer is also intensively reading Dilthey.

In the section "A Few Thoughts on Various Things" (*WEN*, 408, top), we find two verbatim citations from *Weltanschauung und Analyse des Menschen seit Renaissance und Reformation:* from p. 341 Bonhoeffer takes a citation from Giordano Bruno about the friend,[114] a citation standing in the context of the "new life ideal" (341); Bonhoeffer could have borrowed another citation about the affections in Spinoza from p. 429.[115] There Dilthey reflects on "instruction regarding life comportment" (422f.). Bonhoeffer's parents are also aware of his intensive reading of Dilthey during this period. On July 30, 1944, they write to Eberhard Bethge that "in these moving times" their son will "find it hard to concentrate on Dilthey" (*WEN*, 409).

The theme of "living without God" concerns Bonhoeffer in the "Notes" (*WEN*, 412), which were probably written for the *Outline;* in any event, they date from the period when the *Outline* emerged, namely, "July/August 1944" (412). Bonhoeffer notes thetically: "The ouster of God from the world is the disqualification (?) of religion/living without God" (412); he thus believes one must distinguish between Christianity and religion: "But what if Christianity were not a religion at all?" From which he concludes: The "worldly-nonreligious interpretation of Christian concepts. Christianity emerges from the encounter with the concrete human being: Jesus. Experience of transcendence" (412). Here Bonhoeffer alludes to the train of thought he will follow in the first two chapters of the *Outline:* "(1) Stocktaking, (2) What really is Christian faith?" (413f.).

Reading further in the prison letters, one notices that in personal remarks to his friend Bonhoeffer also uses expressions he otherwise uses in connection with the theological "theme." For example, in a letter for Eberhard Bethge's birthday, he speaks about "participation in life": From the number of letters he receives for his birthday, Bethge can "see how many people like you and *take part in your life* and are attached to you" (*WEN*, 419; my emphasis). The expression "being for others" from the *Outline* also occurs in the following sentence: "But there is hardly a more joyous feeling than sensing that one can be something *for others*" (*ibid.;* my emphasis). Here the expression "being for" acquires significance in daily life. Bonhoeffer later writes about what is "human": "God himself lets us serve him in what is human" *(ibid.).* We are able to follow theological ideas even into Bonhoeffer's private remarks in his correspondence, something attesting his consistent theological reference point in life.

On August 21, 1944, he writes to Eberhard Bethge: "We must again and again contemplate the life of Jesus long and calmly in order to see what God promises and what he fulfills. It is certain that we may always live near and in the presence of God, and that this life is a completely new life for us" (*WEN*, 425). Bonhoeffer returns to the concept of "promise" at the end of the letter. First, he explicates the intertwining of life and Christology in a positive and negative formulation.

The positive formulation is: ". . . if a person such as Jesus has *lived*, then and only then do our human lives have *meaning*" (*WEN*, 426; my emphasis). The negative formulation is: "Had Jesus *not lived*, then our *lives* would be . . . *meaningless*" (*ibid.;* my emphasis). The concept of life becomes the central connecting concept between the human existence of Jesus and meaningful Christian human existence, exhibiting thus "life-christological" content; that is, the concept of "meaning" makes the significance of Jesus Christ in life transparent. Bonhoeffer writes concisely: "The unbiblical concept of 'meaning' is of course merely a translation of what the Bible calls 'promise'" (426). The question is whether this constitutes yet another concrete reference to a nonreligiously interpreted biblical concept (cf. above the concept of penitence!). This will similarly be an issue in our interpretation of the *Outline,* on which Bonhoeffer is intensively working at this time.[116] In one of the last signs of life, near the end of 1944, Bonhoeffer writes to his fiancée: "Your prayers and kind thoughts, passages from the Bible, long-forgotten conversations, pieces of music, books — all are invested with *life and reality* as never before" (*Love Letters,* 269; my emphasis).

The accompanying poem, "By kindly, faithful, tranquil powers surrounded," says in the fourth strophe: "But if it be thy will once more to let us / delight in this world and its bright sunshine, / then shall we all these bygone days remember, / then shall our *lives be absolutely thine*" (*Love Letters,* 270 = *WEN*, 436; my emphasis).

2. The Influence of Wilhelm Dilthey on the Tegel Theology

Our presentation of the theme of life in the Tegel correspondence has shown that over the course of this correspondence, the concept of "life" became increasingly important. While at the beginning of the correspondence Bonhoeffer's use of the word "life" was yet unreflected, by the end of 1944 we are dealing with a clearly circumscribed understanding of life. This concept finds its counterconcept in Bonhoeffer's understanding of religion.[117]

While early statements on the theme of life can yet be understood from the perspective of the manuscripts to Bonhoeffer's *Ethics* (1940-1943), this is no longer the case with his understanding of an earthly, christological life, an understanding that is critical of religion (1944). The concept of life becomes a christological concept within the context of a critique of religion. In its christological inclination, the concept of life also acquires cognitive-theoretical significance: For Dilthey, the ground of cognition as understood from the perspective of the philosophy of life is grounded in the question concerning the riddle of life; for Bonhoeffer, this ground of cognition is transformed through a Christology of life into the riddle of Christian life as *participation in Jesus' being*.

a. Dilthey's Significance as a Philosopher of Life as Early as 1929?[118]

Bonhoeffer understands Dilthey as a philosopher of life from a very early period. In *Act and Being,* he appraises Dilthey's critique of Idealism as that of a "philosophy of life determined by history."[119] He apparently already notices the connection between historicism and life as early as his inaugural dissertation, though no theological influence yet exerts itself. Philosophically, Bonhoeffer is following Karl Barth and neo-Kantianism completely at this time. Bonhoeffer's anti-idealistic classification of the "historical philosophy of life" shows how well he already knows Dilthey in 1929; he evaluates this philosophy positively within the framework of the "transcendental attempt" in *Act and Being.*[120] It is precisely this cognitive-theoretical grounding on Dilthey's part, one running counter to German Idealism, that probably constitutes the presupposition for understanding how in Tegel Dilthey's philosophy was able to exert theological influence on Bonhoeffer. Here Bonhoeffer discovers a new side to Immanuel Kant.[121] It is life rather than reason that now stands at the center of philosophical and theological reflection.

Bonhoeffer refers to Dilthey's *Introduction to the Humanities* in his lectures on "Systematic Theology in the 20th Century." In his foreword to the *Introduction to the Humanities,* Dilthey introduces the cognitive-theoretical premise of the philosophy of life, which places " 'life,' . . . the 'whole human being,' 'this willing, feeling, thinking being' in the place of the 'pure,' abstract, unhistorical subject of cognition."[122]

Previously, in the United States (1930/31), Bonhoeffer evaluated and offered a positive estimation of William James and "pragmatism" as a "philosophy of life."[123] In the manuscripts to the *Ethics* (1940-43), Friedrich Nietzsche then apparently plays an important role as an "antipode."[124]

EXCURSUS: P. KÖSTER

In his groundbreaking study, P. Köster demonstrates the philosophical influence Nietzsche exerted on various attempts Bonhoeffer undertakes in the *Ethics*. Köster proceeds in two steps, examining first (367-87) Bonhoeffer's early statements, such as those in lectures on ethics during his stay in Barcelona (375f.). Then, in the second section, Köster examines the fragments to the *Ethics* in detail (387ff.). Regarding possible early influence of Nietzsche's thought, Köster believes the philosopher is "present in the background" (378), but otherwise believes that Barth's influence on the entire complex of Bonhoeffer's critique of Christianity is of significance. "Bonhoeffer follows Barth in radically rejecting any identification of Christianity and morality of the sort theologically grounded on Kant and virtually celebrated in bourgeois society" (379). On the whole, Köster reckons with a "formal reception of Nietzsche" quite in keeping with the time, "but which for that reason must have become suspect to Bonhoeffer's own critical inclinations" (386). As far as the manuscripts to the *Ethics* themselves are concerned, Köster views Bonhoeffer's reference to "beyond good and evil" as having been influenced by Nietzsche (390f.). The critique of ethics taking its point of departure in the "primal condition," Köster believes is based on the premise "that all ethics represents a phenomenon of disaster" (391).

Bonhoeffer allegedly "explains the ethical human desire to know about good and evil as human insistence on autonomous possibilities against God" (392). In this context, Köster sees a proximity to "Nietzsche's development of the 'death of God'" *(ibid.)*. "What for Nietzsche must be considered virtually an intoxicating experience of being forced into super-human greatness, for Bonhoeffer appears as a profoundly contradictory self-constituting of human existence necessarily constructed on the groundlessness of the nihil" (392). Köster shows how Nietzsche becomes an antipode here, how the positive appropriation of Nietzsche's thought becomes a critique of Nietzsche. Autonomy is understood from the perspective of nihilism, a view Bonhoeffer radically modifies in his own interpretation of autonomy and godlessness in the *Letters and Papers from Prison*. Köster refers to this situation under the subtitle "Nietzsche and the West" (402f.; cf. 407f.).

"The chapter 'Inheritance and Decline,' whose conclusion is obscure enough, includes the culmination of Bonhoeffer's explicit critique of Nietzsche in his ethical essays. Nietzsche figures as the culmination in a process critical of Christianity and even ambiguous in its questioning view of the Reformation, a process whose results are nihilism and godlessness" (409). Köster shows clearly how at this time Bonhoeffer is searching for a philosophical conception he can use not just as an antipode, but with whose aid he can better explicate the theological ideas associated with "godlessness." Regarding the adoption of the concept of "life," Köster interprets the *Ethics* fragment "The Ultimate and the Penultimate Things" (410f.) critically, alleging that Bonhoeffer turns "against that irrational and enchanting sound of 'life'" (412). Here, too, Nietzsche remains the antipode. Whereas for him both life and death represent clearly articulated "forms of manifestation" of the "will to power," quite the contrary is the case for Bonhoeffer. "The concept of life occupies the center when Bonhoeffer now materially develops the alleged legitimacy of the natural, taking as his reference point the problem of dealing with corporeal and spiritual human existence, with one's own existence and that of others" (412).

On the whole Köster's study shows that on into the *Ethics* fragments, no real *reception* or appropriation of Nietzsche's thought is discernible. The philosopher of life remains a hidden antipode; but this also means that on into his *Ethics,* Bonhoeffer still has no point of access to the cognitive-theoretical premise of a philosophy of life: He was familiar with it, but did not appropriate it; it remained "irrational enchantment" for him. This confirms further that the repeatedly observed "subjective" element in Nietzsche's philosophy of life was unable to acquire any cognitive-theoretical significance for Bonhoeffer. This does not change until Bonhoeffer encounters Dilthey's "objective," historical philosophy of life.

Toward the end of 1943, several writings by José Ortega y Gasset emerge through which Bonhoeffer might have become acquainted *in nuce* with the significance of Dilthey's philosophy of life. As we saw, Ortega y Gasset occupies a significant and key position in prompting Bonhoeffer to read Wilhelm Dilthey systematically in 1944.

My *interim findings* are that both the significance of a philosophy of life in general[125] and an acquaintance with Dilthey's historical philosophy of life are prefigured and discernible in various of Bonhoeffer's writings, though no systematic *appropriation* of Dilthey's thought is yet underway.

b. The Systematic Influence of Dilthey in 1944

From Tegel, Bonhoeffer asks "what Christianity really is or who Christ really is for us today" (*WEN*, 305). The question regarding Jesus Christ links the Tegel theology with Bonhoeffer's *Ethics*, and the new feature of the *Letters and Papers from Prison* is found in various formulations from Tegel that expand Bonhoeffer's christological understanding by the addition of elements of a critique of religion.[126] Bonhoeffer goes further in his evaluation of maturity and autonomy. Whereas in the *Ethics*, especially in the fragment "Inheritance and Decline,"[127] Bonhoeffer interprets the process leading to autonomy negatively as leading ultimately to nihilism,[128] we find quite the opposite in the *Letters and Papers from Prison*. Bonhoeffer evaluates positively the autonomy of the world, of human beings, and of life, and affirms the process of coming of age. Between the *Ethics* and these positive statements in the *Letters and Papers from Prison*, Bonhoeffer read Wilhelm Dilthey.

Scholars have only marginally discussed the question of Dilthey's influence as a *philosopher of life*. After Eberhard Bethge's ("The Challenge of Dietrich Bonhoeffer's Life and Theology," *Chicago Theological Seminary Register* 51/2 [1961]: 1-38) and then Ernst Feil's (*Die Theologie Dietrich Bonhoeffers* [Munich, 1971], p. 132, n. 20 [note omitted in English translation, *The Theology of Dietrich Bonhoeffer*]) initial, general references to the significance of the philosophy of life for Bonhoeffer, it was T. R. Peters (*op. cit.* [see Introduction] [1976] 133ff.) who provided the first concrete initiative, pointing out that Bonhoeffer's appropriation of Dilthey's thought was not limited to the latter's historicism, but included his philosophy of life as well. Peters did not, however, examine thoroughly the possibility of Bonhoeffer having appropriated elements of Dilthey's philosophy of life, and reckons instead with the continuing significance of Nietzsche's philosophy of life for the entirety of Bonhoeffer's work (133-44). It was only the study of K. Bartl (*Theologie und Säkularität. Die theologischen Ansätze Friedrich Gogartens und Dietrich Bonhoeffers zur Analyse und Reflexion der säkularisierten Welt* [Frankfurt am Main, 1990]) and the book by H.-J. Abromeit (*Das Geheimnis Christi. Dietrich Bonhoeffers erfahrungsbezogene Christologie* [Neukirchen-Vluyn, 1991]) that took things further. Bartl (198ff.) demonstrates Dilthey's relevance to Bonhoeffer's "understanding of reality" as *one* reality, and shows that Bonhoeffer stands close not only to Dilthey's "presentation of history," "but already to his basic concept of life" (204). Bartl does not, however, apply this insight to the understanding of religion in the *Letters and Papers from Prison,* and instead sticks to the theme of his study, namely, "Theology and Secularity." H.-J. Abromeit (125f.) also adduces Dilthey's significance for Bonhoeffer as a philosopher of life, working out the significance of various currents of the philosophy of life for the *Ethics* (126ff.); in the *Ethics,* however, Dilthey is not yet providing Bonhoeffer with any new impulses. Only in the *Letters and Papers* does Bonhoeffer's appropriation of Dilthey emerge through Bonhoeffer's own systematic reading. Abromeit does not address the significance of Dilthey's philosophy of life for the *Letters and Papers,* though he does coin the term "life theology" for the later Bonhoeffer (125), demonstrating thereby the close connection with the philosophy of life, a connection consisting, he alleges, "in the interdependence of understanding and experience undergirding the two" (126).

In summary, we can note that these two initiatives do not throw any new light on the connection between the philosophy of life on the one hand, and the critique of religion on the other; commensurately, they also do not illuminate the significance of Dilthey's *concept of life* for the nonreligious interpretation. They certainly do, however, raise the pertinent general question regarding the possibility of Dilthey's significance for Bonhoeffer as a philosopher of life.

The following discussion will concentrate exclusively on the third writing by Dilthey on which Bonhoeffer worked beginning in March 1944 during his incarceration, and will take as its basis our previous discussion of Dilthey's *Weltanschauung und Analyse des Menschen seit Renaissance und Reformation.*[129] This examination found that the cognitive-theoretical ground of Dilthey's philosophy in *Weltanschauung und Analyse* is the concept of "life." We also saw how Dilthey combines the concept of life with that of history into a certain interpretation of history, namely, historicism. To acknowledge the interdependence of *history* and *experience,* reference has also been made to Dilthey's conception of a *historical philosophy of life* (O. F. Bollnow).

In studying *Weltanschauung und Analyse,* Bonhoeffer probably proceeded chronologically. Several considerations suggest this. We saw, for example, that the citations from Giordano Bruno on the friend and from Spinoza on the affections in Bonhoeffer's "Thoughts on Various Things" (*WEN,* 408) come from the end of Dilthey's volume (*Weltanschauung und Analyse,* 341f.). Bonhoeffer cites these sentences in July 1944, that is, also at the end of his own reading of Dilthey. We can assume that at this time the *whole* of Dilthey is present. In this context, mention of the philosopher and scientist G. Cardano in the *Letters and Papers* and *Weltanschauung und Analyse* is also revealing. In a letter at the end of April 1944, Eberhard Bethge draws his friend's attention to Cardano's significance (cf. *WEN*, 299f.). Bonhoeffer answers Bethge at the beginning of May 1944, that is, when he begins to read Dilthey. "I am not familiar with Cardano. Has he been translated into German?" (315). In the middle of June, Bonhoeffer then remarks to Bethge in an aside: "By the way, Dilthey writes quite a bit about Cardano" (366). Dilthey first mentions Cardano on p. 284.[130] From this one can conclude directly that by mid-June, Bonhoeffer has already read over half — if not more — of *Weltanschauung und Analyse*, while at the beginning of May he is quite obviously just beginning to read Dilthey; in any event, he has not yet come to Dilthey's discussion of the Renaissance philosopher.

Bonhoeffer's mention of G. Cardano shows in an exemplary fashion how carefully he is reading Dilthey's *Weltanschauung und Analyse*. At this point, I would like to mention other names that acquired significance for Bonhoeffer as he read Dilthey: Herbert of Cherbury, Hugo Grotius, Jean Bodin, Michel de Montaigne, Giordano Bruno (cf. *Weltanschauung und Analyse*, 248ff., 279f., 274f., 263f., 297f. = *WEN*, 392f.). This selection is limited to the significant letter of July 16, 1944; Bonhoeffer associates these names with certain themes with whose aid the "one great development . . . toward the autonomy of the world" (392) becomes discernible. These themes include "theology" (representative: Herbert of Cherbury), "morality" (names: Montaigne, Bodin), and "politics" (representative: N. Machiavelli) (cf. *WEN*, 392f.); the name of Grotius is mentioned in connection with the theme "autonomy" in "human society" (*WEN*, 393).

Bonhoeffer is quite obviously systematically organizing *Weltanschauung und Analyse* according to certain thematic groups and name groups from the perspective of autonomy and coming of age. In the letter of July 16, 1944, he then brings together various historical reflections in the different sections of *Weltanschauung und Analyse* (cf. also the parallel letter of June 8). Our previous overall examination of *Weltanschauung und Analyse*, however, revealed that nowhere in his volume does Dilthey himself actually examine "autonomy" or "coming of age" as concepts in and for themselves.[131]

As an example, let us recall how Dilthey understands Grotius. He sees how in the first three decades Pierre Charron, Francis Bacon, and Herbert of Cherbury establish the line of thought which H. Grotius will then carry forward: The "natural system of the moral world" is established

(*Weltanschauung und Analyse,* 276). Dilthey examines the "task" (277), "method" (278), and "concepts" (279) of Grotius and finds that the "universally valid concepts" (278) are "life concepts" (279). These concepts "inhere in the entirety of life and draw from life their persuasive power" (279). The "legal concepts" thus deduced (= "life concepts") (280), following Grotius, are concepts whose "validity does not depend on faith in their grounding within a teleological order resting in God. 'Even if there were no God,' the principles of natural law would maintain their independent and universal validity" (280).

The famous citation of Grotius, which Bonhoeffer renders in Latin,[132] thus appears in the immediate context of the philosophy of life. Dilthey adduces Grotius as a Renaissance legal thinker who takes the concepts of life as his point of departure, thereby renewing "the true intention of Roman jurisprudence" (*Weltanschauung und Analyse,* 279); the concept of justice is a life concept. This also directly explains why Bonhoeffer speaks about *life* without God (cf. *WEN,* 394), and why his historical excurses on the striving for autonomy in various areas basically all end up talking about life.

From Dilthey, Bonhoeffer saw that the statement from Grotius is a statement about life, and "that we must *live* in a world 'etsi deus non daretur'" (*WEN,* 394; my emphasis).

What we find here in the case of Grotius applies as well to the other themes and names mentioned above.[133] Our larger examination of Dilthey's work revealed that all the names enumerated here are associated with the philosophy of life.

Regardless of the sphere in which Dilthey observes the striving to come of age or to attain autonomy, he always begins with human life as it is actually lived in a given epoch. The maturity of the world derives from the maturity of life in the world.

Life as a cognitive-theoretical maxim becomes the historical understanding of a given epoch. The autonomy of life becomes the autonomy of human beings and of the world. Bonhoeffer consciously goes along with this progression, beginning thetically with the conclusion: ". . . it is a great development that leads to the autonomy of the world" (*WEN,* 392). When Bonhoeffer speaks elsewhere about the autonomy of human beings and of life, he lets us know that he is interpreting Dilthey's cognitive-theoretical position — namely, life — christologically: The "appropriation of the world come of age through Jesus Christ" (*WEN,* 375). In the preceding sentence of the letter just cited, Bonhoeffer demands that "the entirety of human life" must be claimed by Christ. The conceptual pairs "mature world" and "worldly life" as well as "world come of age" and "mature life" can thus be used alongside one another.

Bonhoeffer's formulation of the theme of his Tegel theology progresses from the general to the particular, from the initial christological question to the appropriation of earthly life. We can discern the following development in Bonhoeffer's christological understanding of life (my emphasis):

I. Initial question: ". . . who *Christ* really is *for us today*" (April 30, 1944; *WEN,* 305).

II. Basic theme: *"Christ and the world come of age"* (June 8, 1944; *WEN,* 358).

III. Ethical theme: The "*appropriation of the world come of age* through Jesus Christ" (June 30, 1944; *WEN,* 395).

IV. Theme of life: "Jesus lays claim to the *entirety of human life for himself*" (June 30, 1944; *WEN,* 406).

V. Theme: The biblical "blessing is the *appropriation of earthly life for God*" (July 28, 1944; *WEN,* 406).

VI. Ecclesiological conclusion: The church "must tell people of all vocations what *life with Christ* is, what it means "to be for others" (*Outline for a Book; WEN,* 415f.).

From his initial *christological* question (I), Bonhoeffer formulates the basic theme of his Tegel theology (II), applies it ethically (III) (also with respect to "life," IV), and finally gives the theme an exclusive concrete orientation toward *life* (V), including the ecclesiological conclusion of this Christology of life (VI). The essence of the various formulations is thus: Christian life and life come of age.

When we said that Bonhoeffer applies Dilthey's philosophy of life christologically, this alludes to the particular accentuation Bonhoeffer gives to his own reading of Dilthey. Our examination of *Weltanschauung und Analyse des Menschen seit Renaissance und Reformation* repeatedly encountered Dilthey's concept of religion, one he obviously draws into his own philosophy of life. His intention is to show the relationship between life and religiosity in their various manifestations during the Renaissance and Reformation. For example, Ulrich Zwingli's "religiosity" is allegedly "true life" (*Weltanschauung und Analyse,* 226). Dilthey raises the question of "true religion" in connection with Jean Bodin (151), and also admires "the religious vivacity of Luther" (231). On the whole, Dilthey is inclined to engage in criticism whenever religion and life are isolated and opposed to one another (137). The *whole* of life is for him *religious* life: "God wants to be enjoyed" (160). Religion is to be asserted "in life" (237), and Dilthey thus demands a "livable" religion, that is, a religion of the here and now.

Dilthey's *Weltanschauung und Analyse des Menschen seit Renaissance und Reformation* contains no *critique* of religion, something we already explicated in connection with other Dilthey writings; nor, according to Dilthey, can any religion*lessness* come about.[134] In substance, a critique of religion and the notion of religionlessness as two significant motifs of Bonhoeffer's own understanding of religion do *not* derive from Wilhelm Dilthey, although the *critique* of metaphysics — as a further basic motif of *Weltanschauung und Analyse*[135] — exerts considerable influence on Bonhoeffer. Bonhoeffer emphatically followed the critique of metaphysics as grounded in the philosophy of life. The critique of religion, however, is in Bonhoeffer grounded through the critique of religion presented by Karl Barth; this confirms Thesis II, according to which Bonhoeffer takes the theological critique of religion into his Tegel theology and combines it with the historical philosophy of life.

Where Dilthey finds an antithesis between *life* and *metaphysics,* Bonhoeffer juxtaposes *life* and *religion.* Where Dilthey interprets *life and inwardness* from a mutually inclusive perspective, Bonhoeffer does the same with *life and Jesus Christ.*

Under the influence of Bonhoeffer's systematic reading of Dilthey, the concept of life becomes the basic cognitive-theoretical concept. Here the Tegel theology differs from the fragments to the *Ethics.* Although both *in* and *prior* to his *Ethics*[136] Bonhoeffer appropriates elements of the philosophy of life, he does not yet understand these as motifs integral to cognition.[137] The ethical theme is: Christ and the good.[138] It is only in the *Letters and Papers from Prison* that this becomes the theme of Christ and the world come of age.[139] In this context, we again encounter *discontinuity in continuity* in Bonhoeffer's understanding of religion. We discern continuity in his christological questions, and discontinuity with respect to his understanding of the world and of autonomy. In the *Ethics,* Bonhoeffer evaluates mature life and autonomy negatively as apostasy from God, while in the *Letters and Papers* he poses the question of Christ and a world come of age. In Tegel, the ethical alternative "Christ *or* an autonomous world" becomes the relation "Christ *and* the world come of age." Parallel to this discontinuity, the continuity in Bonhoeffer's initial christological question is maintained: *Christ and/or* life come of age.

c. Findings

From the philosophy of life, Bonhoeffer acquired an important impulse for his understanding of life, and the theological understanding of life remains determinative for his reading of Dilthey. Viewed philosophically, life is equivocal; it becomes unequivocal only in view of Jesus Christ. And thus we arrive at the question of *how* this life in *being for others* really looks. This is the boundary question regarding an unequivocal understanding of the concept of *life;* was Bonhoeffer able to define this concept unequivocally? Here we probably become more acutely aware of the fragmentary character of his late theology, and must answer this question with *no.* Bonhoeffer passes on to us this task of searching for the answer. Although various reflections on life in the *Ethics* fragments might help us fill out the concept of life, they, too, are fragmentary. In his fragmentary Tegel theology, Bonhoeffer equipped us with the guiding questions regarding the correct relationship between life come of age and Christian faith — that was his theme, and was the essence of the question of nonreligious interpretation. Both the church and theology will have to struggle ever anew to find the appropriate answer.

C. Findings

1. "Putting It to the Test": Applying the Interpretive Framework to *Outline for a Book*

The "writing" Bonhoeffer intended to compose in connection with his theological correspondence with Eberhard Bethge has been preserved in his *Outline for a Book.* This is no longer merely a letter to his family or friends[140] prompted by a specific, temporally conditioned occasion, but a theological document. The dialogue between Bonhoeffer and Bethge seems to have been concluded, and the time right for a fundamental study. Nor is the addressee of the *Outline* Bonhoeffer's family or friend, but — as we can say with a certain legitimacy — posterity.[141] The *Outline* might be described as a *systematic-theological sketch* which we will decipher in the following section according to the interpretive model of the Tegel correspondence.

Bonhoeffer divides the piece into three chapters: "(1) Stocktaking of Christianity; (2) What really is Christian faith? (3) Conclusions" (*WEN,* 413). These headings already suggest that the *Outline* follows a three-part sequence reflecting the questions: What was? What is? What will be? Bonhoeffer seems to be couching his systematic-theological ideas in a historical-analytical sketch. This means that the discussion of religion is assigned to the first chapter, that is, to that which "was." Human beings were religious, and have now become religionless; and, indeed, we find here reflections on the "religionlessness of the human being come of age" (cf. ch. 1.b = *WEN*, 413). In the second chapter, the theme of religion recedes and is engaged antithetically. Bonhoeffer is apparently concerned with presenting the conclusions from his critique of religion in chapter 1 when in chapter 2.c he writes "interpretation of biblical concepts from this perspective" (414). He seems to be concerned no longer with what was, namely, religion, but with what is. The third chapter, "Conclusions" (415f.), no longer even mentions religion. We will later see what Bonhoeffer uses as a positive replacement for religion.

CHAPTER 1

The first chapter, "Stocktaking of Christianity," begins with the words: "The coming of age of human beings (as already indicated) . . ." (*WEN*, 413). The expression "as already indicated" suggests that Bonhoeffer is here referring to the preceding theological correspondence, apparently not wanting to repeat what he has already said in his letters about the theme "coming of age." And, indeed, he does not repeat it, but continues: ". . . the securing of human life against 'chance'. . . ." These two partial sentences do not bear any immediately discernible relation to one another, and are also separated by a semicolon. Hence one should not too hastily read beyond the introductory sentence. The expression "as already indicated" seems significant; here we are advised to recall the corresponding theological passages from the letters in which Bonhoeffer, drawing on Dilthey, describes the process through which human beings come of age. These include the letters of June 8 (*WEN*, excursus 365f.) and July 16, 1944 (excursus 392f.).

Two terms from chapter 1.a of the *Outline* can show how Bonhoeffer picks up the previous correspondence: "organization" and "blow of fate." Negative reference to "organizations" occurs in the *Thoughts* (cf. *WEN*, 326) in a similar context, while "blows of fate" already occurs in a critical context on February 21, 1944 (cf. 244).

Under 1.b, Bonhoeffer picks up the conclusions of his interpretation of maturity in the form of a disposition: "The religionlessness of the human being come of age. 'God' as a working hypothesis, as a stopgap for our embarrassments, has become superfluous (as already indicated)" (413). This stereotypical formula should again be examined, and possible letters adduced to which Bonhoeffer may be referring. First of all, these again include the two letters of June 6 and July 16, 1944, in which he describes the maturity of the modern human being within a historical argumentative framework. Then come those passages from the correspondence in which he introduces the notion of the working hypothesis "God" (*WEN*, 356 and 393f.). We saw that this reference to the working hypothesis became the collective term for various forms of the critique of religion. This is confirmed here in conclusion. Bonhoeffer finds the notion of the "working hypothesis 'God'" so pregnant that he selects it as a summarizing blanket term in the *Outline*.

In the following chapters (2 and 3), the stereotypical expression "as already indicated" does not recur; that is, in what follows Bonhoeffer is basically offering new arguments. (This omission possibly represents a *formal* indication that he is now thinking and showing the way "forward" rather than "backward," not even with respect to the preceding correspondence.)

Chapter 1 seems to be a necessary negative anticipation of chapter 3. Bonhoeffer explains what the church was: The church was not there for others. "No risk for others" (*WEN*, 414).[142] The expression "for others" is the logical connecting link with chapters 2 and 3.

CHAPTER 2

Chapter 2.b is artfully structured: Bonhoeffer answers the question about the content of faith with the thesis "the experience of God is the encounter with Jesus Christ," and then immediately makes this thesis concrete: "Jesus is there for others. That is the experience of transcendence." The question of chapter 2.b, "Who is God?" thus becomes the question "Who is Jesus Christ?" Bonhoeffer conceives the theological question christologically and expands it into an anthropological question: Who is the human being? Interestingly, the human being as such is not envisioned at all. The human being is the (worldly) Christian, and thus the question "who is the human being" becomes "what is faith?" Hence genuine anthropology is actual only within the christological inquiry.

148

The christological thesis "Jesus *is* there for others" becomes the sentence "faith is participation in this *being* of Jesus."[143] Christology and anthropology are apparently ontically connected. Religiously understood transcendence is not *there for others.* The "counterthesis, one critical of religion," underlying chapter 2 is "religion is *not* there for others."[144]

In a ring composition, Bonhoeffer closes with the second half of the sentence cited above and simultaneously fills out the concept of faith through the understanding of (Christian = new) life: ". . . our relationship to God (= *faith*, see preceding sentence) is a new *life in 'being for others,'* in *participation in Jesus' being.*"[145] Bonhoeffer radicalizes the christological thesis into a statement of faith and ultimately into a life statement. Life and faith are apparently dialectically related: Life can become *being for others* only when through faith it has come to *participate in Jesus' being.*[146] Faith does not remain mere participation in *Jesus' being,* but through participation in *Jesus' being* for others itself becomes *being for others.* Faith is thus the *ontic* presupposition of life. The concept of life radicalizes the concept of faith:

> *Life* as *being for others.*
> *Faith* as participation in *Jesus' being.*
> *Model:* Jesus is *there for others.*

Bonhoeffer had already underscored the significance of ontology[147] for Christology in his lectures on Christology in 1933:[148] ". . . the christological question is essentially an ontological question" (*GS* 3.172). After Christ, one can appropriately ask only "who" are you? That is, the admissible question is the one regarding "the being, essence, and nature of Christ" *(ibid.).* The purpose of the "who-question" is to "disclose the ontological structure of this who" *(ibid.).* At the beginning of his lectures on Christology, Bonhoeffer addresses especially the cognitive-theoretical problem of Christology. The *Outline* (1944) seems to presuppose the cognitive-theoretical insights of the lectures on Christology (1933). In 1933 he is already saying about the person of Christ: "This person is the transcendent" (*GS* 3.167). In 1944 he says about Jesus' humanity: "the person who lives from within the transcendent." He is apparently expanding Christology by the addition of "life," with the cognitive-theoretical grounding of Christology in 1933 becoming the life Christology of 1944; something is added to the simple cognitive-theoretical inquiry regarding the "who?" in the lectures on Christology. Bonhoeffer writes in the *Outline:*

"Jesus' 'being for others' is the experience of transcendence" (*WEN*, 414). The connecting link between the lectures on Christology and the *Outline* is found in the ontic grounding context: "The object of Christology is the personal structure of being of the whole historic Jesus Christ" (*GS* 3.178).

Reference to Christ's "being for others" already appears marginally in the lectures on Christology as well (*GS* 3.195), and does so — as in the *Outline* — initially without any connection with the church.[149] In 1933, the notion of *being for* does not appear as a basic christological statement, but as one among several answers to the question regarding the "place of Christ" (*GS* 3.194f.). "If we ask about the place of Christ, we are asking within the who-structure about the where-structure" (*GS* 3.194). The "where-question" is thus a subquestion of the "who-question." "If we turn the where-question back into the who-question, the answer is: Christ as the one who is there *pro me* is the mediator. That is his essence and his mode of existence. He is in the middle in a threefold fashion" (*GS* 3.195). The first point Bonhoeffer enumerates is ". . . in being for others" *(ibid.)*. Reference to *being for others* is in the lectures on Christology thus a subproblem of the dominating *pro-me* structure. In his formulations of *being for others,* Bonhoeffer probably was not able to draw primarily from his lectures on Christology in 1933, since the notion is not sufficiently developed there. In 1933, the cognitive-theoretical question occupies the foreground; on the other hand, the basic ontic decision in favor of a Christology in *being for others* has already been made. The *pro me*, however, does not simply become *pro aliis*, but is "replaced."[150] This radicalization of Christology in the *Letters and Papers* toward a focus on life is something new and challenging that should not be too hastily traced back to earlier material. The *Outline* no longer contains any trace of the *pro-me* structure that remained determinative into the *Ethics.*[151] Whereas in his lectures on Christology Bonhoeffer is more interested in asking about Jesus' person than about his being, quite the opposite is the case in the *Letters and Papers from Prison.* Between the christological conception of 1933 and the christological statements in the *Outline* of 1944, Bonhoeffer's encounter with Wilhelm Dilthey's historical philosophy of life took place, through whom he was able to relate "Christ *and* life" and to disclose the meaning of the concept of life for Christology. The *new* element of the *Outline* compared with the lectures on Christology or with *Act and Being* is that Bonhoeffer now radicalizes the ontic grounding of Christology *and* confronts it with life come of age.

If we now return to the text of the *Outline,* after the ring composition just observed in chapter 2.c we again find a negation, that is, a statement of what faith is *not,* then the exclamation: "God in human form!" more negations criticizing "religion as metaphysics,"[152] and in conclusion the positive statement: ". . . 'the human being for others!' thus the Crucified. The person who lives from within the transcendent." Bonhoeffer gives concrete reference, from the christological perspective on life, to the exclamation "God in human form!": the person who *lives* from within the transcendent, the person who through faith participates in "Jesus' being" (*WEN,* 414). Here *Jesus' being* means "incarnation, cross, resurrection" *(ibid.).*

In the *Outline,* Bonhoeffer addresses more fundamentally and comprehensively something he has already anticipated in the preceding letters. There he spoke about the believer participating in *Christ's suffering* in the world, that is, about participating in Jesus' being in the sense of the *theologia crucis.* He did not mention incarnation and resurrection, the other themes of Christology. Here in the *Outline,* he now addresses these fundamentals more comprehensively. That is, he is concerned with total participation in Jesus' being in the sense of all the themes of Christology. In an earlier *Ethics* fragment, he already emphasized how important he considered the totality of christological themes to be:

> The unity of incarnation, cross, and resurrection has probably become clear now. Christian life is life with the incarnate, crucified, and resurrected Jesus Christ, whose word as a whole we encounter in the justification of the sinner through grace. Christian life means being a human being through the incarnation, means being judged and pardoned through the cross, means living a new life in the power of the resurrection. The one cannot be had without the other.[153]

Here, too, Christology is accentuated from the perspective of life, these explications emphatically accentuating the thematic unity of Christology; thus, too, there is no *ontological* grounding of faith as participation in Jesus' *being.* Instead, Bonhoeffer formulates *ethically:* "Christian life is participation in the Christ-*movement* in the world."[154] Here in the *Ethics,* Bonhoeffer does not yet establish the connection between Christology and ontology as anticipated in the lectures on Christology. What we do encounter, however, is the important Bonhoeffer concept of "participation," which here in the *Ethics* fragment becomes the connecting link between the ultimate and the penultimate. The ultimate is actualized in the penultimate through "participation in the Christ movement."[155] The concept of participation appears already in *The Cost of Discipleship* of 1937,[156] though here, too, the concept is not conceived ontically as "participation in Jesus' being."

Put briefly: The *Outline* (1944) links the ontic grounding of Christology from the lectures on Christology (1933) with the concept of "participation" from *The Cost of Discipleship* (1937) and the *Ethics* (1940-43). Faith means participating in Jesus' *being (incarnation, cross, resurrection).*

The correspondence already reveals part of the theme, namely, the understanding of faith as the believer's participation in Christ's *suffering* (theme: the cross). It is not until the *Outline* that Bonhoeffer takes his christological insight in a fundamentally systematic-theological direction. (We again have an indication that something he addresses only in certain aspects in the Tegel correspondence is explicated more fully in the *Outline*.)

Chapter 2.c begins with the words: "Interpretation of biblical concepts from this perspective" (*WEN*, 414). We must first ask what these last three words mean. To what do they refer? Formally, they clearly refer to section 2.b. As far as content is concerned, we have observed that this particular section radicalizes the concept of life in its ontological determination from the perspective of faith. Does the expression "from this perspective" thus mean "from the perspective of life as being for others"? This is also suggested by the other observation, namely, that the entire chapter is based on the thesis of a critique of religion: "Religion is not there for others." Bonhoeffer's counterthesis is: "Life means being for others." In the flow of the whole, we thus read: *nonreligious* interpretation of biblical concepts from this perspective — that is, *from the perspective of life as being for others.* The concept of life understood in this way thus becomes the interpretive concept: "Interpretation of biblical concepts from this perspective (creation, Fall, reconciliation, penitence, faith, vita nova, ultimate things)." But how does this interpretation look when applied to the *biblical concepts?* Elsewhere, Bonhoeffer did try to interpret the concept of *penitence* nonreligiously.

In the letter of July 16, 1944 (*WEN*, 391f.), he spoke of the impossibility of performing a "salto mortale" back to the Middle Ages, and of the lone possibility of "honesty." There is no way back to

children's land — at least not through any arbitrary renunciation of inner honesty, but only in the sense of Matt. 18:3, that is, through penitence, that is, through *ultimate* honesty! And we cannot be honest without acknowledging that we must live in the world — "etsi deus non daretur." And precisely this is what we acknowledge — before God! . . . Thus does our coming of age lead to a more genuine acknowledgment of our situation before God. God lets us know that we must live as those who come to terms with life without God. . . . Before and with God, we live without God. (*WEN,* 394)

This theological passage must be cited in full in order that the course of argumentation become clear. We notice first of all that his observation about both God and world begins with human "life" (or better: life *come of age*). From the *perspective* of this "life come of age," he recognizes that "we must live in the world — 'etsi deus non daretur.'" Bonhoeffer links Dilthey's insight with Christology, and introduces the concept of honesty which he already used in earlier writings.[157]

Honesty requires recognition of the true predicament of human life before God. This is *penultimate* honesty, a stocktaking, unrestricted acknowledgment of a world come of age in which "God" is no longer demonstrable. *Ultimate* honesty is penitence. From the perspective of the *Outline,* penitence thus refers to the honest or sincere acknowledgment that one's participation in Jesus' being has in fact not come about! The Christian does penance as a result of the insight (possible only in *faith,* hence "ultimate") that one's *participation in Jesus' being* has not come about, and that this person is thus also *not there for others.* "That is the μετάνοια . . . to allow oneself to be swept along onto the path of Jesus Christ, into the messianic event" (*WEN,* 395). Honesty thus illustrates the concept of participating in Jesus' being in the understanding of penitence.[158] A person lives "before and with God without God" (*WEN,* 394).

Bonhoeffer is obviously taking the Markan passage seriously, incorporating it into his *theologia crucis* in the letter of July 16, 1944 (*WEN,* 394). "The God who is with us is the God who abandons us (Mark 15:34)!" Jesus becomes a God-forsaken person; but by abandoning Jesus, God does not cease to act. "Quite the contrary: *he acts by abandoning Jesus.*"[159] Jesus lives through the crucifixion — without God! Just as the human being Jesus lives without God here, so also the person who through faith gains a portion of Jesus' being so that the person's own life can become being for others; "participation in God's suffering in worldly life" is what constitutes a Christian (395). God is not demonstrable in the world of Jesus, nor in a world that since the Renaissance and Reformation has itself come of age. The historical analysis illustrates a christological point. The situation has become similarly *godless,* and thus *commensurate with Christ.* Thus it is precisely in a godless world that one can speak commensurately about the God of Jesus. In this sense, Bonhoeffer demands: "If one wants to speak about God 'nonreligiously,' one must speak about him such that this does not somehow conceal the godlessness of the world, but rather precisely discloses it, and in so doing casts a surprising light on the world. The world come of age is more godless and for just that reason perhaps closer to God than the world that has not come of age" (396). Bonhoeffer already says quite early: "God is beyond even in the middle of our lives" (letter of April 30, 1944). We should understand similarly the sentence: "Before and with God, we live without God" (letter of July 16, 1944). In the *Outline,* the *theological* dialectic of a God who is both here and beyond (letter of April 30, 1944) becomes the *christological* dialectic of *faith as life,* of faith as participation in *Jesus' being,* and of life as *being for others.*

If we follow the second chapter of the *Outline* further, we find that in chapter 2.d Bonhoeffer first picks up the theme of the cult: "Cult. (Later a more thorough discussion, specifically of the cult and 'religion'!)" (*WEN,* 415). He puts the word "religion" in quotation marks; he counts on the *cult* having a fixed place in the "writing" he is planning later.[160] By contrast, "religion" loses its place, becomes "homeless" — thus the quotation marks? We saw above that the traditional place of religion in the phenomenology of religion was the cult.[161] Bonhoeffer now overcomes the phenomenology of religion by linking his theological critique of religion with the historical analysis issuing in the thesis of religionlessness.[162] He expels religion from his theology. The place of the cult initially remains unoccupied, and Bonhoeffer asks whether this might be filled by the rediscovery of arcane discipline; outside the arcanum is nonreligion, a world come of age, life come of age; there the nonreligious interpretation sets about its work.[163] Arcane discipline and nonreligious interpretation remain mutually related to one another.[164]

This suggests that in chapter 2.d, Bonhoeffer intended to write about arcane discipline as the consequence for the *cult* in a religionless age. This represents a parallel to the letter of April 30, whose question concerning the meaning of the *cult* in religionlessness Bonhoeffer now addresses from a more fundamental angle: He gives the theme of arcane discipline a systematic place under the heading "Cult" (ch. 2.d).

The attendant question is: What does the cult mean in religionlessness? The likely answer is: the reintroduction of arcane discipline.

In chapter 2.e, Bonhoeffer picks up the question repeatedly anticipated in the letters: "What do we really believe?" (*WEN*, 415; cf. 344 and 200). He immediately gives this question a concrete reference with respect to life: ". . . i.e., such that we are attached to it with our very lives?" (415).[165] The two following questions confirm that Dilthey is providing the background here: "Problem of the Apostles' Creed? What must I believe?" (415). Bonhoeffer himself indicates that precisely this line of inquiry derives from *Weltanschauung und Analyse des Menschen seit Renaissance und Reformation*. In his notes from July 1944, he writes: "A confession of faith does not express what someone else 'must' believe, but what one believes oneself. . . . Dilthey 102" (*WEN*, 376).

As we saw, the reference is to *Weltanschauung und Analyse*, page 102. Bonhoeffer incorporates Dilthey's critique of confessions, a critique made from the perspective of the philosophy of life, into the context of the *Outline*. Why? He apparently expects that a confession of faith will relate faith *and* life to one another, and will do so such that "we" really are attached to it with our very *lives*.[166] This "we" is the "we" of the illegal, confessing Dahlemites;[167] these formulations thus become immediately comprehensible in the context of the church struggle in Germany. This ultimately also betrays the polemic against parts of the Confessing Church.[168] Here Bonhoeffer is illustrating a basically systematic-theological point — namely, confessional criticism — in an ecclesiastical-political example from contemporary events.

CHAPTER 3

The critique "religion is not there for others" (from ch. 1) has become the *christological* statement about Jesus, the human being "for others" (in ch. 2), and ultimately (in ch. 3) becomes the *ecclesiological* formula: "The church is a church only when it is there for others" (*WEN*, 415). Again, as between chapter 1 and chapter 2, the formulation *being for others* is the connecting link between chapter 2 and chapter 3, permeating the *Outline* as the basic ontological position. Bonhoeffer has his famous formula concerning the *church for others* culminate in the little-noticed sentence: The church "must tell people of all vocations what *life with Christ* is, what it means 'to be there for others'" (415f.; my emphasis).[169]

In this sentence, Bonhoeffer emphatically correlates the decisive themes of his Tegel theology to one another: church, Christ, human beings, and life. That he no longer addresses "religion" as a theme has a simple explanation: He has left the critique of religion behind in chapters 1 and 2b, and is now speaking about what follows from the historical critique of religion. Where one interprets nonreligiously, *religion* is no longer a question; the concern is with that which replaces religion, namely, *life with Christ.*

The formula *life with Christ* once again shows in an exemplary fashion how Bonhoeffer both appropriates Dilthey's thought and stands in contradiction to it. He adopts Dilthey's *concept of life* and interprets it christologically: *life with Christ.* The nonreligious interpretation is thus a christological interpretation taking its reference point in life; what one might call a "life-christological" interpretation.

Believing means participating in *Jesus' being.* Jesus' being is *being for others.* Accordingly, life means that, *like* Christ, one is there for others. Jesus' function as model acquires meaning in this *like.* In conclusion, Bonhoeffer reflects on the form of the church, on this *like.* The list of attributes ascribed to a *church for others* attests fulcral concepts associated with the philosophy of life, such as "moderation" and "authenticity" (416). Bonhoeffer interprets from a *Christian* perspective concepts deriving from the *philosophy of life.* This list of concepts is subordinated to the basic concept of the "model originating in Jesus' humanity" (416).

The concept of the *model* might also have acquired significance as a result of Bonhoeffer's reading of Dilthey. Our examination of Dilthey[170] revealed how the philosopher of life reflects on the "doctrine of *imitatio Christi* through model and religious experiencing (not doctrine!)" (*Weltanschauung und Analyse,* 504). Dilthey first of all distinguishes clearly between the cognitive character of "doctrine" on the one hand, and a comprehensive "imitation in life." He also speaks in this context about the model. These two observations together make it probable that Bonhoeffer's own "life-christological" reference to the model of Jesus was influenced by the historical philosophy of life. He finally says to Eberhard Bethge: "We must again and again contemplate the life of Jesus . . . in order to see what God promises and what he fulfills" (*WEN,* 425).

The notion of taking Jesus' humanity as a model is concerned with a comprehensive experience, with an experience of the model itself, since "it is not through the concept, but through the 'model' that its [the church's] word acquires emphasis and power" (*WEN,* 416).

On the whole, we find the basic theme of the *Letters and Papers from*

Prison[171] emerging behind the various themes of the *Outline* from chapter 1 to chapter 3: Behind the themes

religion — faith — church

or

critique of religion — nonreligious interpretation — religionlessness

stands the basic theme

Christian faith and life come of age

2. Thesis III

The result of Part III is the thesis: "The nonreligious interpretation is a life-christological interpretation relating Christian faith and life come of age to one another."

CONCLUSIONS

Nonreligious Interpretation and Religious Pluralism?

What does this analysis of the nonreligious interpretation mean for the question of religious pluralism?

Forty years after Bonhoeffer's thesis of religionlessness, the philosophy of religion concluded: "It is not religion that has proved to be an illusion, but the theory of religion."[1] In 1944, Dietrich Bonhoeffer is ahead of his time in renouncing any *theory* of religion; for him, religionlessness means the same as the lack of any theory of religion. He overcomes the dialectical-theological antithesis of religion and revelation. Instead of developing a *concept* of religion, the constructive impulse of a critique of religion remains alive for him through the inclusion of Dilthey's question concerning life come of age. Bonhoeffer is no longer concerned with religion, but with life. The *non*religious interpretation tells us what it means *not* to interpret in the sense of religion. Instead of the development of a theory of religion, we encounter in Bonhoeffer a loose understanding of religion. From this it follows that a dialogue within the framework of religious pluralism not only is possible on the basis of his theology, but is even imperative.

Bonhoeffer scholarship has rescued the demand for a "nonreligious interpretation" over four decades by pointing out that this refers to nothing other than a "christological interpretation." As correct as this observation is, it has remained just as unspecific. What does it mean *concretely* to *interpret christologically?* Our answer to this question is:

159

Nonreligious interpretation of biblical concepts means asking about the relevance of Jesus Christ for modern life come of age, and it means disclosing the meaning of biblical concepts for this earthly life here and now.

Bonhoeffer deciphered the philosophy of life's question concerning the "riddle of life" christologically. For him, the concept of life is a motif in the service of cognition in the Tegel theology, replacing any alleged concept of religion. The demand for a *nonreligious interpretation of biblical concepts* conceals the demand to *live one's faith: To live as to believe* means *believing* through "participation in Jesus' being" *as life* in "being for others."

Notes

INTRODUCTION

1. Letter of May 5, 1944; *WEN* (1985): 313.

2. Several different surveys examine the enormous number of secondary works on Bonhoeffer. Works from the 1950s are covered by R. Schulze in "Hauptlinien der Bonhoeffer-Interpretation," in *EvT* 25 (1965): 681-700; those from the 1960s and 1970s are covered by P. H. A. Neumann in his introduction to the collection *"Religionsloses Christentum" und "nicht-religiöse Interpretation" bei Dietrich Bonhoeffer* (1991), pp. 1-42. The most comprehensive and up-to-date survey of Bonhoeffer scholarship is found in E. Feil's double article "Aspekte der Bonhoeffer-Interpretation," in *TLZ* 117 (1992): 1-16, 81-100. A comprehensive view of German-speaking scholarship will soon be provided by H. M. Rumscheidt in *Religious Studies Review,* while a similar review of English-speaking scholarship will be provided by C. Green; cf. "Recent Bonhoeffer Scholarship in Europe and America," *Religious Studies Review* 123, no. 3 (July 1997): 219-30.

3. Cf. A. MacIntyre, "God and the Theologians," *Encounter* 21 (Nov. 1963): 3-10, no. 3.

4. Cf. A. E. Loen, *Secularization: Science without God?* (London, 1967), pp. 188ff.

5. Cf. B. Jaspert, *Frömmigkeit und Kirchengeschichte* (1986), pp. 76f.

6. Cf. J. Macquarrie, *God and Secularity: New Directions in Theology Today* III (Philadelphia, 1967), pp. 72ff.

7. Cf. W. Hamilton, "A Secular Theology for a World Come of Age," *Theology Today* 18 (1962), no. 440; cf. also J. A. T. Robinson, *Honest to God* (London, 1963; 1991[22]).

8. Cf. C. B. Armstrong, "Christianity without Religion," *CQR* 165 (1964):

175-84; M. D. Hunnex, "Religionless Christianity: Is It a New Form of Gnosticism?" *Christianity* 10/6 (Jan. 7, 1966): 7-99.

9. Cf. P. van Buren, *The Secular Meaning of the Gospel: Based on an Analysis of Its Language* (London: 1963).

10. Cf. K. M. Kodalle, *Dietrich Bonhoeffer. Zur Kritik seiner Theologie* (Gütersloh, 1991).

11. Cf. E. C. Bianchi, "Bonhoeffer and the Church's Prophetic Mission," *Theological Studies* (Baltimore) 28 (1967): 801-11.

12. Cf. G. Krause, "Bonhoeffer, Dietrich," *Theologische Realenzyklopädie* VII (Berlin, 1981): 55-66. Krause repeatedly draws attention to the merely derivative and secondary nature of Bonhoeffer's concepts (cf., e.g., *art. cit.,* 64, nn. 1 and 6).

13. The various interpretive schemata suggest the presence of misunderstandings with regard to Bonhoeffer, and from the perspective of the history of scholarship can be understood as a reaction to the secular interpretation of the 1960s. The assertion "God is dead!" prompted the response "Long live religion!" The declaration of war made by J. A. T. Robinson (*op. cit.,* 1963) or W. Hamilton (*op. cit.,* 1962) was followed by the religious "defensive measures" of those like A. MacIntyre (in *The Honest to God Debate* [Philadelphia, 1963], pp. 215-28), C. B. Armstrong (*art. cit.,* 1964), A. E. Loen (*op. cit.,* 1965), M. D. Hunnex (*art. cit.,* 1966), and J. Macquarrie (*art. cit.,* 1968). At the end of the 1960s, this "religious access" understandably comes to an end. The "secular attempt" failed; history has simply passed it by, and religion is "booming" again. It is quite informative nonetheless to take a look behind the scenes of the 1960s "battles": Quite apart from such "assault" (God is dead!) on the one hand, and "defense" (Long live religion!) on the other, genuine Bonhoeffer research did indeed take place. With regard to the topic of religion as such, this is evident, e.g., within German-speaking scholarship in the monograph by K.-H. Nebe, *Religionslose Interpretation bei Dietrich Bonhoeffer und ihre Bedeutung für die Aufgabe der Verkündigung* (diss., Hamburg, 1963), and in English-speaking scholarship in the S.T.M. thesis of C. Green, *Bonhoeffer's Concept of Religion: An Essay in Interpretation* (New York, 1964); with regard to the "whole" Bonhoeffer, one can mention E. Bethge's pioneering biography (*Dietrich Bonhoeffer: Man of Vision, Man of Courage* [Eng. trans., New York: Harper & Row, 1970; orig. German ed. 1967]). Other studies from the 1960s deal with particular aspects of Bonhoeffer's work or compare him with other thinkers. S. Wiltshire investigated Bonhoeffer's prison poetry ("Dietrich Bonhoeffer's Prison Poetry," *RelLife* 38/4 [1969]: 522-34), while M. Kuske wrote a monograph on the significance of the Old Testament in Bonhoeffer's thinking (*The Old Testament as the Book of Christ: An Appraisal of Bonhoeffer's Interpretation* (Eng. trans., Philadelphia, 1976]). E. B. Borowitz investigated Bonhoeffer's significance for Judaism ("Bonhoeffer's Come of Age," *Judaism* 14 (1965): 81-87. P. de Jong compared Bonhoeffer with A. Camus ("Camus and Bonhoeffer on the Fall," *CJT* 7 (1961): 245-57), and A. Levi found

a parallel with the Catholic theologian A. Delp ("Bonhoeffer and Delp: Papers from Prison," *The Month* [n.s.] 31 [1964]: 328-36).

14. J. Mark, "Bonhoeffer Reconsidered" *Theol* 641 (London, Nov. 1973): 586-93.

15. S. Plant, *The Use of the Bible in Bonhoeffer's Ethics* (diss., Cambridge, 1993), p. 71.

16. T. F. Torrance, "Cheap and Costly Grace," in *God and Rationality* (1971), chap. 3, pp. 56-85, citation on p. 74.

17. G. Ebeling, "The 'Non-religious' Interpretation of Biblical Concepts," in *Word and Faith* (Philadelphia, 1963): 98-161; first in *ZTK* 52 (1955): 296-360, then *MW* II (1956): 12-73.

18. This reduces the Bonhoeffer scholarship of the past forty years to the smallest common denominator; following Ebeling's article (*art. cit.,* 1955), the following scholars can be characterized as having understood the "nonreligious" interpretation as a "christological interpretation": J. D. Godsey, *The Theology of Dietrich Bonhoeffer* (Philadelphia, 1960); E. Bethge, "Bonhoeffer's Christology and His 'Religionless' Christianity," *USQR* 23/1 (1967): 61-77; E. Grin, "Dietrich Bonhoeffer et l'interprétation non-religieuse des notions bibliques," *ETR* 37 (1962): 115-37; K.-H. Nebe (*op. cit.,* 1963); R. H. Fuller, "World Come of Age: A Second Look at Bonhoeffer," in *Conflicting Images of Man* (New York, 1966), pp. 133-63; J. A. Phillips, *The Form of Christ in the World: A Study of Bonhoeffer's Christology* (New York, 1967); R. Ehrlich, "Some Observations on the New Theology and on Dietrich Bonhoeffer and His Ecclesiology," *SJT* 22/1 (March 1969); C. Gremmels, *Mündige Welt und Planung: Eine sozialethische Untersuchung zum Verhältnis von Planung und Geschichte* (1970); E. Feil, *The Theology of Dietrich Bonhoeffer* (Eng. trans., Philadelphia, 1985); G. B. Kelly, *Revelation in Christ: A Study of Dietrich Bonhoeffer's Theology of Revelation* (diss., Louvain, 1972); J. Mark, "Bonhoeffer Reconsidered," *Theol* 641 (1973): 586-93; C. Green, *The Sociality of Christ and Humanity: Dietrich Bonhoeffer's Early Theology, 1927-1933.* American Academy of Religion Dissertation Series 6 (Missoula, Mont., 1975); H.-E. Tödt, "Glauben in einer Religionslosen Welt," *IBF* 1 (1976): 98-106; K. Clements, "Worldliness or Unworldliness?" *SJT* 34 (1981): 531-49; W. Floyd, "Christ, Concreteness, and Creation in the Early Bonhoeffer," *USQR* 39 (1984): 101-14; A. Pangritz, *Dietrich Bonhoeffers Forderung einer Arkandisziplin* (Köln, 1988); E. H. Robertson, *Bonhoeffer's Heritage: The Christian Way in a World without Religion* (London, 1989); S. S. Yu, *Christologische Grundentscheidungen bei Dietrich Bonhoeffer* (diss., Tübingen, 1990); H.-J. Abromeit, *Das Geheimnis Christi: Dietrich Bonhoeffers erfahrungsbezogene Christologie* (Neukirchen-Vluyn, 1991).

I

1. Bonhoeffer relates his impressions of Islam in a letter to his parents from Tripoli on April 9, 1924: "Both religions — Islam and Israelite piety — must of

necessity be explicit religions of the law since national and cultic elements are so strongly mixed, or even coincide, as it were. Only thus can they attain the sharpest delineation from other races and religions. A religion that seeks to be a world religion, however, such as Christianity or Buddhism, cannot in any way be a religion of the law" (*DBW* 9.124).

2. "Luthers Stimmungen gegenüber seinem Werk in seinen letzten Lebensjahren. Nach seinem Briefwechsel von 1540-1546," *DBW* 9.271-305.

3. "Referat über historische und pneumatische Schriftauslegung," *DBW* 9.305-23. Its introductory sentence reads: "The Christian religion stands or falls with faith in the divine revelation that has become actual, tangible, and visible in history" (305f.).

4. *DBW* 9.324.

5. H. Pfeifer, *DBW* 9.324, n. 2, refers to E. Troeltsch, *Psychologie und Erkenntnistheorie.*

6. *DBW* 9.410-30.

7. *DBW* 9.510-16. Because Bonhoeffer had not yet taken his examinations, the sermon had to be checked first by an ordained theologian, and thus bears written remarks (cf. H. Pfeifer, *DBW* 9.510, n. 1).

8. *DBW* 1 (1986).

9. J. von Soosten, *DBW* 1.241, n. 4, refers to R. Seeberg, *Dogmatik,* 1.502ff., and later (n. 6) to *Dogmatik* 2.82ff. concerning "the expression of religion and morality in the conscience . . . of the natural person."

10. The critique of the church as a satisfaction of religious needs is attested within the larger context surrounding the questions of truth and needs in the waning 19th century, e.g., in the work of M. Kähler. With regard to Kähler, J. Wirsching, *Gott in der Geschichte* (Munich, 1963) p. 268, has shown that "the question of truth turns into a question of need: the measure of satisfaction of genuine or alleged needs is the measure of truthfulness." In the present context, this reference to M. Kähler means that a critique of religion in the form of a critique of the church was already present around the turn of the century; this attests a critique of F. Schleiermacher's understanding of religion within an ecclesiological context prior to Karl Barth!

11. "Jesus Christus und vom Wesen des Christentums," *DBW* 10.302-22. Regarding this lecture, Bonhoeffer wrote to his parents November 27, 1928: "I am currently working on my second lecture, which is to be delivered on December 11 and deals with the 'Essence of Christianity.' I had to formulate the topic in an extremely general fashion in order even to provide an overview of the problems" (*DBW,* 10.112). Anyone evaluating this essay is advised to exercise restraint to avoid succumbing to overinterpretation.

12. *DBW* 10.302; several sentences prior to this, Bonhoeffer formulates critically: "Christ is a matter of the church . . . not of life."

13. "Die Tragödie des Christentums und ihr bleibender Sinn," *DBW* 10.285-302.

14. Sermon on Rom. 11:6 (Third Sunday in Lent, March 11, 1928), *DBW* 10.455-60.

15. Sermon fragment on Luke 12:49 (Trinity Sunday, June 3, 1928), *DBW* 10.474-77.

16. Sermon on 2 Cor. 12:9 (Fourteenth Sunday after Trinity, September 9, 1928), *DBW* 10.505-11.

17. *DBW* 2 (1988); *Act and Being* (Minneapolis: Fortress Press, 1996).

18. E. Feil, *The Theology of Dietrich Bonhoeffer,* p. 169.

19. "The Question of the Human Being in Contemporary Philosophy and Theology. Inaugural Lecture on July 31, 1930," *DBW* 10.357-78. In this lecture, Bonhoeffer discusses the anthropological perspective in the choice between philosophy and theology. "Two great possibilities emerge: Human beings try to understand themselves from the perspective of their *work* or their *limitations*" (358).

20. "The Theology of Crisis and Its Attitude toward Philosophy and Science," *DBW* 10.434-49, 435.

21. Cf., e.g., *WEN,* 356f. The concepts "religion" and "metaphysics" appear in immediate proximity first in the essay "Concerning the Christian Idea of God" (1932), *DBW* 10.423-33, which states that "no religion, no ethics, no metaphysical knowledge may serve man to approach God" (433).

22. "Studienbericht für das Kirchenbundesamt," *DBW* 10.262-80.

23. Concerning the significance of American philosophy in the larger sense, cf. the "Studienbericht über das zweite Semester," *DBW* 10.281-82, 281: "A [. . .] large part of my work consisted in reading American philosophy in 'extra work' with Professor Lyman."

24. Concerning criticism of I. Kant from the perspective of a philosophy of life, cf. already W. Dilthey, "Preface" to *Introduction to the Human Sciences,* [partial] Eng. trans., ed. R. A. Makkreel and Frithjof Rodi, in *Wilhelm Dilthey Selected Works,* vol. 1 (Princeton: Princeton University Press, 1989), 1.50: "No real blood flows in the veins of the knowing subject constructed by Locke, Hume, and Kant, but rather the diluted extract of reason as a mere activity of thought." [In the following discussions, the German original is cited for material not included in the English translation. Trans.]

25. This essay also repeatedly mentions the connection between religion and individualism. The concept of "religious individualism" is for Bonhoeffer a key concept in understanding and critiquing American theology, which in his view has an "individualistic understanding of life" (270); he also found that American Protestantism had a "churchless individualistic character," and that there was no confessional development because of this "general religious individualism" (276). Even the thinking of Fundamentalism he found to be "basically individualistic." "Yet even if religiously this position is unequivocally caught up in a process of dissolution, its strength is still almost unbroken in the social and ethical thinking of even enlightened Americans" (277).

26. In a letter from December 1930, Bonhoeffer exercises extreme reserve in commenting on the church's reception of James: "James's wisdom concerning

the finite God resides deep within most theologians and pastors, who find it profound and modern and do not at all sense the cheeky thoughtlessness of such talk" (letter to Superintendent M. Distel, December 19, 1930; *DBW* 10.219-21; citation on 221).

27. "Das social gospel" [sic], *GS* 1.104-12, citation on 108.

28. *Ibid.,* 110.

29. Edited by O. Dudzus as a compilation of student notes, *GS* 5.181-227; the new edition of the lectures, edited by E. Amelung, essentially follows the notes of Joachim Kanitz, *DBW* 11.139-213.

30. *DBW* 11.145 (the following page numbers also refer to this edition).

31. Published as a compilation of student notes in *GS* 5.227-75; according to the copy by Hanns Rüppell in *DBW* 11.239-303. The following pagination refers to the Dudzus compilation and is complemented where appropriate by the Rüppel copy.

32. Cited according to the Rüppel copy, *DBW* 11.253; concerning the critique of religion, cf. also 277-80.

33. *GS* 3.270-85.

34. Cf. E. Feil, *The Theology of Dietrich Bonhoeffer,* pp. 169f.

35. *DBW* 3 (1989).

36. I. Tödt and M. Rüter in *DBW* 3.163f.; in my opinion, Friedrich Nietzsche is already present in the background of the lecture "Your Kingdom Come" in Bonhoeffer's reference to provincialists; cf. F. Nietzsche, "On Provincialists," in *Thus Spoke Zarathustra.*

37. "Recent Theology: A Discussion of Recent Systematic-Theological Publications," *GS* 5.300-340. This lecture, too, is preserved only in student copies; cf. the foreword by the editor, O. Dudzus, *op. cit.,* pp. 300-302.

38. *GS* 3.166-242.

39. This corresponds to the view of E. Feil, *The Theology of Dietrich Bonhoeffer,* pp. 107ff., according to which the topic of religion reaches a temporary high point in Bonhoeffer's work in the year 1932, and then recedes in the following years (with the *Christology* and *The Cost of Discipleship*). Feil compares the writing of *The Cost of Discipleship* with Luther's withdrawal to the monastery (128), and E. Bethge, *Dietrich Bonhoeffer. Christ, Theologe, Zeitgenosse* (Munich, 1967), p. 760, pregnantly characterizes the relationship between *The Cost of Discipleship* and the *Ethics* as "the world for Christ" and "Christ for the world." According to E. Feil, it is only in the *Ethics* and the Tegel correspondence that Bonhoeffer's treatment of religion and of the attendant understanding of the world reaches its real culmination (*The Theology of Dietrich Bonhoeffer,* pp. 138ff. and 160ff.).

40. Hegel is also treated under the subtitle of docetic heresies, which hold that "Christ God is substance, Jesus man is *accidens*" (*GS* 3.209). There is probably some connection here with Bonhoeffer's Hegel seminar during the same semester (cf. *Internationales Bonhoeffer Forum* 8 [1988]: 96).

41. Published as student notes under the title *Dietrich Bonhoeffers Hegel-Seminar 1933. Nach Aufzeichnungen von Ferenc Lehel,* edited by I. Tödt, *Inter-*

nationales Bonhoeffer Forum 8 (Munich, 1988). The Hungarian student Ferenc Lehel attended Bonhoeffer's classes in 1933. His (fragmentary) notes are the only material that has been preserved from this dogmatic-philosophical class and have been published in this historical-critical edition along with the Hegel volumes discussed.

42. For example, Bonhoeffer's comment on Hegel's statement "in devotion . . . God is for me" (vol. 12.145) is "God's advent to me. To know God as to be known by God" (*Bonhoeffers Hegel-Seminar 1933,* p. 15). Bonhoeffer underlined the expression "for me" *(ibid.)* from the Hegel citation; it was apparently important to him — in the sense of the Lutheran "pro me"? Lehel recollects that Bonhoeffer was concerned with a "theological reception of Hegel," esp. with respect to Lutheran elements in Hegel's philosophy. The catch phrase from Tegel concerning "being drawn in," one that was so important to Bonhoeffer, was similarly borrowed from Hegel (cf., e.g., *WEN,* 395).

43. Cf. *GS* 4.17-153; *DBW* 11.375-466.

44. *DBW* 11.378.

45. *DBW* 11.388.

46. *Ibid.,* 389.

47. *Ibid.,* 437.

48. *Ibid.,* 438.

49. *Ibid.,* 440.

50. *GS* 4.89.

51. *Ibid.,* 4.142.

52. *Ibid.,* 4.126.

53. *Ibid.,* 3.303-24.

54. Although the expression "autonomy" is indeed attested earlier in Bonhoeffer's writings, it is used there in connection with his portrayal of other theologians or philosophers, e.g., of Luther (1926: *DBW* 9.380), I. Kant or M. Heidegger (1930: *DBW* 2.133), F. Gogarten (1932: *GS* 5.286, 322), and W. Stapel (1932: *GS* 5.333). Without explicitly using the term "autonomy," the historical considerations in Bonhoeffer's sermon cited above (June 12, 1932) have been placed into an anthropological argumentative framework that understands as "autonomous" the development of the human being who thinks in a commensurately modern fashion. The word "autonomy," however, does not occur in this passage.

55. Bonhoeffer's reference to "autonomous self-understanding" from *Act and Being* (*DBW* 2.133) already appears in this negative light; there he turns against a doctrine of revelation dictated by ontology and Transcendental Philosophy.

56. The concept of "honesty," of significance for the Tegel correspondence, is also attested in this lecture (*GS* 3.305). In connection with his explications of a Christianity that needs to be justified before the world, Bonhoeffer writes that "it is now merely a question of honesty that one completely loses all interest in this construction and turns away from it. This evocation of the Christian message

leads directly to paganism, whence it also follows that the difference between German Christians and so-called neo-pagans is merely one of honesty" (304f.).

57. *GS* 4.202-4.

58. *Ibid.,* 4.187-89.

59. *Ibid.,* 4.427-34.

60. *GS* 3.325-34.

61. *DBW* 4 (1989).

62. "Luthers Stimmungen gegenüber seinem Werk in seinen letzten Lebensjahren. Nach seinem Briefwechsel von 1540-1546," *DBW* 9.271-305; citation on 300.

63. Bonhoeffer continues on the same page: "Christianity without discipleship is always Christianity without Jesus Christ; it is idea, myth." This sentence is found almost verbatim in the diary selections of Kierkegaard edited by W. Kütemeyer and published in 1943 (p. 163); cf. T. Vogel, *Christus als Versöhner. Eine kritische Studie zum Problem des Verhältnisses von Gesetz und Evangelium im Werke Sören Kierkegaards* (1968), p. 299.

64. With regard to this citation, M. Kuske and I. Tödt remark that "the catch words in this sentence allude to National Socialism, to which large parts of the church were accommodating themselves" (*DBW* 4.102, no. 10).

65. So M. Kuske and I. Tödt, *DBW* 4.241, no. 4, and 299, nn. 7 and 8. The editors adduce Bonhoeffer's criticism of Hegel from the lectures on "Christology" (cf. *GS* 3.211f.).

66. *DBW* 4.242, no. 11.

67. M. Kuske and I. Tödt refer to E. Troeltsch, *Soziallehren,* 125 (cf. *DBW* 4.261, no. 72).

68. See n. 63 above.

69. *Life Together: Prayerbook of the Bible. Dietrich Bonhoeffer Works,* vol. 5 (Eng. trans., Minneapolis: Fortress Press, 1996) = *DBW* 5 (1987).

70. Cf. in this regard G. L. Müller and A. Schönherr: "The inner connection between worldliness and arcane discipline explains perhaps why precisely the *Letters and Papers from Prison* and *Life Together* have become the most widely read and familiar of Bonhoeffer's books" (*DBW* 5.143). (Sentence not quoted in the English *DBW,* cited according to the German *DBW.*)

71. Cf. A. Pangritz, *Dietrich Bonhoeffers Forderung einer Arkandisziplin* (Köln, 1988), pp. 209f.

72. Diary entry on June 18, 1939, *GS* 1.300.

73. "Protestantism without Reformation," composed in August 1939, *GS* 1.323-54.

74. *Life Together: Prayerbook of the Bible. Dietrich Bonhoeffer Works,* vol. 5, pp. 141-77.

75. Cf. also the attempts to interpret the Old Testament christocentrically; cf. in this regard E. Bethge, *Dietrich Bonhoeffer. Christ, Theologe, Zeitgenosse,* p. 766, and generally also M. Kuske, *The Old Testament as the Book of Christ: An Appraisal of Bonhoeffer's Interpretation* (Eng. trans., Philadelphia, 1976), pp. 33ff.

76. *GS* 3.421-25.

77. The concept of "coming of age" is also found in a nontheological context as early as 1933. In the lecture "The Leader and the Individual" (*GS* 2.22-38), Bonhoeffer demands that a leader guide followers to "genuine maturity" rather than to "self-incapacitation" (36).

78. *DBW* 6 (1992).

79. Cf. the tabular survey in *DBW* 6.16-17.

80. Cf. *DBW* 6.84, no. 81.

81. Letter of December 5, 1943 (*WEN*, 176).

82. Letter of January 29 and 30, 1944 (*WEN*, 223f.; *ibid.* also the following citation).

83. Cf. *DBW* 4.117f.; concerning the interpretive problem, cf. G. Class, *Der verzweifelte Zugriff auf das Leben* (Neukirchen, 1994), pp. 159ff., 233f.

84. Letter of June 25, 1942, *GS* 2.419-21.

85. Here Bonhoeffer writes: "Let me quickly formulate once more the topic with which I am concerned: Jesus Christ's claim on the world come of age" (*WEN*, 375).

86. This context also illuminates the sense of the sentence from April 30, 1944, which underscored the correct relationship between transcendence and immanence: "God is transcendent even at the center of our lives" (308).

87. Concerning the "religious act," Bonhoeffer writes that "it is not some religious act that makes a Christian, but participation in God's own suffering amid worldly life" (*WEN*, 395).

88. Cf. E. Bethge, *Dietrich Bonhoeffer*, 780.

89. Cf. *ibid.*

90. See A.1 above.

91. See A.2 above.

92. See A.3 above.

93. R. Bernhardt, *Der Absolutheitsanspruch des Christentums. Von der Aufklärung bis zur pluralistischen Religionsauffassung* (Gütersloh, 1993²), p. 68.

94. Cf. *DBW* 9.324, n. 2, where Bonhoeffer is indirectly criticizing E. Troeltsch's doctrine of the "religious a priori," a critique that continues from *Act and Being* on into the Tegel theology (cf. *DBW* 2.51f.; *WEN*, 305), and yet seems to be disrupted by the *Ethics*. In the ethics-fragment "Inheritance and Decay," Bonhoeffer seems to be presupposing the doctrine of the "religious a priori" by suggesting that "western godlessness," precisely as "western," is not denying the "theoretical existence of a God." "Rather, it is itself religion, religion born of enmity toward God" (*DBW* 6.113). The anthropological "locus" of religion does not remain unoccupied; "not until his prison letters does Bonhoeffer overcome this *horror vacui*" (P. Köster, "Nietzsche als verborgener Antipode in Bonhoeffers 'Ethik,'" *Nietzsche-Studien* 19 [1990] 367-418, citation on 407).

95. Cf. the lectures on Christology (1933), *GS* 3.166-242 (here: 170). According to the previous assertion, precisely the "how-question" would have to be the "religious question."

96. Cf. *WEN,* 305.

97. Positive statements about religion are not found only in writings Bonhoeffer composed as a student, that is, not just in reports and seminar papers *before* 1927. Just as with the statements critical of religion, so also does a survey of the positive statements reveal that the latter do not in fact stand in any discernible connection, but rather seem to be merely strewn about. Quite unburdened by the criticism of religion, Bonhoeffer repeatedly relates "religion and morality"; this occurs first in 1926, after he first was able to speak in concurrence about the commonality of "the religious possession" (*DBW* 9.418) in a paper for A. von Harnack. In 1927 this same coupling reappears — and again in a positive context — in the dissertation he wrote for R. Seeberg (*DBW* 1.68). In an altered form, the reference to the "religious possession" as "possession of God" then recurs in 1928 in a sermon (*DBW* 10.296). The coupling "religion and morality" occurs in 1928 in the variant "morals and religion" (cf. *DBW* 10.475).

98. "The History of Systematic Theology in the 20th Century," lecture from the winter semester of 1931/32, *GS* 5.181-227, citation on 219 (my emphasis). In this sentence I am following the Dudzus compilation.

99. Cf., e.g., the concept of person in *Sanctorum Communio* from 1927 (*DBW* 1.130, n. 68), where we see Bonhoeffer struggling to establish conceptual clarity. Both sociality and individuality are posited in the concept of person. As late as 1944 in the *Letters and Papers from Prison,* Bonhoeffer is still seeking an unequivocal definition of certain concepts. On January 23, 1944, he reflects on the concept of friendship: "It must probably be understood as a sub-concept of the concept of culture and education, while brotherhood falls under the concept of church and camaraderie under that of work and of the political" (*WEN,* 216). This conceptual analysis acquires significance for Bonhoeffer because "friendship" does not have any divine mandate at its disposal, and thus cannot be incorporated into the doctrine of mandates in his ethics; cf. *DBW* 6.392ff., 397f.

100. Cf. *Church Dogmatics,* I/2, §17, 280ff.

101. In the study *Gedanken über die religiöse Problematik der Gegenwart im Licht der Theologie der Religionen* (Frankfurt am Main, 1986), I. Asouzu has recently considered the outline of a "theology of religions." In this study, Asouzu presents various recent religio-philosophical conceptions and understands them as issuing into the view of religion presented by Pannenberg (50ff.), which he then expressly affirms (103f.). According to Asouzu, one of the most significant features of Pannenberg's concept of religion is the "anthropological method" he follows (52ff.). In a subsection, Asouzu then explicates the "special position occupied by human beings in the cosmos" as a theme in Pannenberg's philosophical anthropology (57f.). Similarly, in the section on the "anthropological method," he deals with the connection between Pannenberg and William James (61f.); this connection is found not only in the anthropological procedure as such, but also in the fact that for both, religion constitutes an essential constituent part of their philosophical systems.

102. W. Pannenberg, *Systematic Theology,* vol. I (Eng. trans., Grand Rapids:

Wm. B. Eerdmans, 1996), pp. 119ff. The formulation of the topic (namely, of religion*s*) already suggests that the concern is not just with "the Christian concept of religion," something the specifically Christian doctrine of the Trinity also presupposes.

103. This results in awkward circumscriptions, such as "the existence or working of God or the gods" (*op. cit.,* p. 152), "the reality and operation of God or of the gods" (cf. *op. cit.,* p. 157, where the English translation has — significantly — been smoothed over to read "divine reality and operation"), to mention but two examples. Commensurate with a commitment to nonchristological language, "Jesus Christ" is not even mentioned explicitly in chapter 3, while Jesus of Nazareth is mentioned twice at the end of the chapter.

104. He also includes the topic of religion*s,* whereas Bonhoeffer speaks of religion*s* only in isolated instances in sermons, and even there always in a critical connection with piety; cf. 1931 (*DBW* 11.388); 1935 (*GS* 4.187); 1938 (*GS* 4.431). The critique of religion, following the position of dialectical theology, includes the critique of religions (cf. I. Asouzu, *op. cit.,* p. 41).

105. Cf., e.g., "Weltanschauung und Analyse des Menschen seit Renaissance und Reformation," *Gesammelte Schriften* II (^{2}1921).

106. In the three volumes of his *Systematic Theology,* we find that taking Augustine as his point of departure is important for Pannenberg within the framework of an ecumenical theology. To mention but one example, cf. from vol. 3 (original German edition) the discussion of his understanding of the sacraments (265ff., here esp. 268, 284, 287f.). Cf. also in this connection Pannenberg's work on the ecumenical document *Lehrverurteilungen — Kirchentrennend?, I. Rechtfertigung, Sakramente und Amt im Zeitalter der Reformation und heute,* ed. K. Lehmann and W. Pannenberg (1986). The question remains whether, first, this is an appropriate understanding of Reformational theology — and even of Catholic theology (Trent!) — (cf., e.g., the discussion of "justification," *op. cit.,* pp. 35ff. and 59f.), and whether, second, this "backward salto mortale" in the sense of historical development is not rather a "desperate step that can be taken only by sacrificing intellectual honesty" (cf. Bonhoeffer, *WEN,* 393f.).

107. *WEN,* 426.

108. *Ibid.,* 306.

109. Concerning the "cult" as a religious phenomenon, cf. G. van der Leeuw, *Phänomenologie der Religion* (Tübingen, 1933; 1977^3), pp. 509f. According to Pannenberg, it is the cult that "overcomes our separation from the deity" (*op. cit.,* p. 173). Pannenberg is following Hegel insofar as it is Hegel who allegedly conceives the concept of the cult most broadly within the study of religion *(ibid.).*

110. A. Pangritz, "Aspekte der 'Arkandisziplin' bei Dietrich Bonhoeffer," *TLZ* 119 (1994), cols. 755-68, citation 765.

111. Cf. *WEN,* 328.

112. Cf. A. Pangritz, *art. cit.,* col. 764.

113. In the German edition of my book, *Glauben als Leben. Dietrich Bonhoeffer und die nichtreligiöse Interpretation biblischer Begriffe* (Frankfurt am

Main: Peter Lang, 1996), I have on pp. 255-345 discussed virtually the entirety of scholarship on the topic of religionlessness.

114. Here a series of important studies can be mentioned that have investigated the influence of Barth on Bonhoeffer: J. D. Godsey, *op. cit.* (1958), see introduction above; E. Bethge, "The Challenge of Dietrich Bonhoeffer's Life and Theology," *Chicago Theological Seminary Register* 51/2 (1961): 1-38; W. O. Fennel, "Dietrich Bonhoeffer: The Man of Faith in a World Come of Age," *CJT* 8 (1962): 172-80; E. Grin, "Dietrich Bonhoeffer et l'interprétation non-religieuse des notions bibliques," *ETR* 37 (1962): 115-37; D. Jenkins, *Beyond Religion: The Truth and Error in "Religionless Christianity"* (1962); W. Lillie, "Worldliness of Christianity," *ET* 75 (1963/64): 132-37; J. Richmond, "Dietrich Bonhoeffer's Attack on Christian Existentialism," *RMS* 8 (1964): 92-108; W. J. Peck, "A Proposal concerning Bonhoeffer's Concept of Person," *ATR* 50 (1968): 311-29; H.-E. Tödt, "Glauben in einer Religionslosen Welt," *IBF* 1 (1976): 98-106.

115. With regard to Bonhoeffer's reception of philosophy in connection with his Tegel theology, I would like to mention esp. E. Feil and C. Gremmel's study of Bonhoeffer's dependence on Dilthey (*op. cit.,* see introduction above); this was then continued by D. Hopper, *A Dissent on Bonhoeffer* (Philadelphia, 1975); G. L. Müller, *Für andere da. Christus-Kirche-Gott in Bonhoeffers Sicht der mündig gewordenen Welt* (Paderborn, 1980); E. G. Wendel, *Studien zur Homiletik Dietrich Bonhoeffers. Predigt-Hermeneutik-Sprache* (Tübingen, 1985); B. Jaspert, *op. cit.* (1986), see introduction above; E. H. Robertson, *op. cit.* (1989), see introduction above; K. Bartl, *Theologie und Säkularität. Die theologischen Ansätze Friedrich Gogartens und Dietrich Bonhoeffers zur Analyse und Reflexion der säkularisierten Welt* (Frankfurt am Main, 1990); and H.-J. Abromeit, *op. cit.* (1991), see introduction above. In addition to the influence of Dilthey, other aspects of Bonhoeffer's treatment of philosophy have also been researched: J. Richmond, *op. cit.* (1964) (see above) illuminated Bonhoeffer's reception of Kierkegaard, while H. Mottu, "Feuerbach and Bonhoeffer: Criticism of Religion and the Last Period of Bonhoeffer's Thought," *USQR* 25/1 (1969): 1-18, focused on Bonhoeffer's dependence on Feuerbach. D. Thomasma, "Dietrich Bonhoeffer: Religionless Christianity," *RUO* 39 (1969): 406-25, investigates Kierkegaard's and Nietzsche's influence on Bonhoeffer. H. Obayashi, "The World Come of Age: Cultural Fact or Faith's Demand?" *USQR* 26/1 (1970): 99-116, and S. Picken, "Kant and Man's Coming of Age," *SJT* 26/1 (1973): 63-70, illuminate Kant's influence on Bonhoeffer. P. H. Ballard, "Bonhoeffer on Providence in History," *SJT* 27 (1974): 268-86, focuses on the influence of German Idealism; D. Hopper, *op. cit.* (1975) on that of Dilthey. G. B. Kelley, "Bonhoeffer's Nonreligious Christianity: Antecedents and Critique," *Bijdr* 37 (1976): 118-45, and T. R. Peters, *Die Präsenz des Politischen in der Theologie Dietrich Bonhoeffers* (Munich, 1976) both address the influence of Nietzsche. S. R. Sutherland, "Ethics and Transcendence in Bonhoeffer," *SJT* 30 (1977): 543-54, investigates the influence of Kant on Bonhoeffer.

II

1. E. Bethge, *Dietrich Bonhoeffer*, p. 52.

2. Cf. *ibid.*, pp. 50f.

3. Cf. *NL*, p. 195.

4. In a letter of August 31, 1925, Paula Bonhoeffer asks her son Dietrich: "Could you send along to me here in Kissingen the volume by Barth which you sent to Uncle Hans" (*DBW* 9.155), referring to Hans von Hase, to whom Bonhoeffer had loaned *Das Wort Gottes und die Theologie* (*ibid.*, nn. 4f.).

5. E. Bethge, *Dietrich Bonhoeffer*, p. 51.

6. In *Das Wort Gottes und die Theologie. Gesammelte Vorträge* (Munich, 1924), pp. 70-98; cf. also English translation *The Word of God and the Word of Man* (New York, 1957).

7. Cf. B.-E. Benktson, "Kristus och den myndigvordna världen," *STK* 40 (1964): 65-113.

8. E. Bethge, *Dietrich Bonhoeffer*, p. 51.

9. R. Widmann, cited according to E. Bethge, *Dietrich Bonhoeffer*, p. 54; cf. also *DBW* 9.157ff.

10. Cf. *NL*, p. 194; in a report, Bonhoeffer himself mentions, e.g., Karl Barth, "Menschenwort und Gotteswort in der christlichen Predigt," *Zwischen den Zeiten* 3 (1925): 119ff., and Barth's essay "Das Schriftprinzip der reformierten Kirche," *Zwischen den Zeiten* 3 (1925): 215ff. (cf. *DBW* 9.305, n. 1).

11. See Part I.A.

12. Concerning Holl's influence on Bonhoeffer, cf. J. von Soosten, *Die Sozialität der Kirche. Theologie und Theorie der Kirche in Dietrich Bonhoeffers "Sanctorum Communio"* (Munich, 1992), pp. 159ff.

13. *DBW* 9.350; the inserted citation comes from Barth's *Römerbrief*, p. 462; cf. the reference in *DBW* 9.350, n. 67.

14. *DBW* 9.377; Bonhoeffer references his quotation as coming from Barth's *Römerbrief*, 134f.; *ibid.*, n. 65 of the seminar paper.

15. *DBW* 9.443f.; citation from Barth's *Römerbrief*, p. 255; cf. the reference in *DBW* 9.444., n. 15.

16. H. Pfeifer, *DBW* 9.628.

17. *DBW* 1 (1986).

18. In R. Seeberg, *Dogmatik*, 1.152, we read that "faith appropriates into itself the dominion of God coming from above, and love, ascending from below to above, gives itself over to the creation of the Kingdom of God." Seeberg recognizes two levels of the religious community, "a double movement." "Religion shows itself to be a concern of humankind insofar as it establishes community" (152). Above this there is the "second, higher" level *(ibid.)*. Hence Seeberg, too, understands his view as beginning "from above," even though he identifies religion with Christianity. These citations are found in the first chapter of his *Dogmatics* under the subtitle "The Essence of Religion and the Demonstration of Chris-

tianity as the Absolute Religion" (15-222), an examination occupying over two hundred pages! This could not fail to leave some impression on Bonhoeffer.

19. E. Troeltsch, *The Social Teaching of the Christian Churches* (Eng. trans., Louisville, 1992) 69ff., in his presentation of the Pauline understanding of the church, equates the "independent religious community" on the one hand, and the "cultic congregation" on the other (70). "The religious community is the Body of Christ into which men are incorporated through Baptism, and through which they are fed and nourished by the Supper of the Lord" *(ibid.)*.

20. J. von Soosten, *DBW* 1.262, n. 71, refers to Karl Barth, *Römerbrief*, 211ff., 314ff., 346ff., 375ff. These pages correspond to chaps. 7 and 9–11 of the commentary.

21. Karl Barth, *Der Römerbrief* (1922) (Zurich; reprint of 13th ed. 1984).

22. In *Christus und die Religion* (1967), p. 59, Benktson suspects the presence of such a dialectic of grace and religion; but contra Benktson, cf. already H.-J. Kraus, *Theologische Religionskritik* (Neukirchen-Vluyn, 1982) p. 37, who alternatively views the *Letter to the Romans* from the perspective of "faith or religion" *(ibid.,* p. 7).

23. A. Ritschl, *Rechtfertigung und Versöhnung,* III (1888), p. 508.

24. Cf. *ibid.,* pp. 105, 124, 274.

25. Elsewhere in *Sanctorum Communio,* Bonhoeffer refers in a basically positive fashion to Ritschl; cf. *DBW* 1.88, n. 10; 105, n. 24; 150, n. 92; 166, n. 110. In these passages, he is adducing Ritschl as an example; elsewhere, he draws from Ritschl in opposing Schleiermacher, cf. 112, n. 32. Bonhoeffer cannot follow Ritschl's distinction between the Kingdom of God and the church, since he considers this distinction "both theologically and sociologically untenable" (147, n. 85; cf. also 198).

26. When Bonhoeffer later criticizes religion under the aspect of partiality, he doubtless is not drawing from Ritschl's concept of religion!

27. In his own footnote to this sentence, Bonhoeffer advises the reader to compare the "appropriate explications in Karl Barth, 'Auferstehung der Toten,' 1924, pp. 97f." (*DBW* 1.98, n. 15).

28. *DBW* 1.111, n. 29; concerning the lack of any concrete concept of person, cf. 130, n. 68.

29. J. von Soosten, *DBW* 1.265, n. 117; here also the reference to the connection between *Sanctorum Communio* and the *Letter to the Romans,* pp. 435ff.

30. With regard to the topic "love of one's neighbor," Bonhoeffer goes beyond R. Seeberg, whose *Dogmatics* (vol. II, pp. 524ff.) stops with the determination of the mutual relationship between faith and love. "In faith, Christians are sanctified; in love, they sanctify themselves through the impulses they receive in faith" (528). Neither is any explicit treatment of the topic "love of one's neighbor" found in the ethical section of the *Dogmatics* (cf. §§33ff. in vol. II, 229ff.; cf. similarly the reference to ethics on 527).

31. Contra the *Letter to the Romans,* which Bonhoeffer cites in brackets, Bonhoeffer writes (110, n. 28) critically "that love genuinely loves the other

person, and not the One in the other — who perhaps does not even exist (double predestination! *Barth,* p. 437) — that precisely this love for the other person as the other person is supposed to 'glorify God' (438). What gives *Barth* the right to say that the other is 'in and for himself infinitely of no consequence' (437) if God commands us to love precisely that person? God has made our 'fellow in and for himself' infinitely important, and for us there is no other 'in and for himself of our fellow.'" In what follows, Bonhoeffer then follows, contra Barth, the *Lutheran* interpretation of love of one's neighbor given by Rudolf Bultmann; cf. *op. cit.,* p. 111, n. 28.

32. Concerning the relationship Barth-Bonhoeffer in the light of the Reformed and Lutheran traditions, cf. A. Pangritz, *Karl Barth in der Theologie Dietrich Bonhoeffers — eine notwendige Klarstellung* (Berlin, 1989), pp. 31ff. Pangritz sees Barth's influence on Bonhoeffer commencing as early as Bonhoeffer's seminar papers in 1925 and 1926 (25) and remaining essentially determinative even into the cell at Tegel. Neither, according to Pangritz, do *Sanctorum Communio* and *Act and Being* cloud the close theological relationship between Barth and Bonhoeffer (31f.). Pangritz interprets Bonhoeffer's reserved attitude toward Barth in *Sanctorum Communio* against the background of the Berlin Luther scholarship: K. Holl (32). Bonhoeffer steps up as a Lutheran against the *extra Calvinisticum*, an attitude culminating in *Act and Being: "God is free not of human beings, but for human beings" (DBW* 2.85). Pangritz remarks that "without a doubt, here a Lutheran is protesting against the Reformed *non capax*" (35).

33. Karl Barth, *Der Römerbrief,* p. 428.

34. Neither does the influence of Barth's *Dogmatics in Outline* (*DBW* 1.172ff.) alter anything in this regard.

35. H. Pfeifer, *DBW* 9.2.

36. *DBW* 10.316.

37. *DBW* 10.319.

38. Karl Barth, *Der Römerbrief* (1922), p. 32. Concerning the expression "religion as unbelief," cf. Barth's explications in *Church Dogmatics,* I/2, 297ff.

39. *DBW* 10.457. Bonhoeffer may previously have read Barth's commentary on Romans regarding this passage, in which the repeated "grace *alone*" is quite noticeable (cf. *Der Römerbrief,* 381). The editors of *DBW* 10 observe a "strong resonance" (457, n. 7) of Barth's early essay collection "Das Wort Gottes und die Theologie," and refer the reader to pp. 8ff. and 24-31 there.

40. *DBW* 10.509.

41. Karl Barth, *Der Römerbrief* (1922), p. 241.

42. *DBW* 10.509.

43. Karl Barth, *Der Römerbrief* (1922), p. 212.

44. *DBW* 10.513.

45. H.-R. Reuter, *DBW* 2.7 in the German edition, refers to the seminar report from the summer semester of 1925 (*DBW* 9.305ff.).

46. Cf. H.-R. Reuter, *DBW* 2.33, n. 1.

47. J. H. Burtness, "Als ob es Gott nicht gäbe," *IBF* 6 (1983): 167-83, citation on 168.

48. E. Seeberg apparently passed on to Bonhoeffer E. Troeltsch's reference to the religious a priori. Concerning more recent discussion, cf. F. W. Veauthier, "Das religiöse Apriori: Zur Ambivalenz von E. Troeltschs Analyse des Vernunft-elementes in der Religion," *Kant-Studien* 78 (1987): 42-63.

49. H. R. Reuter remarks in *DBW* 2.172: "Bonhoeffer indeed incorporated some of the basic positions of his systematic teacher, Reinhold Seeberg, into the flow of the course of his thinking. But while he did so in such a way that Seeberg did not feel that he had fallen entirely by the wayside in respect to the protagonists from Münster, Marburg, and Jena (55ff., 101ff.), Bonhoeffer actually radicalized Seeberg's and Lütger's semi-critique of idealism" (172).

50. Here Bonhoeffer is referring to R. Seeberg, *Dogmatik II,* pp. 506ff. (cf. *DBW* 2.52, n. 36).

51. Karl Barth, *Gesamtausgabe II. Akademische Werke 1927. Die Christliche Dogmatik im Entwurf. 1. Band: Die Lehre vom Wort Gottes* (Zurich, 1982).

52. The following page numbers refer to the edition cited in n. 51.

53. *DBW* 10.357-78.

54. According to Barth's *Gesamtausgabe* (see n. 51 above), this citation is found on p. 383. The citation from §17 of *Dogmatics in Outline,* as well as the religio-critical §18, which was important in *Act in Being,* belongs to the third section, "The Outpouring of the Holy Spirit" (380ff.). Barth's *Dogmatics in Outline* continues to be of significance for Bonhoeffer.

55. *DBW* 10.440; following citations in *op. cit.*

56. In the present study, we cannot explore more deeply the extent to which Barth interprets from the perspective of a theology of revelation the "thing in itself" which in Neo-Kantianism functions as a boundary term, nor how Barth modifies phenomenalism into a theological premise. These are issues for Barth scholarship, whereas the present study is examining how Bonhoeffer understood Barth. Concerning a philosophical understanding of Barth, cf., e.g., U. Browarzik, *Glauben und Denken* (Berlin, 1970), pp. 95ff., esp. 232f.

57. Both philosophers try to undo the self-limitation of philosophy under-taken by Kant: Fichte by means of the "absolute ego," and Hegel by means of the dialectic of history: The moment the Idealists shoved the 'thing-in-itself' aside, Kant's critical philosophy was destroyed.

58. E. Bethge, *Dietrich Bonhoeffer,* p. 129.

59. E. Bethge, *Dietrich Bonhoeffer,* p. 132: "According to the story current among Bonhoeffer's later students, he had quoted at Barth's seminar Luther's saying that the curses of the godless sometimes sound better in God's ear than the hallelujahs of the pious, whereupon the delighted Barth asked who had made this contribution to the discussion, and this was the beginning of their personal acquaintance."

60. Letter of July 24, 1931, *DBW* 11.(18-22)19; following citations are also from *DBW* 11.

61. Cf. Barth's letter to Bonhoeffer of February 4, 1933, *Gesammelte Schriften* 2.40-41, here 41: "In the era of *Reichskanzler* Hitler, Wobbermin will doubtless be stylistically more appropriate in Schleiermacher's old position than I. I hear that you stuck your neck out on my behalf."

62. E. Bethge, *Dietrich Bonhoeffer,* p. 133.

63. Letter to Karl Barth of December 24, 1932: "Here at year's end, I would like to thank you once more for everything I have received from you over the course of this year. The evening here in Berlin and then the incomparably wonderful hours with you on the Bergli belong to the moments in this year that will abide" (*GS* 2.39).

64. Letter of September 9, 1933, *DBW* 13.11-15, here 13f.

65. Letter to Karl Barth, October 24, 1933, *GS* 2.130-34, here 132.

66. Barth's letter of response, November 20, 1933, *DBW* 13.31-34, here 31.

67. Edited by O. Dudzus as a compilation of student notes, *GS* 5.181-227; the new edition of the lectures, edited by E. Amelung, uses the notes of Joachim Kanitz, *DBW* 11.139-213. I essentially follow this edition.

68. In this passage, the Dudzus compilation reads that "Christianity *was* identified with religion" (*GS* 5.285; my emphasis).

69. E. Feil, *The Theology of Dietrich Bonhoeffer,* p. 105. Unfortunately, Feil ends his observations at this point concerning Bonhoeffer's historicizing understanding of religion, one allegedly evident as early as 1931/32; Feil then later juxtaposes it antithetically to the systematic-theological critique of religion.

70. The question is "whether everything is not simply based on an illusion" (Dudzus compilation, *GS* 5.187).

71. W. J. Peck, "A Proposal concerning Bonhoeffer's Concept of the Person," *ATR* 50 (1968): 311-29, already drew attention to a connection between the Feuerbach questions of 1931/32 and the Tegel correspondence from early summer of 1944. Whereas Bonhoeffer's early writings (from *Sanctorum Communio* to *The Cost of Discipleship*) deal essentially with the first Feuerbach question, his *Ethics* and *Letters and Papers from Prison* provide an answer to the second; according to Peck, "the notion of religionless Christianity is Bonhoeffer's answer to Feuerbach's second question" (328).

72. Letter of June 8, 1944, *WEN,* p. 358. (This is the only passage in the Tegel correspondence that mentions Troeltsch.)

73. Cf. *DBW* 10.408-10; concerning the scope of his study of James, cf. *DBW* 10.269.

74. The concepts of "life" and "psychology," which acquire such significance in the Tegel correspondence with reference to W. Dilthey, still appear in a negative light here; this may derive from the particular declivity of this lecture: It is only through Karl Barth that the Feuerbach question concerning the dissolution of theology into anthropology is first answered. Still, Bonhoeffer probably did derive something from James's philosophy, otherwise he no doubt would not have studied virtually the entirety of the American pragmatist's work (cf. *DBW* 10.269). At

this point, we can only surmise that Bonhoeffer's acquaintance with James relativized the philosophical influence of neo-Kantianism (mediated through Barth), opening Bonhoeffer up to the "life philosophy" that then becomes important in the Tegel theology.

75. O. Dudzus writes concerning this section: "In his presentation of the secularization process of culture, one almost feels displaced into the world of the famous letters from the *Letters and Papers from Prison*" (*GS* 5.182).

76. Bracketed material according to the Dudzus compilation, *GS* 5.210.

77. *GS* 5.219; my emphasis. Here I am following the wording of the Dudzus compilation. The text according to *DBW* 11.199 reads: "There can no longer be any general *grounding of religion*" (my emphasis). In fact, however, the copy of this passage by Joachim Kanitz which served as the basis for *DBW* 11 reads: "[German:] keinen allgem. Begr. v. Rel. kann es mehr geben" (*NL* B 1.1). For grammatical reasons (namely, the orthography "kein*en*" rather than "kein*e*"), the abbreviation *Begr.* can only be rendered masculine singular accusative = *Begriff,* "concept," rather than feminine singular accusative *Begründung,* "grounding" (see *NL* B 1.1).

78. Sermon on Colossians 3 (1932), *DBW* 11.435-53, here 437.

79. *GS* 5.300-340.

80. Bonhoeffer writes about E. Schaeder: "The first attack against Karl Barth was launched from the position of religious inwardness" (*GS* 5.304).

81. *GS* 3.170.

82. With regard to the influence of philosopy on Bonhoeffer, the seminar on Hegel confirmed the tendency of playing Kant off against German Idealism (here esp. against Hegel; cf. *Dietrich Bonhoeffers Hegel-Seminar 1933. Internationales Bonhoeffer Forum* 8 [Munich, 1988]: 19).

83. Barth does admittedly continue his "presence" during the time of *The Cost of Discipleship* as well. In a letter to him from Finkenwalde, Bonhoeffer confesses that "basically the entire time was an ongoing, silent debate with you, and for that reason I had to remain silent for a while" (letter of September 19, 1936, *GS* 2.283-87, here 284).

84. Cf. the compilation of individual statements critical of religion from *The Cost of Discipleship* and *Life Together* above (Part I.A.2 above).

85. "Protestantism without Reformation," composed in August 1939, *GS* 1.323-54.

86. If we understand the word *still* historically, the question arises whether this constitutes a linking of a historically articulated critique of religion with that of dialectical theology.

87. Diary entry on June 16, 1939, *GS* 1.300.

88. Diary entry on June 18, 1939, *GS* 1.300.

89. Eberhard Bethge in personal written communication to me on February 2, 1992.

90. So P. Köster, "Nietzsche als verborgener Antipode in Bonhoeffers 'Ethik,'" *Nietzsche-Studien* 19 (1990): 367-418, here 407.

91. The editors of *DBW* 6 point out other terminological reverberations from Barth; Bonhoeffer speaks about the world that "is preserved until it is ready for its end" (*DBW* 6.146). His reference to the "breaking up of the world" derives allegedly from the essay volume *Das Wort Gottes und die Theologie,* and recurs in one of Bonhoeffer's sermons from 1934 (*GS* 5.560) as well as in *The Cost of Discipleship,* 255; cf. *DBW* 6.146, n. 35.

92. Afterword of the editorial circle of the *Ethics* (*DBW* 6.424).

93. Cf. the letter of June 8, 1944 (*WEN,* 359); Barth also later positively evaluated Bonhoeffer's *Ethics;* cf. *Church Dogmatics* III/4, e.g., pp. 14f., 21f., 404.

94. Cf. *WEN,* 223f. We saw earlier how Bonhoeffer picks up and radicalizes as a critique of religion his own observation from his *Ethics* (*DBW* 6.143) that in "serious situations" he was more inclined to engage in "penultimate behavior," e.g., to "say nothing" rather than to offer "biblical" words of comfort.

95. The premise of A. J. Wesson, "Bonhoeffer's Use of 'Religion,' " *London Quarterly and Holborn Review* 192 (1967): 43-53, is that the understanding of religion in *Widerstand und Ergebung* is articulated in three basic concepts: "inwardness, conscience, and metaphysics" (45). Wesson suggests that the concept of "inwardness" is a culmination of the "thinking in two spheres" from the *Ethics.* If the concept of inwardness had emerged from the *Ethics,* as Wesson assumes, then Bonhoeffer could not have appropriated it from Wilhelm Dilthey, as E. Feil argues (*The Theology of Dietrich Bonhoeffer,* pp. 180f.). "Inwardness" would have emerged through a process of "conceptual continuity" and would not represent a neologism prompted by Bonhoeffer's reading of Dilthey. Our intention is not to anticipate prematurely the discussion of Dilthey at this point, but merely to point out the connection between the *Ethics* and the *Letters and Papers from Prison.*

96. Letter to P. W. Herrenbrück, December 21, 1952, *Die mündige Welt* 1 (1959): 122.

97. *Theologie und Sozialismus* (Munich, 1985³), pp. 245f.

98. *Revelatory Positivism? Barth's Earliest Theology and the Marburg School* (Oxford, 1988), pp. 313f.: ". . . the term 'revelatory positivism' is best deleted from the theological dictionary." Fisher is expressly following F.-W. Marquardt (cf. his introduction, pp. 1ff., esp. 6, n. 6).

99. R. Prenter, "Dietrich Bonhoeffer und Karl Barths Offenbarungspositivismus," *Die Mündige Welt* 3 (1960): 11ff. For E. Feil, *The Theology of Dietrich Bonhoeffer,* p. 176, "this positivism of revelation consists of an abstract state in a worldlessness and an absence of history in which Barth was irrevocably mired." R. T. Osborn, "Positivism and Promise in the Theology of Karl Barth," *Interpretation* 25/3 (July 1971) 283-302, follows R. Prenter (288f.), approves of his presentation of Barth's doctrine of revelation in *The Letter to the Romans* (289), but then criticizes Prenter's presentation of Barth's understanding of revelation in the *Church Dogmatics* (290). On the whole, Osborn views Bonhoeffer's critique as being directed against Barth's christocentric doctrine of revelation (298).

100. J. H. Burtness, "Als ob es Gott nicht gäbe. Bonhoeffer, Barth und das lutherische finitum capax infiniti," *Internationales Bonhoeffer Forum* 6 (Munich,

1983): 167ff., esp. 172: "From *Act and Being,* where the passionate Lutheran comes to blows with the staunch Calvinist over the *finitum capax sive incapax infiniti,* to the Tegel correspondence, where Bonhoeffer charges Barth with 'revelatory positivism' (May 5, 1944), Bonhoeffer maintains a critical position alongside his enduring concurrence." G. B. Kelly, "Bonhoeffer's 'nonreligious' Christianity: Antecedents and Critique," *Bijdr* 37 (1976): 118ff., believes the Lutheran *finitum capax infiniti* may offer a possible explanation for Bonhoeffer's charge of revelatory positivism (133f.), and concludes with respect to Barth that "God's revelation in Christ stands over and against the world" (135).

101. Cf. H. Ott, *Wirklichkeit und Glaube I: Zum theologischen Erbe Dietrich Bonhoeffers* (Zurich, 1966). "In substance," Bonhoeffer "may be called a Barthian. . . . But with regard to his style, diction, conceptual methodological intentions, he takes a path in his early writings differing characteristically from that of Karl Barth" (113). As far as revelatory positivism is concerned, from the methodically correct "basic assertion . . . he constructs a system of assertions which, to the extent the basic presupposition, the axiomatic assertion is correct, must all be true in the same way and with the same import. Thus a monolithic block emerges" (110). And "indeed, methodologically the *Church Dogmatics* derive everything from one systematic christological principle" (113).

102. Cf. T. R. Peters, *Die Präsenz des Politischen in der Theologie Dietrich Bonhoeffers. Eine historische Untersuchung in systematischer Absicht* (Munich, 1976), p. 172: "A self-enclosed, positivistic theology of revelation along with its corresponding church are incapable of providing orientation for action, indeed, they do not even facilitate any committed perception of social processes."

103. H.-J. Abromeit, *Das Geheimnis Christi. Dietrich Bonhoeffers erfahrungsbezogene Christologie* (Neukirchen-Vluyn, 1991), p. 168.

104. Bonhoeffer refers in his letter of June 8, 1944, to the originality of his conceptual construction when he writes " 'revelatory positivism,' as I express myself" (*WEN,* 359). G. Krause, "Bonhoeffer, Dietrich," *Theologische Realenzyklopädie* VII (1981), pp. 55-66, here 64, n. 1, finds the expression "revelatory positivism" already formally attested in the writings of church historian E. Seeberg, adducing in support Seeberg's first volume of *Luthers Theologie* from the year 1929, albeit without examining the content of the term as Seeberg uses it. The expression "revelatory positivism" is attested only twice in the relevant chapter in Seeberg's book, namely, Chapter II.4, "God and his Revelation," pp. 182ff. (185 and 218); its content derives from a coupling of Luther's understanding of revelation in the doctrine of the Lord's Supper with "Occamistic positivism" (216). "Luther conceives the Spirit not abstractly = rationally . . . but rather concretely = historically; the Spirit does not exist in and for itself, but rather always in a concrete manifestation, in the word, in the sacrament, and in God's saints, that is, in the church" (216). Revelatory positivism is associated with concrete historicness. According to E. Seeberg, Luther changes Christ "into a historic and concrete form" (200). The dependency Krause assumes for the expression "revelatory positivism" on E. Seeberg's book on Luther is thus refuted at least from the

perspective of content. Of course, we cannot exclude the possibility that Bonhoeffer was familiar with Seeberg's book; Bonhoeffer received his doctorate under the tutelage of E. Seeberg's father, R. Seeberg, in 1927. Yet if the concept of revelatory positivism had acquired significance for Bonhoeffer as a result of his having read Seeberg, we would already have encountered some evidence of this earlier, perhaps in *Sanctorum Communio, Act and Being,* or the lectures on Christology, rather than in the letters from prison in the early summer of 1944, seventeen years after the publication of Seeberg's book. Furthermore, the composition of the concept of revelatory positivism is theologically undefined. Bonhoeffer uses the combination "revelation-positivism" differently than does E. Seeberg. Whereas the latter understands "Occamistic positivism" as being "concrete-historic," the positivism criticized in connection with Karl Barth refers in the broader sense to "the relationless quality of the statements of faith . . . by virtue of which they must simply be accepted as that which is merely given (posita) with no additional grounding" (cited from R. Prenter, *art. cit.,* p. 13). Not only is the understanding of positivism different, so also is the understanding of revelation underlying the revelatory positivism which E. Seeberg derives from the Luther exegesis. According to him, "natural knowledge of God . . . is to be viewed as a preliminary stage of supranatural knowledge" (206). "Natural knowledge of God is also a gift of God" (203; cf., e.g., 202f. or 207). Precisely this evaluation of *theologia naturalis* makes any use of the word "revelatory positivism" from the Seeberg book useless for Bonhoeffer against Karl Barth, since Bonhoeffer and Barth unanimously reject natural theology in any case. Hence even though the expression "revelatory positivism" itself does indeed appear in E. Seeberg's work, its theological meaning is not prefigured there. "Revelatory positivism" is attested formally prior to Bonhoeffer, but not with the same content.

105. Cf. *WEN,* 303ff., 311ff., 355ff.

106. G. B. Kelly, *art. cit.* (1976): 130 (see Part I).

107. D. Jenkins, *Beyond Religion* (Bloomsbury, 1962), pp. 26ff., observes a relationship between *Church Dogmatics* I/2 and Bonhoeffer's understanding of religion according to *Letters and Papers from Prison;* this idea is then picked up by J. A. Phillips, *The Form of Christ in the World* (London, 1967), pp. 202f. [published in the United States as *Christ for Us in the Theology of Dietrich Bonhoeffer* [New York, 1967]). The premise of C. E. Krieg, "Bonhoeffer's Letters and Papers," *RelS* 9 (1973): 81-92, is that Barth and Bonhoeffer initially concur in their critique of religion. Then, however, Bonhoeffer turns against Barth, who he alleges is characterized by a fundamentally "religious" attitude and fails to draw the appropriate conclusion from the critique of religion. "Barth describes religion as man's attempt to have and possess God, in contrast to genuine faith which is a gift of grace. In other words, for Barth religion is a perversion of a faithful response to grace. Bonhoeffer is sympathetic to Barth's distinctions at this point. Nevertheless, Barth, too, is doing 'religious' theology according to Bonhoeffer. Barth's greatest shortcoming, as far as Bonhoeffer was concerned, was that he offered no nonreligious interpretation of biblical concepts" (81).

108. The premise of A. Pangritz, *Karl Barth,* p. 88, is that the charge of revelatory positivism might have been "coined" with an eye on Barth's "Tambach Lecture" of 1919, though one would have to "question whether Bonhoeffer did not fundamentally misunderstand the Tambach Lecture" *(ibid.).* Pangritz thus initially remains with F.-W. Marquardt's thesis of a misunderstanding, though he then offers other explanatory models for Bonhoeffer's objection, e.g., that he was directing his charge against H. Asmussen (82ff.), was incensed at Barth's dialectical evaluation of religion in the second edition of the *Letter to the Romans,* and then also in the *Christian Dogmatics* and *Church Dogmatics* (108).

109. B.-E. Benktson, "Kristus och den myndigvordna Världen," *Svensk teologisk kvartalskrift* 40 (1964): 94ff.

110. G. Sauter, "Zur Herkunft und Absicht der Formel 'Nicht-religiöse Interpretation biblischer Begriffe' bei Dietrich Bonhoeffer," *EvT* 25 (1962): 283ff. Five years after Sauter, A. J. Wesson, "Bonhoeffer's Use of Religion," *London Quarterly and Holborn Review* 192 (1967): 50f., established a conceptual connection between *Church Dogmatics* I/2 and *Widerstand und Ergebung.* One element of Bonhoeffer's critique of religion, namely, the "deus-ex-machina concept," might be found in Barth's section "The Problem of Religion in Theology" (280ff.) from *Church Dogmatics* I/2 §17. Unfortunately, Wesson does not follow up on these insights. Cf. also E. Grin, *art. cit.* (1992) (see introduction above).

111. Although Bonhoeffer was also familiar with the first edition of Barth's commentary on Romans, he consistently references the second edition (cf., e.g., *DBW* 1.109, n. 28; 97, n. 71; *DBW* 2.75, n. 1; *DBW* 10.457, n. 8; 459, n. 13; *WEN,* 359).

112. *WEN,* 359.

113. *WEN,* 359, my emphasis.

114. *WEN,* 312, 359.

115. B. E. Benktson, *art. cit.* (1964) (see above): 94ff.

116. Karl Barth, *Das Wort Gottes und die Theologie. Gesammelte Vorträge,* vol. 2 (Munich, 1920), pp. 70f.

117. Karl Barth, *Das Wort Gottes und die Theologie,* p. 94.

118. Sauter, *art. cit.* (see above): 291 (citation from *WEN,* 305).

119. Wilhelm Dilthey, "Weltanschauung und Analyse des Menschen seit Renaissance und Reformation," *Gesammelte Schriften,* 2.337.

120. One striking formal observation concerns the conjunction *then* (emphasized in the text), which always introduces criticism of Barth. The question is whether Bonhoeffer was thinking of §17 of *Church Dogmatics* I/2, where he observed the change from a critique of religion (in section 2 of §17) to a positive evaluation of religion from the perspective of a theology of revelation (in section 3), which he then designates "revelatory positivism."

121. R. Gruhn, "Religionskritik als Aufgabe der Theologie," *EvT* 39 (1979): 234-55, citation on 255.

122. Cited according to Karl Barth, *Gesamtausgabe* 14 (Zurich, 1982): 306ff.; here 317.

123. *Church Dogmatics,* I/2 (Eng. trans., New York, 1956), p. 326.

124. *Church Dogmatics,* pp. 280, 298.

125. *Church Dogmatics,* p. 296.

126. *Church Dogmatics,* p. 295.

127. This would also explain why in the passages from the *Ethics* attesting Barthian terminology, this terminology actually derives from *Sanctorum Communio* and thus from the early Barth.

128. Cf. also C. Green, *The Sociality of Christ and Humanity: Dietrich Bonhoeffer's Early Theology 1927-1933* (Missoula, Mont., 1975), p. 309: ". . . there is no sense in which his [Bonhoeffer's] contemporary reinterpretation of Christianity involves any rehabilitation or justification of religion as he defines it. In this his position is different from Barth who, after his attack on all religion (including Christianity) as unbelief, presents a view of Christianity as 'true religion' under the rubric of the doctrine of justification by grace."

129. A dialectic of arcane discipline and religionlessness is also mentioned by R. G. Smith, *The New Man: Christianity and Man's Coming of Age* (New York, 1956); E. C. Bianchi, "Bonhoeffer and the Church's Prophetic Mission," *Theological Studies* (Baltimore) 28 (1967): 801-11; H. Mottu, *art. cit.* (1969) (see Part I); G. B. Kelly, *art. cit.* (1976) (see Part I); J. Mark, "Bonhoeffer Today," *Theol.* 718 (1984): 272-76; and A. Pangritz, *Forderung* (1988).

130. Cf. *WEN,* 312.

131. R. Prenter, *art. cit.* (1960) (see above): 11-41.

132. Prenter's methodology here was quickly criticized. R. G. Smith writes that "Prenter, for all his anxiety to do justice both to Barth and Bonhoeffer, does not, it seems to me, succeed in being entirely convincing. It is doubtful whether Bonhoeffer can really be understood on the basis that he is one of Barth's school" (Introduction to *World Come of Age* [London, 1967], p. 10).

133. B.-E. Benktson, *art. cit.* (1964) (see above): 83, first presents Bonhoeffer's critique of religion with respect to the working hypothesis "God," and then transitions to the nonreligious interpretation in Bonhoeffer with the words: "Thus his [Bonhoeffer's] ideas revolve around the necessity of a new, nonreligious interpretation of biblical concepts" (83). The word "thus" underscores for Benktson the tight bracketing of a critique of religion on the one hand, and the nonreligious interpretation on the other.

134. Cf. B.-E. Benktson, *Christus und die Religion* (Stuttgart, 1967), p. 59. So also K.-H. Nebe, *'Religionslose' Interpretation bei Dietrich Bonhoeffer und ihre Bedeutung für die Aufgabe der Verkündigung* (diss., Hamburg, 1963), pp. 165f., who does clearly work out the difference between Tillich's and Barth's understandings of religion (170ff.) while still understanding Barth's concept of religion from the *Letter to the Romans* to the *Church Dogmatics* I/2 as being "dialectical" (165).

135. H.-J. Kraus, *Theologische Religionskritik* (Neukirchen-Vluyn, 1982), p. 20.

136. H.-J. Kraus, *Theologische Religionskritik,* p. 33, draws attention to the

appropriate question, though without answering it correctly in the sense of our own analysis (34ff.).

137. Bonhoeffer reflects on the connection between revelatory positivism and incarnational theology when on May 5, 1944, he writes that "revelatory positivism makes it too easy for itself by ultimately erecting a law of faith and by sundering that which is actually a gift for us through the incarnation of Christ" (*WEN*, 312).

138. Concerning the interpretation of this clause, cf. A. Pangritz, *Karl Barth* (Berlin, 1989), pp. 82ff., whose premise is that the expanded polemic is being directed against H. Asmussen and Lutheran circles within the Confessing Church. This is allegedly also suggested by the connection with Rudolf Bultmann in the letter of June 8, 1944, beyond whom Bonhoeffer yet wishes to go (similarly on May 5). By contrast, H. Asmussen defends "the present positivistic-theological position against Bultmann's alleged demonic nature" (85).

139. Concerning religion as a historic entity in Barth, cf. earlier discussion of Barth in this study.

140. Cf. in this regard the examination of all the statements from Tegel that were critical of religion (see Part I above, section 3).

141. For a characterization of Dilthey's philosophy as a "historical philosophy of life," cf. O. F. Bollnow, *Dilthey. Eine Einführung in seine Philosophie* (Stuttgart, 1955²), p. 35.

142. Cf. the letters of January 14, 1944 (*WEN*, 210, the first mention of Dilthey, then 212 and 229); February 5, 1944 (235: "From Klaus I received Dilthey's *Von Deutscher Dichtung und Musik* [*On German Poetry and Music*]"); Bonhoeffer also received Dilthey's *Das Erlebnis und die Dichtung* (Eng. trans., *Poetry and Experience,* ed. R. A. Makkreel and Frithjof Rodi [Princeton: Princeton University Press, 1985]) from his father (cf. *NL* 216); in his letter of March 2, 1944, Bonhoeffer writes to his parents: "Could you please send me Dilthey's *Weltanschauung und Analyse des Menschen seit Renaissance und Reformation* [*World-view and Analysis of Man since the Renaissance and Reformation*]?" (255).

143. C. Gremmels, *Mündige Welt,* pp. 13f.

144. E.g., *Weltanschauung und Analyse des Menschen seit Renaissance und Reformation* (Leipzig/Berlin, 1921²), pp. 90ff.

145. Of course, Bonhoeffer is concerned with establishing the correct understanding of immanence and transcendence, wherein he is dependent on Dilthey; but in Part III we will inquire whether it is not precisely Dilthey's understanding of *life* that exercised considerable influence on statements such as these.

146. In C. F. von Weizsäcker, *Weltbild der Physik,* Bonhoeffer could read the sentence: "Even if the details of Laplace's hypotheses were in part incorrect, still all researchers in the natural sciences must make it their goal to render the *hypothesis God* superfluous in their particular sphere of *work*" (cited after Gremmels, p. 26; my emphasis). It is certainly conceivable that Bonhoeffer compressed the words "(sphere of) work (of the) hypothesis God" into "working hypothesis

God" (26, n. 3). The expression "working hypothesis" does indeed already occur once in 1941 as an aside in one fragment to Bonhoeffer's *Ethics* (*DBW* 6f.106), but here it is the *"ratio"* that becomes a "working hypothesis." This does not prefigure the terminological development "working hypothesis God" of the sort that will become important throughout *Widerstand und Ergebung.*

147. Concerning the equally possible connection with Hegel in this passage, see Part I above.

148. Cf., e.g., "Religionsloses Christentum und nichtreligiöse Interpretation bei Dietrich Bonhoeffer," *TZ* 25 (1968): 40-48. He first treats the connection with Dilthey in the essay "Der Einfluss Wilhelm Diltheys auf Dietrich Bonhoeffers Widerstand und Ergebung," *EvT* 29 (1969): 662-74, and then more extensively in *The Theology of Dietrich Bonhoeffer,* pp. 178ff. Cf. also "Das Weltverständnis Dietrich Bonhoeffers," *EvT* 32 (1972): 511-29, esp. 518f. concerning Dilthey's influence on Bonhoeffer. More recently, cf. his book *Religio* (1986), where he demonstrates that "into the middle of the 16th century" the concept of religion "did not have that particular function the term acquired in modern times" (273). This book is of significance for Bonhoeffer scholarship insofar as it shows un-equivocally that it was only in modern Protestantism that one attributed to the concept of religion the meaning that makes the 20th-century critique of religion (at the end of modernity?) historically comprehensible.

149. E. Feil, *The Theology of Dietrich Bonhoeffer,* pp. 178ff.

150. This book by Dilthey bears the dedication of Bonhoeffer's father, who wanted to give it to his son for his birthday on February 4, 1944. Bonhoeffer, however, already mentions reading Dilthey since January 14, 1944 (*WEN,* 210; cf. also 212). The concurrence of the Lessing citation in the letter of January 23 and Bonhoeffer's own enumeration of all the books he received for his birthday (letter of February 5, 1944, 234f.) except for this particular book suggests that Bonhoeffer "must already have possessed his father's gift and had read it earlier" (Ernst Feil in personal correspondence with me).

151. Cf. E. Feil, *The Theology of Dietrich Bonhoeffer,* p. 179.

152. Cf. E. Feil, *The Theology of Dietrich Bonhoeffer,* pp. 179f., 183.

153. Cf. E. Feil, *The Theology of Dietrich Bonhoeffer,* pp. 180f.

154. Scholars have not determined the source from which Bonhoeffer derives the Latin version "etsi deus non daretur." Dilthey (*Weltanschauung,* 280) cites this in a German version (English: "even if there were no God"). The original version in H. Grotius, *De jure belli ac pacis libri tres. Prolegomena* 11.7, reads: "etiamsi daremus, quod sine summo scelere dari nequit, non esse deum" ("Even if we were to give [= let ourselves be heard saying] — which cannot be done without great sacrilege — that there is no God"). Bonhoeffer uses a construction with Latin *datur;* Grotius also twice uses Latin *datur.* We conclude that Bonhoeffer was familiar with the citation in its original, longer Latin version, and under the influence of the (shortened) German rendering in Dilthey constructed the Latin form we now have from him. A glance at the original manuscript of the letter of July 16 underscores this observation: Bonhoeffer cites Grotius (*NL* A 195/174),

"that we must live in the world — 'etsi deus non daretur. . . .'" The two periods following the citation indicate to the reader that this is an abbreviation! Abbreviations of citations and a rendering of originals from memory are customary in Bonhoeffer's writing (cf., e.g., the citation of Barth's *Letter to the Romans* in *Sanctorum Communio, DBW* 1.134). A familiarity with Grotius can be presupposed within Bonhoeffer's educational milieu.

155. E. Feil, *The Theology of Dietrich Bonhoeffer,* p. 183.

156. Cf. Dilthey, *Gesammelte Schriften,* 8.184: "Cognition cannot get behind life." In *Gesammelte Schriften,* 5.12, Dilthey writes about Kant: "To me this seems to establish the basic problem of philosophy for all time." In an abbreviated form, we can say that Dilthey tried to accomplish for the humanities what Kant did for the natural sciences. The *Critique of Pure Reason* becomes a "critique of historical reason." Wolfram Hogrebe describes the difference between the natural sciences and the humanities using an example: "The natural scientist *explains* the term 'water' by analyzing the (molecular) structure of this material (H_2O); the scholar in the human sciences *understands* the term 'water' through recourse to those particular relationships in which water possesses meaning *for* human beings" (*Deutsche Philosophie im XIX Jahrhundert. Kritik der idealistischen Vernunft* [1987], p. 138).

157. Cf. also Dilthey, *Leben Schleiermachers,* II.2.508f., where under the subtitle "Schleiermacher as Reformer of Theology" (508) Dilthey tries to integrate Schleiermacher's concept of religion into his own historical philosophy of life. Thus, e.g., does he relate religiosity and worldview (509). The connection between Schleiermacher and Dilthey can also be understood from the perspective of their common philosophical background, namely, Kant, whose concept of "transcendental apperception" becomes Schleiermacher's concept of "feeling" (after the *Christian Faith* 1830/31) and Dilthey's concept of "life." Concerning the relationship between Kant and Schleiermacher, cf. Dilthey's "Schleiermacher, der Kant der protestantischen Theologie," in *Leben Schleiermachers,* pp. 531ff..

158. Given their substantive proximity, one can mention Schleiermacher's and Dilthey's concepts of religion under a common denominator; cf. K. E. Welker, *Die grundsätzliche Beurteilung der Religionsgeschichte durch Schleiermacher* (Leiden, 1965); concerning the concept of religion, see pp. 33f.; summary on p. 99; concerning Schleiermacher's influence on Dilthey, see esp. pp. 67 and 161.

159. It is certain that Bonhoeffer read this sentence in Dilthey, since the Lessing citation in the letter of January 1 is itself found on p. 92 of Dilthey's work, i.e., merely six pages after this sentence.

160. *Gesammelte Schriften,* I (²1922); [partial] English translation *Introduction to the Human Sciences,* ed. R. A. Makkreel and Frithjof Rodi, in *Wilhelm Dilthey: Selected Works,* vol. 1 (Princeton: Princeton University Press, 1989). In the following discussion of this work, the German original is cited for material not included in the English translation.

161. Cf. *DBW* 11.146; cf. n. 31 of the editor, E. Amelung.

162. *DBW* 11.146. The Dudzus compilation relates more fully concerning

Dilthey: ". . . but esp. Dilthey in his systematic grounding of the humanities" (*GS* 5.186). A glance at the table of contents of the *Einleitung in die Geisteswissenschaften* reveals that Dilthey does indeed address the topics Bonhoeffer mentions, and even does so in the same order, namely, natural sciences (14ff.), historical sciences (21ff.), psychology (64ff.), sociology (86ff.), theology (134ff.).

163. Cf. *Weltanschauung und Analyse des Menschen seit Renaissance und Reformation,* 54: "religionless morality"; Dilthey does not speak here, as in *Introduction to the Human Sciences,* of a "process of understanding" or a "religionless age."

164. Cf. the lectures on "Systematic Theology in the 20th Century" according to *DBW* 11.139-213, esp. 145f.; he assumes here that religion had a historic beginning, when it replaces another concept, namely, faith.

165. In the lectures of 1931/32, Bonhoeffer adduces Paul de Lagarde in addition to Dilthey in this passage. He writes (*DBW* 11.145): "Paul de Lagarde, *The Relationship of the German State to Theology, Church, and Religion.* He considers the decisive antithesis to be that between religion and Reformational faith." It is interesting that for Lagarde, this antithesis is *historically* grounded. He himself writes: "Protestantism is a historical construction that can be correctly evaluated only on the basis of a study of the 16th century, not on that of public opinion of the waning 19th century" (*Deutsche Schriften von Paul de Lagarde. Gesamtausgabe,* pp. 40-83, citation on 42). Luther's understanding of faith and Schleiermacher's concept of religion thus diverge *historically.*

166. Sermon on Colossians 3:1-4 (Third Sunday after Trinity 1932), *DBW* 11.435-43.

167. Here, too, associated with a critique of the empirical concept of science: "In the final analysis, the most exact scientific methods would have to reach the goal, would have to impose order on our chaos. How much more trustworthy, how much more promising is this scientific drive, pushing feverishly onward, than that sober expression 'in the name of God, amen,' which says nothing" (*DBW* 11.439).

168. *DBW* 11.440. Bonhoeffer gives this religious thematic material a contemporary political-historical edge in the sermon when he alludes to the government of Papen: "We read that an administration is proclaiming that an entire people is to be snatched from the brink of collapse — by means of the Christian worldview" *(ibid.).* His listeners are to be called back not to religion — "that is nothing" (442) — nor to the "Christian worldview" (441), but rather to faith "in the living God." "That is our disobedience, that is our flight, that is our disastrous apostasy: the more devout we become, the less do we want to hear that God is dangerous, that he will not tolerate being mocked, and that we human beings must die if we really do want to deal with the living God" (441).

169. *DBW* 11.441.

170. The following discussion cannot examine the philosophical and theological scope of these concepts. We will focus exclusively on whether the individual

concepts were of significance for Bonhoeffer's *critique* of religion *prior* to his Tegel theology.

171. *DBW* 10.682; my emphasis. As an example of the appearance of metaphysics in a nontheological context, one can adduce the lecture on "The Leader and the Individual" from 1933, where Bonhoeffer remarks critically concerning the "spirit of the people" and "metaphysical depths": "The spirit of the people — one imagines — produces the leader from within its own metaphysical depths and elevates him to the greatest heights" (*GS* 2.32).

172. *GS* 5.303f.; my emphasis. In the same context, Bonhoeffer also speaks critically of "religious inwardness," whence he alleges the "first attack against Karl Barth was conducted" (*op. cit.,* p. 304).

173. Cf. also the juxtaposition of inwardness and Christology, one not, however, involving any critique of religion (*DBW* 5.22): "Our community cannot determine what a person is as a Christian within himself, in all inwardness and piety; rather, it is what a person is from the perspective of Christ that is determinative for our brotherhood."

174. Cf. also E. Feil, *Theology of Dietrich Bonhoeffer,* p. 234, n. 164.

175. Cf. *DBW* 11.145.

176. *DBW* 11.189; material in brackets from *GS* 5.212.

177. *GS* 3.303-24.

178. The question is "Christ *or* the autonomous human being," not "Christ *and* the world come of age." (See Part I.A above.)

179. Concerning "relational Christology," cf. Eberhard Bethge, "Christologie und 'religionsloses Christentum,'" *Glaube und Weltlichkeit* (1969), who emphasizes "relational" as an element of Bonhoeffer's Christology (92f.).

180. *Evocation of New Testament Texts, GS* 3.303-24.

181. Cf., e.g., Wilhelm Dilthey, *Das Erlebnis und die Dichtung,* pp. 18-123.

182. Bonhoeffer replaced "questions of faith" with "religious matters." The question arises whether this attests an intention toward a critique of religion within the *Ethics* that can be articulated historically.

183. The connection between "penitence" and "honesty" is a new element in the Tegel theology; a comparison with, e.g., one of Bonhoeffer's sermons on the Day of Penitence (November 19, 1933) reveals that the concept of "honesty" appears not at all there, while "penitence" is mentioned frequently (*GS* 4.154f.). The connection between penitence and honesty does not yet appear.

184. Here we have one of the few concrete models of nonreligious interpretation of biblical concepts. Bonhoeffer interprets another biblical concept nonreligiously, "promise," with the word "meaning": "The unbiblical concept of 'sense or meaning' is merely a translation of what the Bible calls 'promise'" (*WEN,* 426).

185. Bonhoeffer's reference to "ultimate questions" constitutes a certain exception, since it represents a clear instance of discontinuity. In 1944, he remarks critically that "the so-called 'ultimate questions' — death, sin — still remain, for which one needs God and the church and the pastor" (*WEN,* 357). In a sermon

from 1933 he evaluates the task of the church in a reverse fashion, and does so with virtually the same words. Responding to the allegedly "ultimate question" "Where will we be after death?" Bonhoeffer says: "And the church claims to provide an answer to this impossible human question. Indeed, the church exists because it knows the answer to this ultimate question" (*GS* 4.160). Regarding the topic "ultimate questions," Bonhoeffer is apparently drawing completely different conclusions for the church in 1944 than he did in the sermon of 1933. This represents a genuine alteration in his train of thought.

186. *Church Dogmatics* I/1, 1. The publication of *Church Dogmatics* I/1 took place — as did Bonhoeffer's lecture — in 1932.

187. Here Bonhoeffer rejects an understanding of the church as a religious community.

188. *DBW* 11.33. Cf. in this context also Bonhoeffer's "Thoughts on the Baptism of Dietrich Wilhelm Rüdiger Bethge" from May 1944, where Bonhoeffer predicts that "the day will come when people are again called to preach the word of God such that this changes and renews the world" (*WEN*, 328).

189. Cf. in this regard W. J. Peck, "The Significance of Bonhoeffer's Interest in India," *HTR* 61 (1968): 431-50, esp. 440f. Peck understands the entire complex of nonreligious interpretation from the perspective of Bonhoeffer's plans to travel to India. As we will see, however, Bonhoeffer incorporates the East-West perspective as a kind of second level of argumentation *into* the historical understanding of religion.

190. Bonhoeffer concisely outlines the difference between Kant and Hegel with the terms "transcendental philosophy" and "philosophy of identity": "Transcendental philosophy would be: consciousness directs itself toward [the] thing in itself. . . . In Hegel, a statement of identity. . . ." (*Hegel*, p. 19; here also an explanation of the connection between Spinoza and Hegel).

191. Cf. also the letter of February 20, 1944: "It is always a small, inner struggle to hold in all sobriety to what is actual, to rid oneself of all illusions and fantasies, and to be satisfied with the given" (*WEN*, 241).

192. Genuine "this-worldliness" *(Diesseitigkeit)* "no longer takes its own suffering seriously, but rather God's suffering in the world, . . . and I believe that is faith, that is μετάνοια; thus does one become a human being, a Christian" (*WEN*, 402).

193. The theme of suffering is also attested prior to 1944, e.g., in the biblical study "Temptation" from 1938.

194. In the letter of April 30, 1944, Bonhoeffer begins with a "question" that is "bothering" him "incessantly" (*WEN*, 305), and then develops this question in recurring, almost stereotypical formulae: ". . . a few more words on the thoughts . . ." (311); "thoughts that have concerned me recently" (356); "to continue with the theological topic" (373); "a couple of thoughts on our topic" (377-92); "a few more introductory remarks on the theological topic" (395). The "thoughts" that become the "theological topic" finally prompt his plan to write a piece now preserved as his "Outline for a Book" (413f.).

195. Eberhard Bethge distinguishes in a lecture between various of Bonhoeffer's "behavioral conditions," ". . . the 'pacifist,' the 'prophet,' the 'Pietist,' the putschist." Lecture at the Bonhoeffer Conference in Eisenach 1992, printed in *IBK Rundbrief* 38 (May 1992): 7-19, citation on 16.

196. E. Feil, *The Theology of Dietrich Bonhoeffer*, 182f.; cf. also *idem*, "Ende oder Wiederkehr der Religion? Zu Bonhoeffers umstrittener Prognose eines 'religionslosen Christentums,'" *IBF* 7 (1987): 27-49, esp. 37f.

197. E. Feil, *The Theology of Dietrich Bonhoeffer*, p. 177.

198. K. Barth, *Unterricht in der christlichen Religion. Erster Band. Prolegomena 1924. Karl Barth Gesamtausgabe* 17/II, Akademische Werke (Zurich, 1985), citation on p. 224.

199. Cf. in this context Barth's lecture on L. Feuerbach from the year 1926, in *Die Theologie und die Kirche. Gesammelte Vorträge* 2.212-39 (1928). In this lecture, Barth challenges his listeners to "admit that Feuerbach's interpretation of religion is correct across the board" (*ibid.*, 238).

200. Cf. *DBW* 11.145f.

201. Cf. *DBW* 11.435ff.

202. *GS* 1.300.

203. *DBW* 6.113.

204. Cf. *GS* 2.420.

205. First in the letter of April 30, 1944 (*WEN*, 305ff.).

206. Concerning this concept: Bonhoeffer himself understands pragmatism, as established by William James and expanded into instrumentalism by John Dewey, as the "philosophy of life" (*DBW* 10.271).

207. *DBW* 10.268.

208. Cf. *DBW* 10.408f.

209. "Conclusions to the Varieties of Religious Experience," *The Writings of William James*, ed. J. J. McDermott (Chicago, 1977), pp. 758ff.

210. "Conclusions to the Varieties of Religious Experience," pp. 762f.

211. "Conclusions to the Varieties of Religious Experience," p. 767.

212. Cf. *DBW* 10.668, same orthography 668.

213. James, too, considers religion to be of significance only since the 17th century, and in a longer excursus distinguishes between modern and premodern thinking, identifying the concept of religion itself as deriving from the modern period. In the process, he draws a line in metaphysics from Aristotle to Augustine and into late scholasticism, finding that their mechanistic worldview has become obsolete in modernity.

214. Cf. R. K. Wüstenberg, "Bonhoeffer on Theology and Philosophy," *ANVIL* 12/1 (1995): 45-56.

215. Bonhoeffer similarly often adduces philosophers who are critical of German Idealism, such as L. Feuerbach (1931/32 in the lecture on *Systematic Theology of the 20th Century*), S. Kierkegaard (1937 in the *Cost of Discipleship*), and F. Nietzsche (1940f. in the *Ethics*).

216. Contra H. Müller, *Von der Kirche zur Welt* (1956), who observes "qualitative leaps" and "contradictions" in Bonhoeffer's theology (p. 9).

III

1. *WEN*, 396.

2. *WEN*, 396.

3. Concerning C. F. Meyer as a philosopher of life, cf. O. F. Bollnow, *Die Lebensphilosophie* (Berlin, 1958), p. 96.

4. Bollnow, *Lebensphilosophie*, p. 36, finds a close connection between these two philosophers from the perspective of "pure subjectivity" as this relates to the philosophy of life.

5. Concerning Feuerbach as a philosopher of life, cf. Bollnow, *Lebensphilosophie*, pp. 77f.

6. Bonhoeffer mentions Heidegger in Tegel only peripherally, and does so explicitly in a letter to his father. Basically, however, existential ontology appropriates premises from the philosophy of life and carries them forward (so Bollnow, *Lebensphilosophie*, p. 129). Concerning the problem of delimiting existentialism from the philosophy of life, cf. H. Fahrenbach, "Lebensphilosophische oder existenzphilosophische Anthropologie? Plessners Auseinandersetzung mit Heidegger," *Dilthey-Jahrbuch* 7 (1990/91): 71-111.

7. Concerning his significance for the philosophy of life, cf. Bollnow, *Lebensphilosophie*, pp. 48f.

8. Bonhoeffer possibly also read L. Klages from the perspective of the philosophy of life; concerning Klages as a philosopher of life, cf. Bollnow, *Lebensphilosophie*, pp. 51f.

9. Here Bonhoeffer quotes: " 'Whoever has pondered the depths, loves what is most alive,' Hölderlin on Socrates." Concerning F. Hölderlin in the context of the philosophy of life, cf. Bollnow, *Lebensphilosophie*, p. 103.

10. Concerning his significance for the philosophy of life, cf. Bollnow, *Lebensphilosophie*, approximately pp. 60f.

11. Cf. also E. Bethge, *Dietrich Bonhoeffer* [German edition] (Munich, 1967), p. 1053, Appendix G; here he lists the philosophical works Bonhoeffer read in Tegel. Three books by Ortega y Gasset appear: *History as System, On the Nature of Historic Crises,* and *On the Roman Empire.* While Bonhoeffer had already read the latter after October 1943, he studied the first two in May 1944.

12. Cited in the following according to the German edition, *Gesammelte Werk-Ausgabe. Band* IV (1956), pp. 366ff.

13. In *Gesammelte Werke* 4.414ff.

14. Cf. also E. Bethge, *Dietrich Bonhoeffer* [German edition] p. 1053, Appendix G.

15. According to Bollnow, *Lebensphilosophie*, p. 44, the Spanish philosopher

of culture Ortega y Gasset is to be classified directly among the representatives of the philosophy of life.

16. *Gesammelte Werke,* 4.427ff.

17. *Gesammelte Werke,* 4.428.

18. F. W. Kantzenbach, *Programme der Theologie* (Munich, 1984³), p. 245.

19. Bollnow, *Lebensphilosophie,* p. 44.

20. Cf., e.g., Bollnow, *Dilthey,* p. 26.

21. Cf. *Weltanschauung und Analyse des Menschen seit Renaissance und Reformation* (= *Gesammelte Schriften* II), e.g., pp. 17, 18, 20, 43, and 50.

22. *Weltanschauung und Analyse,* p. 20.

23. *Weltanschauung und Analyse,* e.g., pp. 20, 40, 58f., 136f., 144f., 247, 298, 322, 359, 394f., 414f., and 441.

24. O. Marquard, "Leben und Leben lassen," *Dilthey-Jahrbuch* (1984): 132, summarizes Dilthey's critique of Nietzsche as follows: ". . . because Nietzsche tried to bypass history in order to take nature and life as his basis, he for all practical purposes defined life and human nature through something that is merely historical, namely, the Renaissance ideal of human beings." By contrast, Dilthey begins with history "in order to see human nature" *(ibid.).*

25. Wilhelm Dilthey, *Gesammelte Schriften,* 8.224.

26. G. Kühne-Bertram, "Bibliographie der populären Lebensphilosophie des 19. Jahrhunderts in Deutschland," *Dilthey-Jahrbuch* I (1983): 289ff., 291.

27. O. Marquard, *art. cit.,* p. 135, who also speaks of "Dilthey's anthropological philosophy of life" *(ibid.,* p. 136).

28. Concerning the concept of experience in Dilthey, cf. Bollnow, *Lebensphilosophie,* pp. 26f.

29. Concerning "religious experience," cf. also *Weltanschauung und Analyse des Menschen seit Renaissance und Reformation,* p. 509: "The experience" of "baptism and eucharist."

30. Concerning the concept of "imitating" "Christ's own life," cf. *Weltanschauung und Analyse des Menschen seit Renaissance und Reformation,* p. 514.

31. Concerning C. Gremmels and E. Feil, see Part IIB above.

32. H.-U. Lessing, "Lebensphilosophie und Metaphysik. Anmerkungen zu Kurt Magers Dilthey-Kritik," *Dilthey-Jahrbuch* IV (1986/87): 269-73, citation on 270. Concerning Bonhoeffer's critique of the Archimedean point, cf. his citation of Archimedes in the *Outline for a Book* (*WEN,* 413; see also 270 and the "Drama Fragment," *DBW* 7.71, n. 66).

33. A. Degener, *Die Lebensphilosophie Wilhelm Diltheys* (1932), p. 6.

34. *Die Lebensphilosophie Wilhelm Diltheys,* p. 7.

35. Archival numbers A.76 to A.81 refer in the *Nachlass Dietrich Bonhoeffer* (edited by D. Meyer [Munich, 1987]) to those letters reproduced only in part or not at all in previous editions of the *Letters and Papers from Prison (Widerstand und Ergebung),* and which will be published first in full within the framework of the *Dietrich Bonhoeffer Werke (DBW).* As editor of *DBW* 8, C. Gremmels granted me access to this material. I examined eight letters from Eberhard Bethge to

Dietrich Bonhoeffer in the form of transcriptions, letters reproduced in *Widerstand und Ergebung. Neuausgabe* with considerable omissions. These include a letter from the end of March 1944 (cf. *WEN*, 272), letters from May 5, June 3, and August 24, 1944 (cf. *WEN*, 308f., 346f., and 429), and those from August 26, September 21, and September 30, 1944 (cf. *WEN*, 430f., 431f., 433). (The postscript from August 28, 1944 is not included in *Widerstand und Ergebung. Neuausgabe*.) In addition, I had access to the originals of many of Bonhoeffer's letters already published in *Widerstand und Ergebung. Neuausgabe* as well as the *Outline for a Book* in a *non*-transcribed version. In this section (Part III) I will return to this material, which comes from the microfilm archive of the University Library of Cambridge, U.K.

36. Concerning this complex (*WEN*, 12-14), cf. the parallel statements in the fragments to the *Ethics*, "Ethics as Shaping" (*DBW* 6.63-66). Concerning the reference to "misanthropy" (*WEN*, 19), cf. the dramatic fragment *DBW* 7.21-71, esp. 64f.

37. Adalbert Stifter initially became important for the friendship between Eberhard Bethge and Bonhoeffer; during the period when no correspondence was possible between the two friends (from Bonhoeffer's arrest in April 1943 until November 1943), Bonhoeffer underlined various passages in Stifter, thus revealing something about his friendship with Bethge (cf. Eberhard Bethge, "My Friend Dietrich Bonhoeffer's Theology of Friendship," lecture in Boston, 1993).

38. Letter of November 21, 1943 (*Love Letters from Cell 92: The Correspondence between Dietrich Bonhoeffer and Maria von Wedemeyer 1943-45,* ed. Ruth-Alice von Bismarck and Ulrich Kabitz; Eng. trans., Nashville: Abingdon Press, 1995, pp. 118f.); here Bonhoeffer is quoting from a Stifter anthology; cf. the editor's reference, *Love Letters,* p. 120, n. 3.

39. Concerning this hitherto unidentified citation, cf. Adalbert Stifter, *Witiko* (1953), p. 28; to the question whether Witiko is the "right man," the answer is given: "'Whether I am the right man?' the knight answered, 'well, I don't know yet; but I want to do the whole of what I am able to do in the world.'" Here, too, Bonhoeffer is apparently quoting from memory.

40. *WEN,* 225; in a letter from the end of November 1943, Bonhoeffer speaks about the character of totality attaching to life; on the one hand, he speaks about "the piece of one's own life" (168), and on the other writes that "precisely with that which one is and receives, a person is a whole" (168f.).

41. Cf., e.g., the fragment "Inheritance and Decay" (*DBW* 6.91ff.); in this study, the "church" represents the historical guarantor of "order" in contradistinction to the world, which is moving toward "nothingness" and "the absence of history." "With the shattering of biblical faith in God and of all divine commandments and ordinances, human beings are destroying themselves. An unrestrained vitalism emerges containing the dissolution of all values and ending only in ultimate self-destruction, in nothingness" (115). The church represents those values that have been lost in the world. (Bonhoeffer may have borrowed these

ideas from R. Schneider, *Macht und Gnade,* which he read in Ettal; cf. *DBW* 6.477.)

42. "Fragments from Tegel," *DBW* 7.21-71.

43. *DBW* 7.73-191.

44. This "we" probably represents Bonhoeffer's own tradition. Bonhoeffer himself is speaking in Christopher; cf. R. Bethge and I. Tödt, *DBW* 7.12ff.

45. *DBW* 7.67.

46. *DBW* 7.57.

47. R. Bethge and I. Tödt, *DBW* 7.57, n. 19.

48. *DBW* 7.180.

49. *DBW* 7.74.

50. *DBW* 7.75.

51. The considerable evidence of an appropriation of the philosophy of Nietzsche during this period also attests the influence of the philosophy of life on Bonhoeffer; cf. the references provided by the editors in *DBW* 7.22, 38, 157, 181f.

52. Cf., e.g., the concept of "distress," which Bonhoeffer would like to leave "uninterpreted" (*WEN,* 228), and which then also does *not* appear on the list of terms to be interpreted (see *Outline, Widerstand und Ergebung. Neuausgabe,* p. 414 bottom; see also the list on p. 313); cf. further the concept of "memory": "For Luther, a bolt of lightning suffices to change his entire life" (228); cf. also the concept of "life comportment" (224), for which Bonhoeffer simply was unable to find any "religious" words during a nighttime bombing raid; and cf. finally the letter of March 1, 1944, according to which one's "life comportment" is strengthened by "life impulses" (251).

53. Other statements by Bonhoeffer are probably to be understood similarly, such as that on March 9, 1944: "In my months here I have tried to determine the extent to which the people here still believe in anything 'suprasensual' " (*WEN,* 259). The question raised by the *Outline for a Book* regarding what is "really" believed is in any case prefigured in the Tegel correspondence (cf. 415).

54. C. Gremmels, editor of *DBW* 8, suggests in this volume that the nonreligious interpretation was also considerably motivated by Eberhard Bethge himself (communication from Professor Gremmels at the International Bonhoeffer Conference in New York, 1992).

55. Letter of March 11, 1944 (*Love Letters,* pp. 199ff.); here Bonhoeffer is reflecting on the meaning of life: ". . . it's real life, just as it flows from the hand of God" (201f.). The letter concludes with the formulation cited earlier, which reads in full: "There will be times when we're drawn to fundamentals of our own accord, but God subsists not only in fundamentals but in everyday life as well" (153).

56. Bonhoeffer is writing this sentence following a citation from Lessing he excerpted from a book by Dilthey (cf. Ernst Feil, *The Theology of Dietrich Bonhoeffer,* p. 182). As far as Bonhoeffer's appropriation of Dilthey's thought is concerned, this raises the question whether at this time Bonhoeffer was possibly

already reading Dilthey as a "philosopher of life." Is the concept of life being developed here in part under the influence of Dilthey?

57. Without overinterpreting such a statement, we do notice that the terms "to order" and "to live (out)" do not contradict one another here. This may represent an attempt to integrate the philosophy of life into the ethics of order.

58. This admiration for the element of totality attaching to the life of his parents' generation, along with the "tensile strength" accompanying such totality, attracts Bonhoeffer's attention even into the most personal remarks in his correspondence with Maria von Wedemeyer; on August 13, 1944, he writes: "I've recently, and with great enjoyment, reread the memoirs of Gabriele von Bülow-Humboldt. She was separated from her fiancé for three whole years, shortly after her engagement! What immense patience and forbearance people had in those days, and what great 'tensile strength' [*Spannungsbogen*]!" (*Love Letters,* p. 260).

59. Cf. Wilhelm Dilthey, *Das Erlebnis und die Dichtung,* e.g., p. 10.

60. Cf. Wilhelm Dilthey, *Von deutscher Dichtung und Musik* (1957[2]), pp. 195ff.

61. Concerning the thematic complex, cf. the critical remarks of A. Pangritz, *Polyphonie des Lebens. Zu Dietrich Bonhoeffers "Theologie der Musik"* (Berlin, 1994), pp. 76f.

62. Concerning J. W. Goethe, cf. Dilthey, *Das Erlebnis und die Dichtung,* pp. 124ff., "Goethe and the Poetic Imagination." Dilthey classifies Goethe within the context of the philosophy of life; cf. pp. 126f., "Life." Dilthey opens this section with the words: "Poesy is the portrayal and expression of life. It expresses experience, and portrays the external reality of life" (126). It is improbable that Bonhoeffer could have missed the significance Dilthey attributes to life in this particular book.

63. Concerning the understanding of "chivalry" cf. in *Witiko,* e.g., pp. 61ff.; the scene portrayed at the beginning of the book is revealing concerning this anticlerical Christian attitude: "He [Witiko] then rode down into the forest that lay before him. . . . After a while he came to a red cross. He stopped at the cross, said a small prayer, and then rode on" (23).

64. With respect to possible objections from feminist theologians, let it be noted here that Bonhoeffer is probably emphasizing "man" simply because he is speaking to his friend Eberhard Bethge. Concerning this thematic material, cf. H. Kuhlmann, "Die Ethik Dietrich Bonhoeffers — Quelle oder Hemmschuh für feministisch-theologische Ethik?" *Zeitschrift für Evangelische Ethik* 37 (1993): 106-20.

65. I believe that in passages such as these we can find a key to understanding Bonhoeffer's Tegel theology. Bonhoeffer tries to make faith transparent for daily life. Faith becomes a matter of *experience;* he reflects theologically on whatever is being experienced at a particular time, in the process drawing theology itself into the nexus of experience. That which is experienced is experienced from a Christian perspective. In his *Ethics* he begins to take seriously life here and now: There is no world reality apart from the reality of Christ (cf. *DBW* 6.35, 43, 53); only

within life itself can Christ be experienced as the human being *for others,* as Bonhoeffer will ultimately write in his *Outline for a Book.*

66. With regard to the topic of religion, I have spoken of *discontinuity in continuity* (cf. Part II.B).

67. Concerning the triadic formula, cf. C. Zimmermann-Wolf, *Einander beistehen. Dietrich Bonhoeffers lebensbezogene Theologie für gegenwärtige Klinikseelsorge* (Würzburg, 1991), p. 327.

68. A similar christologically slanted question also appears in two fragments of the *Ethics.* In the fragment "Christ, Reality, and the Good," Bonhoeffer concludes: "It is thus a matter of participating in the reality of God and the world in Jesus Christ" (*DBW* 6.40). In the section "Ethics as Shaping," he writes: "The question how Christ might acquire shape among us today and here . . . conceals other difficult questions: what do 'among us,' 'today,' 'here' mean?" (*DBW* 6.87). These two passages from the fragments to Bonhoeffer's *Ethics* from 1940 seem to indicate the path at whose end we find the question of April 30, 1944. The question of shaping or forming "among us" becomes "for us"; the question of the "how" of Christ's form becomes the concrete question of "who" Christ is for us today. On the other hand, the dimension of actuality concerning the "today" addressed by these questions seems to link the *Ethics* with the *Letters and Papers from Prison.*

69. Cf. in this regard the Lectures on Christology, in which Bonhoeffer distinguishes between a who-question and a how-question (*GS* 3.168f.). A look at the original manuscript of the letter shows how important this who-question was for Bonhoeffer on April 30. Here we read: "What continually occupies my attention is the question what Christianity really is for us today ["today" crossed out] or who Christ really is for us today" (*NL* A 162/96). Bonhoeffer thus originally wanted simply to ask "what Christianity really is for us today," but then obviously noticed while writing that the question was insufficient in this form, and that it needed to be made more concrete through the who-question, the question of Christ himself! This explains the crossed-out "today" after "Christianity" and emphasizes the special significance of the following clause. It is possible that in the who-question Bonhoeffer is consciously picking up on his own formulation from the Lectures on Christology.

70. Cf. esp. the fragment "Christ, Reality, and the Good" (*DBW* 6.31-61); Bonhoeffer assumes that "the decision over life as a whole" is made "with regard to one's relationship" with the ultimate reality (33). This concept of the "whole of life" is more than a "life theme" (35); he argues: If "the good is the real itself," then the "good cannot be an independent life theme" (*ibid.*). When in the *Letters and Papers from Prison* Bonhoeffer speaks about the good and about life, he is referring — in the language of the *Ethics* — to the "real" and the "whole of life."

71. In that letter, Bonhoeffer challenged us to love God "in our lives and in the good he gives to us" (*WEN,* 242).

72. Cf. the manuscript "The Ultimate and Penultimate Things," *DBW* 6.137ff.

73. I do not believe it is accidental that Bonhoeffer chooses the concept of life here; he could just as easily have said "in the middle of our *being*," "in the middle of our *existence*," or "in the middle of our *world*" — as he did in the *Ethics:* In the manuscript "Christ, Reality, and the Good," *DBW* 6.31ff., we read in contrast to the *Letters and Papers from Prison:* "Christ died for the world, and only *in the middle of the world* is Christ Christ" (53; my emphasis). Nor does the original manuscript of the letter of April 30, 1944, contain any corrections of the sort involving the ensuing formulations concerning the church; Bonhoeffer seems to have made the formulations about life with a calm hand, with no cross-outs or reworkings (cf. *NL* A 162/100).

74. Date of the accompanying letter; cf. *WEN*, 411f.

75. *WEN*, 309; in the original letter, which was obviously smoothed out for publication in *Widerstand und Ergebung. Neuausgabe,* this line reads: ". . . to understand and comprehend things, people, and relationships, and to do so in a somewhat vague fashion 'from a human perspective,' if you can imagine what this might mean" (*NL* 80).

76. In the original, this reads: ". . . concentrated in the personal experience of marriage and love to Renate" (*NL* 80).

77. On September 30, 1944, Bethge yet writes to his friend: "When I can finally tell you about my most recent intellectual and worldly experiences!" (*WEN,* 433). The reflection on personal experiences is maintained into September 1944.

78. The basic wording occurs already in the fragments to the *Ethics;* cf. *DBW* 6.404. We will later examine whether this is saying the same thing substantively and theologically.

79. By contrast, God's transcendence, correctly understood, focuses on the concept of life: "God is beyond even in the middle of our lives" (*WEN,* 306).

80. Similar formulations can be found already in the *Drama Fragment* (1943), where Bonhoeffer has Christopher say: "Our self-evident truths have been tested by many generations, and have proven themselves in life hundreds and even thousands of times" (*DBW* 7.68).

81. Cf. also the reference to a "life goal" already in *Sanctorum Communio* (*DBW* 1.193), apparently made under the influence of A. Ritschl and yet unreflected.

82. Eberhard Bethge, "Das Erbe der Bekennenden Kirche. Transport über die Wenden," *IBK Rundbrief* 38 (1992): 1-19, reference on 17.

83. The future(-prophetic) statements about the unreligious language that will yet come should not mislead us into displacing the entire complex of religionlessness into the future. Bonhoeffer's interest is essentially systematic-theological, not apocalyptic; from the outset, he is concerned with the question focused on the present, namely, who Christ is for us *today* (cf. *WEN,* 305), and with the fact that it is for the church to tell people what *life with Christ* in the here and now means (cf. 416).

84. Bonhoeffer previously explains how the christological notion of "not

separate, and yet distinct" of the Definition of Chalcedon parallels the relationship in music theory between *cantus firmus* and counterpoint.

85. An "earthly" interpretation focusing on life is for Bonhoeffer a "christological" interpretation. To his friend Eberhard Bethge, he suggests reading Canticles in this sense as an "earthly love song," remarking: "That is probably the best 'christological' interpretation" (*WEN*, 345).

86. Cf. esp. *GS* 3.194-200; reference to Christ as the "center" in the lectures on Christology might be influenced by E. Brunner, *Der Mittler* (cf. there, e.g., pp. 304 and 317). "God comes to human beings in the mediator," so Brunner (304). Bonhoeffer speaks of Christ as "the rediscovered middle, the middle between I and I and between I and God" (*GS* 3.194f.). One notices that neither Brunner nor Bonhoeffer (1933) speaks about Christ as the "middle (or center) of life." Here Bonhoeffer's understanding of Christology seems to be modified with respect to its actualization, something we will examine more closely in connection with Bonhoeffer's *Outline for a Book*.

87. Previously unpublished material indicated by an ellipsis as an omission in *Widerstand und Ergebung. Neuausgabe*, to be inserted between "wurde bald steril" [*soon became sterile*] and "Also wie ist es . . ." [*So, how is it . . .*] in the printed section *WEN*, 348 (*NL* A 80/181f.).

88. It is no doubt futile to ask source-critically concerning passages such as these whether Bonhoeffer had the Bethge letter before him and adopted the latter's formulations. This possibility cannot be excluded, since both were reflecting on the *same* topic. Bonhoeffer emphasized that the issue was "his and Eberhard Bethge's theme" (= *our* theme; cf., e.g., *WEN*, 377, 392). On the other hand, it is of significance for later readers when Bethge's own contribution acquires sharper contours; these questions of origin should not, however, cause us to lose sight of the real systematic-theological topic of concern to them both.

89. I am also citing this clause according to the transcribed archival material available to me; according to *WEN*, 348, this reads simply "participates in the multidimensionality." According to the archival material (*NL* A.80/181f.), however, Bethge is speaking about participation in the "multidimensionality *of life*," which is of considerable importance for the present study (my emphasis).

90. See Part II.B above.

91. Bonhoeffer is probably not thinking just of the "simple man" (358); his reference to the "simple man" finds its counterpart in the "intellectual" or "degenerate" *(ibid.)*. He is using this expression as an illustration; cf. also the "religionless worker" in *WEN*, 306, or in the *Novel* his portrayal of those who "try to lead their lives in work, family, suffering, and happiness" (*DBW* 7.176); concerning the "mode" of "psychologizing," cf. the *Drama* in *DBW* 7.66.

92. W. Hamilton, " 'The Letters Are a Particular Thorn.' Some Themes in Bonhoeffer's Prison Writings," *World Come of Age* (London, 1967), pp. 131-68, observes in this letter Bonhoeffer's emergent "non-eschatological (vision)" (140), and refers to the close bracketing of this letter with the earlier lectures on Christology (1933). Whereas in other letters Bonhoeffer allegedly spoke somewhat

"unclearly" with regard to Christology, here he exhibits much more clarity: "Here we find that it is the suffering, the dereliction, and the cross that are the signs of the full acceptance of Jesus of the world. This passage reminds us of many passages of much earlier 1933 christology lectures, delivered at the University of Berlin, where the humiliation-christology of Luther was very much to the fore" (143). In our interpretation of the *Outline*, we will examine more closely the connection with the Christology lectures.

93. Here the considerable extent to which Bonhoeffer understands the New Testament from the perspective of the Old becomes clear; cf. M. Kuske, *The Old Testament as the Book of Christ: An Appraisal of Bonhoeffer's Interpretation* (Eng. trans., Philadelphia, 1976), pp. 96ff.

94. A parallel here is Bonhoeffer's reflection on ultimate questions and distress on June 30, 1944 (*WEN,* 374). Rather than being sought in the "middle of life," God becomes the "answer to life questions, a solution to life trials and conflicts." Here Bonhoeffer is also able to employ critically the concept of life, namely, where in conceptual combinations such as "life distress, life conflicts, life questions" God simply becomes the "ultimate question" and functions as the "deus ex machina" (*WEN,* 374). The notion of the wholeness of life is missing here; in the *Ethics,* he similarly is already criticizing the concept of *life themes,* since Christ understood as the "center of life" is more than merely a *theme.*

95. Cf., e.g., the *Ethics* fragment "Christ, Reality, and the Good" (*DBW* 6.53): ". . . only in the middle of the world is Christ Christ." In this connection, we must ask whether the following doctrine of mandates intends to demonstrate precisely this christological "center" in the world with the aid of the four mandates (*ibid.,* 54f.). H.-J. Abromeit, *op. cit.* (1991), p. 134, remarks: "Quite in the Lutheran tradition, Bonhoeffer suggests taking the doctrine of mandates as an interpretive framework for human life."

96. Cf. Bollnow, *Lebensphilosophie,* pp. 107f.: *happiness* as a "joyous and life-affirming basic attitude" that also developed against the "attitude of existential philosophy" (cf. the clear parallel in Bonhoeffer's letter of July 8!); concerning the concept of *authenticity,* see Bollnow, *op. cit.,* p. 88; Bollnow includes *energy* (*ibid.,* 56f.) among the categories of life, called "life concepts" in Dilthey *(ibid.).*

97. Bonhoeffer also speaks to his fiancée Maria von Wedemeyer about the Christian life come of age; he demands: ". . . every Christian should be *sui juris* and obedient solely to God and his word, not to other people and their ideas" (*Love Letters,* p. 229). Here, too, Bonhoeffer seems not to formulate this theme first with respect to the world come of age, but with respect to a Christian life come of age.

98. *WEN,* 376; there follows a direct reference to Dilthey's *Weltanschauung und Analyse des Menschen seit Renaissance und Reformation,* p. 102: "Episcopius at t[he] Synod of Dort for the Arminians[,] Dilthey 102" (*WEN,* 376).

99. Cf. Wilhelm Dilthey, *Weltanschauung und Analyse des Menschen seit Renaissance und Reformation,* e.g., pp. 19ff.

100. Cf. in this regard the formulation from the *Outline* in which Bon-

hoeffer challenges the church to tell people of all vocations "what life with Jesus means" (*WEN*, 416).

101. Cf. the letter of June 8, 1944. The rejection of existential philosophy might be motivated by the philosophy of life; the former emerged historically from the larger context of a philosophy of life, and early encountered "difficulties and limitations," as Bollnow writes (*Lebensphilosophie,* pp. 1f.). Here one might examine more closely the line from Dilthey to Heidegger to Gadamer. One must at least ask at this juncture whether Bonhoeffer is anticipating a basic critique and is giving preference to the full life concept over the concept of existence; cf. also the concepts deriving from the philosophy of life which Bonhoeffer uses: "energy," "happiness," "wholeness," etc., as well as his intensive reading of Dilthey. Bonhoeffer's observation on May 5 is probably also to be understood in the sense of a critique of the concept of existence in favor of that of life, namely, that Bultmann did not go far enough (*WEN*, 311) — the existential-philosophical interpretation is insufficient. For the rest, existentialism probably also falls under Bonhoeffer's basic criticism of "individualism." One question would be whether Bonhoeffer possibly begins to refer to the "individual" instead of to "individualism"; cf. also already *The Cost of Discipleship* (*DBW* 4.87, 89f., 92ff.), in part probably traceable back to Kierkegaard, e.g., *DBW* 4.87, n. 2.

102. This letter shows with particular clarity that the terms "nonreligious" and "worldly" are to be used together. Nonreligious interpretation and worldly interpretation obviously refer to the same thing. For our own interpretation, this is of interest esp. because terminologically, too, Bonhoeffer no longer seems bound to a concept of religion (cf. Thesis I).

103. Thus the subtitle suggested by S. F. Wiltshire, "Dietrich Bonhoeffer's Prison Poetry," *RelLife* 38.4 (Winter 1969): 522-34, here 526.

104. I read "His" in German beginning with an uppercase character (German: *Seinem*) as in the poem above; in my opinion, a closer look at the original manuscript also confirms this; see *NL* A 195 (175).

105. *DBW* 6.71; my emphasis.

106. Here one finds a crucial typographical error in *Widerstand und Ergebung. Neuausgabe,* where we read "a human being." The original reads "the" human being; cf. *NL* A 195 (175 bottom), and given Bonhoeffer's theology, only this particular reading makes sense, esp. with respect to his ethics! This typographical error has been corrected in the paperback edition of *Widerstand und Ergebung* (since the 14th edition, 1990; cf. 193 there).

107. In the *Outline for a Book,* we will have occasion to examine in detail the relationship between faith, life, and model. Here the *Outline* is artfully structured, precisely formulating and delimiting these concepts in a ring composition.

108. J. Mark, "Bonhoeffer Reconsidered," *Theol* 641 (Nov. 1973): 586-93, citation on 593.

109. Cf. C. Gremmels, *Mündige Welt,* pp. 40f.

110. So S. F. Wiltshire, *art. cit.* (see introduction above) (1969): 530f.;

following Eberhard Bethge's tripartite division of Bonhoeffer's life into "theologian-Christian-contemporary" (cf. the subtitle of his Bonhoeffer biography), she assumes a tripartite division in the "Stages on the Path to Freedom." She writes about the third stage: "It was the final stage of his life (1939-45), as a fully contemporary man, that brought Dietrich Bonhoeffer to the last two subjects of his poem — suffering and death" (531).

111. Concerning the reference to an "earthly Christology," cf. esp. *WEN*, 345, 351.

112. In our discussion of the *Outline,* we will return to the Tegel Christology, inquiring of its relationship to Bonhoeffer's earlier christological statements.

113. Bethge himself is probably also retracting these ideas when under the impression of Bonhoeffer's letter here he writes from Italy on August 24: "By the way, with a keen ear reawakened by your ideas about happiness and blessing, I am now reading with particular joy Proverbs, Canticles, Ecclesiastes. And this entire complex now makes more sense to me." (This letter is printed only in excerpts in *WEN*, 429; the sentences cited come from archival material and are part of the Bethge letters made accessible to me in transcriptions.)

114. Cf. E. Feil, *The Theology of Dietrich Bonhoeffer,* p. 236, n. 189.

115. Cf. C. Gremmels, *Mündige Welt,* p. 13, where the two citations are compared synoptically with Dilthey.

116. Cf., e.g., the letter of August 23, 1944: "I am currently working on the 'Stocktaking of Christianity'. . . . Sometimes I am shocked at my own sentences, esp. in the first, critical section. This is why I am already looking forward to being able to write something positive" (428). Here Bonhoeffer seems to be alluding to the second and third chapters of the *Outline,* in which he reflects on the conclusions his critique of religion have for faith and for the church.

117. We saw the development from the *indirect* juxtaposition of the "fullness of life" and the "religious imagination" at the end of 1943 (cf. *WEN*, 189) to the *direct* antithesis between the "religious act" and the "act of life" in the middle of 1944 (cf. 396). Bonhoeffer's reading of Dilthey took place in between.

118. One probably cannot speak of any enduring influence of Dilthey on the student Bonhoeffer prior to 1929, e.g., in seminar papers or reports; cf. E. G. Wendel, *Studien zur Homiletik Dietrich Bonhoeffers. Predigt-Hermeneutik-Sprache* (Tübingen, 1985), p. 91.

119. *DBW* 2.49.

120. *DBW* 2.49.

121. Concerning the philosophical relationship between Kant and Dilthey, cf. S. Giammusso, "Der ganze Mensch. Das Problem einer philosophischen Lehre vom Menschen bei Dilthey und Plessner," *Dilthey-Jahrbuch* VII (1990-91): 112-38. Giammusso shows how Dilthey allegedly goes beyond Kant by means of the concept of life. The doctrine of categories, so Giammusso, becomes anthropology in Dilthey (123). The categories reside in life, which is itself to be interpreted; rather than being "applied to life a priori as something alien to it," they reside

"in the essence of things themselves" (*ibid.;* Dilthey citation from *Vorrede zu Gesammelten Schriften,* 7.232).

122. H.-U. Lessing, "Lebensphilosophie und Metaphysik. Anmerkungen zu Kurt Magers Dilthey-Kritik," *Dilthey-Jahrbuch* IV (1986/87): 269-77, 269 (various citations from Dilthey, *Vorrede zu Gesammelten Schriften,* 1.xviii).

123. *DBW* 10.271.

124. Cf. P. Köster, "Nietzsche als verborgener Antipode in Bonhoeffers 'Ethik,'" *Nietzsche Studien* 19 (1990): 367-418. (Pagination in the following excursus refers to this essay.)

125. In addition to the concepts deriving from the philosophy of life such as "totality," "happiness," "experience," "authenticity," "strength," and "meaning," one might mention others as well that acquired significance for Bonhoeffer: "understanding" as the technical mastery of life (L. Klages); life as "suffering" (Nietzsche in the context of tragedy!); "boundary" (G. Simmel); concerning these terms, cf. Bollnow, *Lebensphilosophie,* pp. 55, 71, 33; finally the concept of "truth," which already acquired significance for Bonhoeffer in connection with William James's pragmatic philosophy of life; at the end of 1943, he examines "What is meant by 'telling the truth'?" (*WEN,* 385ff.); cf. the letter of November 17, 1943, *WEN,* 149 (in this regard also T. R. Peters, *op. cit.* [Part I.C] [1976], pp. 149f.); Nietzsche also traces "truth" back to the notion of purposiveness.

126. In the *Ethics,* Bonhoeffer formulates: "Jesus is not a human being, but the human being" (*DBW* 6.71). In Tegel, he picks up precisely this formulation from the *Gestalt* ethics and applies it to a critique of religion: "Being a Christian does not mean being religious . . . it means being a human being; Christ creates in us not a type of human being, but rather the human being" (*WEN,* 395).

127. *DBW* 6.93ff., esp. 113f.

128. The only positive aspect in this fragment involves the liberation of *ratio;* cf. *DBW* 6.107f.

129. See A.2 above.

130. He then speaks more extensively about Cardano in *Weltanschauung und Analyse des Menschen seit Renaissance und Reformation,* pp. 416f. and 429ff. Since Bonhoeffer says he is reading *a great deal* about the philosopher, it is also conceivable that he is already referring to these later passages.

131. Scholars have repeatedly noticed that Bonhoeffer, too (motivated by Dilthey), variously concluded his historical excursuses by focusing on the thematic material of life (cf. my discussions of the letters of June 8 and July 16, 1944). Bonhoeffer was studying *Weltanschauung und Analyse des Menschen seit Renaissance und Reformation* intensively at this time.

132. Concerning the origin of the Latin version, cf. the discussion above, Part II.B.1.

133. One notices that the mention of names is important for both Dilthey and Bonhoeffer. Dilthey explicates his "historical philosophy of life" with the aid of such names (Bruno, Montaigne, Bodin, etc.), while Bonhoeffer similarly explicates his "nonreligious interpretation" with the aid of such names, whereby

biblical names acquire significance alongside the philosophers taken from Dilthey, e.g., Paul (306ff., 369), Cornelius, Jairus, Nathanael (396), etc.

134. Cf. *Einleitung in die Geisteswissenschaften* [German edition], p. 138, according to which the notion of a "religionless condition" is historically incomprehensible.

135. Cf. *Weltanschauung und Analyse des Menschen seit Renaissance und Reformation,* pp. 20, 40, 58f., 136f., 144f., 247, 298, 322, 359, 394f., 414f., 439f., esp. 441, 458f., 469, 480, 472, 494f., and 498. With respect to other writings as well, Dilthey scholarship at large finds "no link with the metaphysical tradition" in Dilthey; so S. Giammusso, "Der ganze Mensch. Das Problem einer philosophischen Lehre vom Menschen bei Dilthey und Plessner," *Dilthey-Jahrbuch* VII (1990-91): 121.

136. In addition to P. Köster, who examines Nietzsche's influence as an antipode in Bonhoeffer's *Ethics* fragments, one might also mention H.-J. Abromeit, *Das Geheimnis Christi* (Neukirchen-Vluyn, 1991), pp. 125ff. In contrast to Köster, Abromeit does not examine the significance of any particular philosopher (of life) on Bonhoeffer, but rather the significance of the philosophy of life for Bonhoeffer's *Ethics* (esp. pp. 126f.). He also speaks of a "life theology" in Bonhoeffer (125), though not of a "life christology." Concerning the elements of the philosophy of life in Bonhoeffer's life theology, Abromeit observes that "life is *lived,* but not *thought.*" He also asserts that for Bonhoeffer, "the concept of life, a rather unclear concept from the human perspective, corresponds to a clear statement of position from the perspective of revelation theology" (130). Abromeit juxtaposes life and revelation, life and thought, something I find quite in keeping with the *Ethics,* confirming indirectly my own thesis concerning Dilthey's significance for the *Letters and Papers from Prison,* since for Dilthey, life is not merely *lived* — as it is, for example, in Nietzsche's philosophy of life — but also *thought.* This corresponds to the "objective element" in Dilthey's philosophy of life. On the other hand, Bonhoeffer's Tegel theology no longer contains any juxtaposition of life *and* revelation or of life *and* thought. He speaks not of revelation *or* life (as in the *Ethics*), but of Christ *and* the world come of age. Bonhoeffer is interested in establishing relationships, not in juxtaposing things antithetically. Life does not remain simply "irrational enchantment" (cf. P. Köster, "Nietzsche als verborgener Antipode in Bonhoeffer's 'Ethik,' " *Nietzsche-Studien* 19 [1990]: 412), but interpreted christologically is a ground of cognition. Abromeit himself does not examine the influence of the philosophy of life in the *Letters and Papers from Prison,* but merely alludes to the names of Dilthey and Ortega y Gasset (cf. pp. 125f.). I consider his observations concerning the significance of the concept of life in the *Ethics* to be fundamental, not least because these observations lend sharper contours to the difference between the *Ethics* and the *Letters and Papers from Prison:* The understanding of life, "in and for itself," is qualified negatively, similar to the understanding of the world or of autonomy. Only when the "concept of life" is filled "christologically" (133) is the understanding of life placed into a positive light. We thus observe an element of continuity in Bonhoeffer's christo-

logical questioning in the *Ethics* and the *Letters and Papers*. Discontinuity obtains in the evaluation of a mature understanding of life.

137. P. Köster, "Nietzsche als verborgener Antipode in Bonhoeffer's 'Ethik,'" *Nietzsche-Studien* 19 (1990): 367-87, already draws attention to the significance of the philosophy of life *prior to* the *Ethics;* T. R. Peters, *Die Präsenz des Politischen in der Theologie Dietrich Bonhoeffers* (Munich, 1976), pp. 127ff., also suspects that Bonhoeffer read Nietzsche quite early; he discerns the latter's presence not just in Barcelona (as does Köster), but already in *Sanctorum Communio* (135f.). He also finds Nietzsche to be of significance in *Act and Being* (137f.) and finally in a lecture given in 1932 (138f.); he also finds evidence in the *Ethics* and in the *Letters and Papers from Prison*. Although Peters does also observe the antipodal character of Bonhoeffer's reading of Nietzsche, he does not present this view as clearly as does Köster; still, it is probably also clear for Peters that Bonhoeffer cannot share his cognitive-theoretical premise in the *Letters and Papers from Prison* with either Nietzsche or William James (concerning James, cf. Peters, *op. cit.,* pp. 145f.). For this, Bonhoeffer's systematic reading of Dilthey in Tegel was necessary.

138. Cf. the *Ethics* fragments "Christ, Reality, and the Good" and "History and the Good" (in two versions), *DBW* 6.31ff.; 218ff. or 245ff. Concerning the significance of the manuscript from the perspective of the philosophy of life, cf. H.-J. Abromeit, *Das Geheimnis Christi* (Neukirchen-Vluyn, 1991), pp. 126ff.

139. Only once in the *Ethics* does Bonhoeffer make any reference to "maturity" or "coming of age," namely, when he speaks about "maturity [or coming of age] in faith" (*DBW* 6.402); nor does the antithetical juxtaposition of life and religion appear in the *Ethics*.

140. Eberhard Bethge alludes to this in a remark made at the Bonhoeffer Conference, Friedrichrode (September) 1993.

141. This observation corresponds with an additional, formal one: Compared with other handwritten documents by Bonhoeffer, the manuscript of the *Outline* is quite legible, was composed in Roman characters, and has very little material crossed out. This suggests that Bonhoeffer had already composed preliminary versions (now lost), and that the manuscript we now have actually represents a "final version." The third chapter esp. contains complete, almost "programmatic" sentences (cf. W. Huber, "Ein Dienst für die Zukunft der Kirche. Überlegungen im Anschluss an Dietrich Bonhoeffers 'Entwurf einer Arbeit,'" *IBG Rundbrief* 42/43 (1993): 23-45, citation on 23f.

142. The concept "risk" is ethically qualified; cf. the *Ethics* manuscript "History and the Good (Second Version)" (*DBW* 6.245-98, esp. the section "The Structure of Responsible Life" [256ff.]).

143. Citations *WEN,* 414; my emphasis.

144. No ontic content is ascribed to religion, confirming Thesis I: Within Bonhoeffer's theological conception, religion has become homeless. Religionlessness has emerged historically. Religion no longer has a place, and has lost its being.

145. *WEN,* 414; my emphasis.

146. Life and action emerge from faith and are grounded in it. The indicative and the imperative are thus related ethically such that the imperative calls one back to the indicative but cannot have any independent meaning alongside the indicative of faith. The connection between faith and life is ontic, not moral.

147. Concerning the relationship between "ontology" and "Christology," cf. H. Dembowski, *Grundfragen der Christologie* (Munich, 1993³), pp. 243ff. Dembowski shows that christological reference to "being for the other person" stands opposed to traditional ontology. "God is not the highest being; but in the way he discloses himself in Christ he is existence for the other person" (244f.). Bonhoeffer himself writes: "Encounter with Jesus Christ. The experience that this represents a reversal of human existence insofar as Jesus is only 'there for others' " (*WEN,* 414). He himself thus grounds his understanding of Christ ontologically in Jesus' "being for others" (!); a person should be "swept up" precisely into the "otherness" of Jesus' being; his understanding of being is thus "relational" in contrast to the conceptual schema of substance metaphysics (concerning "relational ontology," cf. G. Ebeling, *Dogmatik des christlichen Glaubens,* vol. 1 [Tübingen, 1987³], pp. 215 and 233).

148. *GS* 3.166-242 (the following page references also refer to this edition).

149. *Act and Being* already discusses ecclesiology and ontology, albeit in a different form, namely, as an *inner-ecclesiastical* model for solving the philosophical problem of "act and being": initially in connection with the "ontological attempt" in *Act and Being (DBW* 2.53ff., esp. 62ff., 72f.); then, in summarizing the issues of act and being, Bonhoeffer is concerned with defining the church as a unity of act and being in its "being in Christ" (149f.). He does not yet mention "Jesus' being for the world" or a "church for others." Ontology remains completely focused on ecclesiology. " 'Faith' is grounded in being in the communion of Christ" (153).

150. E. Feil, *The Theology of Dietrich Bonhoeffer,* p. 93, quite rightly points out that a "significant change" takes place in the *Letters and Papers from Prison;* whereas from the lectures on Christology to the *Ethics* the "pro nobis" recurs, this formula is now replaced by a "pro aliis" *(ibid.).*

151. E. Feil, *The Theology of Dietrich Bonhoeffer.*

152. In this section, the critique is articulated consistently in the critique of religion: *Religion is not there for others.*

153. "The Ultimate and Penultimate Things," *DBW* 6.137ff., citation 150.

154. *DBW* 6.151; my emphasis.

155. With respect to the concept of life, in this *Ethics* manuscript the penultimate is related to the ultimate as eternal life is to earthly life = new life; cf. *DBW* 6.150.

156. *DBW* 4.300f.; here Bonhoeffer discusses the "imago dei" character within Christology and its meaning for discipleship: "The Image of Christ" (297f.). In this context, he says: "No one will find the lost likeness of God again except by gaining a portion in the figure of the incarnate and crucified Jesus Christ. God's pleasure rests in this image alone" (300f.). Bonhoeffer is concerned

with discipleship against the background of Luther's conformatio Christology (donum-exemplum), and thus with gaining a portion in the figure of Christ; there is no reference here to participation in being in any fundamentally ontological sense. (Bonhoeffer seems rather to be thinking toward the formation Christology of the *Ethics*.) The question of the shape of discipleship in life is important for the theme of the book *The Cost of Discipleship*, and this explains the significant statements on Jesus and life in what follows; cf., e.g., 303f. There is not yet any connection between Christology and ontology on the one hand, and the philosophy of life on the other. All the same, the themes of Christology and life are being approached, though it is only through Dilthey that the concept of life can become the determinative concept of the christological conception. Here, too, the *Outline* of 1944 develops more fundamentally ideas anticipated earlier.

157. Concerning the history of this concept, see Part II.B.1 above.

158. Cf. also the interpretation of biblical "promise" = (nonreligious) "meaning" (*WEN*, 426).

159. W. Schmithals, *Das Evangelium nach Markus. Ökumenischer Taschenbuchkommentar* 2/2 (1979): 696. In connection with his exegesis of Mark 15:33, Schmithals refers explicitly to this Bonhoeffer passage (*ibid., 698*).

160. Probably in connection with arcane discipline; cf. the letter of April 30, 1944, in which Bonhoeffer poses the question: "In religionlessness, what do the cult and prayer mean? Does arcane discipline acquire new importance here?" (*WEN*, 306).

161. See Part I.B.2 above.

162. See Part II, Thesis II.

163. Here, too, Bonhoeffer does not intend to establish a subdivision into "two spheres." The interdependence of arcanum and the nonreligious continues: Nonreligious *faith as life* is juxtaposed with arcane *faith as prayer*. The one interprets the other.

164. See Part I.B.2 above.

165. Bonhoeffer notes in this context "obsolete questions of controversy, spec. interconfessional; the Lutheran-Reformed — (in part also Catholic) antitheses are no longer genuine" (415). In view of our contemporary ecumenical discussion, we must ask whether Bonhoeffer was not far ahead of his time. It was not until a few years ago — almost fifty years after the *Outline* — that the attempt was undertaken to examine the full implications of Reformational-Catholic antitheses; cf. *Lehrverurteilungen — kirchentrennend?*, ed. by K. Lehmann (Freiburg im Bresgau/Göttingen, 1986). On the other hand, we must also ask whether Bonhoeffer had thought substantively in the direction of this document; here, as we saw, he attempted to effect a counterbalance on the basis of Augustinian theology (see Part I.B.2 above).

166. Cf. also the formulation of the Heidelberg Catechism: "First Question: What is your sole comfort in life and in death?" Cited after *Der Heidelberger Katechismus*, ed. O. Weber (1983²), p. 15.

167. Communication from Eberhard Bethge at the Bonhoeffer Conference in Friedrichroda, September 1993.

168. Concerning the polemic against the Confessing Church, cf. A. Pangritz, *Karl Barth*, pp. 82ff.

169. Bonhoeffer demands in this context that "pastors must live exclusively from the voluntary gifts of the congregations" (*WEN*, 415), expressing here a practice quite common in the Confessing Church. In 1944, however, Bonhoeffer is also anticipating the end of the *Volkskirche;* he could not conceive that after the war a restoration could take place so quickly (cf. his statement in 1942, *GS* 2.435). Bonhoeffer already expressed criticism of the church taxation system in 1927 in *Sanctorum Communio.* In the original version, the sentence deleted from the printed version reads: "It is probably undeniable that obligatory collection of taxes by the state constitutes an abuse" (*Sanctorum Communio,* p. 287, n. 385).

170. See A.2 above.

171. See B.2 above.

Conclusions

1. H. Lübbe, *Religion nach der Aufklärung* (Graz, 1986), p. 14.